MW01286740

The

Whole Language / OBE

Fraud

Books by Samuel L. Blumenfeld

*How to Start Your Own Private School
And Why You Need One*

The New Illiterates

How to Tutor

The Retreat from Motherhood

Is Public Education Necessary?

Alpha-Phonics: A Primer for Beginning Readers

NEA: Trojan Horse in American Education

The Whole Language / OBE Fraud

For ordering information see last page of book.

THE
WHOLE LANGUAGE / OBE
FRAUD

Samuel L. Blumenfeld

THE PARADIGM COMPANY

Boise, Idaho

Copyright © 1995 by Samuel L. Blumenfeld. All Rights Reserved.
No portion of this book may be reproduced without permission of
the publisher, except by a reviewer or journalist who may quote
passages in a review or article.

First Printing January, 1996

The Paradigm Company
P.O. Box 45161
Boise, Idaho 83711
208-322-4440

Library of Congress Cataloging in Publication Data

Blemenfeld, Samuel L.
    The whole language/OBE fraud: the shocking story of how America
is being dumbed down by its own education system / Samuel L.
Blumenfeld.
        p. cm.
    Includes bibliographical references and index.
    ISBN 0-941995-09-7
    1. Reading (Elementary)–Language experience approach–United
States. 2. Competency based education–United States. 3. Education–
United States. I. Title.
LB1573.33.B58 1996   95-26059
372.41–dc20   CIP

To

June and Peter Watt

**Fellow Toilers in the Vineyard of
Educational Freedom**

With Affection and Appreciation

Foreword and Acknowledgments

This book is, in many ways, a sequel to *The New Illiterates* which was published in 1973. In that book I traced the history of the reading problem in America, which was basically a story of the struggle between the advocates of intensive phonics and the advocates of the look-say, whole-word method. I had hoped then that the educators would return to their senses and once more teach American children to read in the proper phonetic manner with its long track record of success. But I did not understand that there was a hidden agenda behind the look-say method which precluded a return to intensive, systematic phonics as the principal means of teaching children to read.

In other words, it eventually became clear to me that our public educators were using education as a means of promoting a social and political agenda without making that agenda known to the parents who were entrusting their children to the schools. In fact, most parents still assume that the public schools do want their children to become fully literate in the traditional sense.

Over the years, this battle of methods has turned, for many of us, into a crusade for intensive, systematic phonics, a struggle to give our children the great benefits of literacy which can only be acquired through proper phonetic instruction. One of the great pleasures of this crusade is in having met so many dedicated individuals who have been willing to share with me the fruits of their research, without which this book could not have been written. Geraldine Rodgers, who spent many years in the classroom teaching children to read, has written a monumental, yet unpublished, history of reading instruction which she graciously made available to me. Hopefully, someday it will be published.

Charlotte Iserbyt has been sending me materials for years. As a former senior staff member in the U.S. Department of Education, she had access to information revealing the cozy relationship that many educators have developed with those who have grant-giving power in the federal bureaucracy.

Others who have provided moral support, shared information and contributed their expertise on educational matters over the years include Kathy Diehl, Mike Brunner, Bob Sweet, Betty Russinoff, Arnold and Barbara Simkus, Ros Haley, Ed Miller, Jeanne Sussman, Sarah and Lynn Leslie, Bettina and Sidney Dobbs, Bettye Lewis, Marion Dalton, Barbara Cueter, Debbie Nalepa, Phyllis Schlafly, Jan Mickelson, Charlie Richardson, Jim and Dori Charles, Marianna Thomas, Marva Collins, Virginia Birt Baker, Anna Lee Bear, Bill Coulson, Hughs Farmer, Vandalyn Hooks, Pat Groff, Donna Hearne, Andy and Shirley Lane, Barbara Morris, Jack Maguire, Tom Parent, Paul Lindstrom, Mary Pride, Jack Phelps, Marla Quenzer, Marian Hinds, Bettina Rubicam, Alice Steele, Rita and Jack Shapiro, Bob Unger, Lawrence Dawson, David Drye, Laura Rogers, Jolene McGreery, Maggie and Guy Wickwire, Betty Zutt and others who have sent me letters and clippings, too numerous to mention. I am especially grateful to Dr. R. J. Rushdoony and the Chalcedon Foundation for their unstinting support of my writing and research over the years in this field of literacy and the teaching of systematic phonics.

I also wish to pay tribute to Neil McCaffrey, Jr., publisher of my first four books, who died in December, 1994. Neil got me started on this educational crusade, and I am grateful for the encouragement he gave me.

I have also been helped in various ways by a host of wonderful people abroad: Mona McNee and Martin Turner in Britain; Rona and Harry Joyner, Ros and David Phillips, Margaret Ratcliffe, Babette and Charles Francis, Fred Nile, Dr. Susan Moore, Peter Frogley, Margaret and Ian Dickson, Hunter Calder, Steve Gustafson, and Ian Hodge in Australia; Claire Aumonier and Tom Nicholson in New Zealand.

Many of the chapters in this book were first published as articles in *The Blumenfeld Education Letter.* Therefore, the reader will find some repetition of ideas and quotations. In the interest of getting this book out before we are overwhelmed by the cultural revolution in progress, I decided that a little repetition might not be such a bad idea. Also, for sources of the quotations used in the book, please refer to the Notes.

There is no question but that we shall be engaged in this struggle over educational methods, goals and outcomes for the foreseeable future. In fact, the Congress passed legislation in March 1994 that virtually federalized whole language and Outcome-Based Education, making them mandatory for public primary schools. In other words, the Congress of the United States has officially mandated by law the dumbing down of American children. How long it will take to reverse this horribly perverse situation is anyone's guess. Hopefully this book will reach enough legislators so that they will become aware of what they have unwittingly done and will seek to undo the harm their legislation will cause to millions of innocent, trusting, and unwary children.

August 1995

Blessed is he that readeth...
Rev. 1:3

What thou seest, write in a book...
Rev. 1:11

Contents

Introduction

Sometime in the late 1980s, a new reading program, called Whole Language, began to invade the primary schools of America. It was touted as a real breakthrough in reading instruction, one that would radically change our view of what reading and language learning are *really* all about. Marvelous results were promised: children would become excited about books and learn to read practically on their own; children would become excited about writing and would actually write their own books before they even knew how to spell!

We were also told that the new method had been used successfully in New Zealand and Australia for some time and was producing wonderful results. Teachers were excited, principals were excited, and school boards were excited. It seemed as if America had finally found a way out of its literacy crisis. Reading scores, it was anticipated, would soon begin to rise.

But those of us who have been involved in the reading instruction controversy for the last twenty-five years were more than skeptical. We knew who the promoters of whole language were: the same professors of reading who had been knocking intensive phonics for years, the same professors who had defined reading as "a psycholinguistic guessing game." We knew that whatever kind of reading program they dreamed up, it would be based on whole-word, look-say methodology.

What we didn't know, however, was that whole language is also based on an entirely different view of language which is contrary to the view that has prevailed in Western civilization since the invention of the alphabet, a view which today bears the label of "deconstruction."

What we also didn't know is that whole language has become an integral part of the school reform or restructuring movement known as Outcome-Based Education. OBE has been written into every state education reform bill passed in the last few years, thus making whole language virtually state-mandated. And with the enactment of Goals 2000 into law, whole language will, no doubt, be mandated nationally.

Meanwhile, we began to hear from concerned parents complaining that their children were not learning to read in these new whole-language classrooms, that they were unable to sound out words, that they were misspelling words and not being corrected by their teachers. The parents had gone to the schools and spoken to the teachers and were told not to worry.

The parents were also alarmed over the stories their children were reading at school: gruesome, gory, nightmarish stories about witchcraft, the occult, the macabre, stories with satanic overtones. All across the country, parents were standing up at school-board meetings and complaining, but to little or no avail.

Regardless of increased parental complaints, whole language continued to make its way into school district after school district until it has now become the dominant philosophy of reading instruction in American education. In many ways, the whole-language juggernaut is like a computer virus wiping out all past knowledge and practice of traditional, time-tested reading instruction. Whole-language teachers haven't the faintest idea what intensive, systematic phonics is about, let alone how to teach it. In fact, if a teacher so much as hints that he or she prefers intensive phonics as the means of teaching reading that teacher would probably be ostracized from the reading instruction community. For the most part, teachers of intensive phonics have had to go underground or keep a very low profile in order to keep doing what they know is right. To be politically correct in primary education, you have to be an enthusiastic proponent of whole language, or else. The pressure to conform has become irresistible.

And because we have had so many inquiries about whole language and Outcome-Based Education, it became obvious to this writer that a book was needed to answer the myriad questions being asked. Although we've written many newsletters on these subjects and have discussed them on many radio interview programs, they are far too complex for short talk-show answers alone. A deeper, more extensive knowledge of the reading instruction controversy is essential if one is to make sense of all of this. Not only must parents have this knowledge but teachers and school boards as well.

Every year, four million six-year-olds enter the first grade expecting to be taught to read. Their parents expect them to be taught to read, and when they are not, they wonder why. This book explains why.

By now, everyone is aware of the U.S. Education Department's revelation that 90 million American adults have literacy skills so poor that they can barely make it in our high-tech economy. Thus, it is important for the American people to realize that the new reading instruction program will not improve the situation, but make it worse, much worse.

And that is why this book is entitled *The Whole Language/OBE*

Fraud. The fraud is the great deception being perpetrated by the professional educators upon the children of America, all of whom want to be taught to read but are being turned into reading cripples condemned to lives of frustration, academic failure, stunted intellectual growth and destroyed ambition.

Considering the billions of dollars the American people are pumping into the education system of this country, they deserve better than the predetermined failure they are getting in return.

Meanwhile, as reading scores continue to decline, some school districts are having second thoughts about their whole-language programs. They are considering adding more structured phonics at the primary level. But the simple fact is that mixing whole language with phonics doesn't work because there are two mutually exclusive reflexes involved. And so, parents must be aware of the pedagogical details involved in the teaching of reading or else fall prey once more to consumer fraud.

1. A Bit of Important History

Back in 1955, Dr. Rudolf Flesch wrote a book which has since become a classic in education literature, *Why Johnny Can't Read.* In that book American parents were told for the first time why their children were having such a difficult time learning to read. Most of the parents had been taught to read by way of the centuries-old alphabetic phonics method, and they assumed that the schools were still using the same time-tested method. Thus it came as somewhat of a shock when they found out that their children were being taught to read by a new and very different method.

Flesch revealed that in the early 1930s, the professors of education changed the way reading is taught in American schools. They threw out the alphabetic phonics method, which is the proper way to teach anyone to read an alphabetic writing system, and put in a new whole-word, look-say, or sight method that teaches children to read English as if it were an ideographic writing system, like Chinese. Flesch explained that when you impose an ideographic teaching method on an alphabetic writing system, you get reading disability.

Flesch, incidentally, was not the first to make this observation about the new method. The first professional researcher to do so was Dr. Samuel T. Orton, a neuropathologist who had studied cases of reading disability in Iowa in the late 1920s. He came to the conclusion that the cause of the children's problems was the new sight method of teaching reading, and he wrote an article on the subject which appeared in the Feburary 1929 issue of the *Journal of Educational Psychology*, entitled "The 'Sight Reading' Method of Teaching Reading as a Source of Reading Disability." Dr. Orton wrote:

> I wish to emphasize at the beginning that the strictures which I have to offer here do not apply to the use of the sight method of teaching reading as a whole but only to its effects on a restricted group of children for whom, as I think we can show, this technique is not only not adapted but often proves an actual obstacle to reading progress, and moreover I believe that this group is one of considerable educational importance both because of its size and because here faulty teaching methods may not only prevent the acquisition of academic education by children of average capacity but may also give rise to far reaching damage to their emotional life.[1]

Unfortunately, Dr. Orton's warning fell on deaf ears, and the professors of education launched their new textbooks on the education market, the most famous of which were the Dick and Jane basal readers. It didn't take long for reading problems to begin to appear. Parents began to hear of a new reading disorder called dyslexia, which many children were coming down with. In its issue of April 10, 1944, *Life* magazine ran a major article on the subject, reporting:

> Millions of children in the U.S. suffer from dyslexia which is the medical term for reading difficulties. It is responsible for about 70% of the school failures in 6- to 12-year-age group, and handicaps about 15% of all grade-school children. Dyslexia may stem from a variety of physical ailments or combination of them—glandular imbalance, heart disease, eye

or ear trouble—or from a deep-seated psychological disturbance that "blocks" a child's ability to learn. It has little or nothing to do with intelligence and is usually curable.

The article went on to describe the case of a little girl with an I.Q. of 118 who was being examined at the Dyslexia Institute of Northwestern University. After her tests, the doctors concluded that the little girl needed "thyroid treatments, removal of tonsils and adenoids, exercises to strengthen her eye muscles." The article concluded:

> Other patients may need dental work, nose, throat or ear treatment, or a thorough airing out of troublesome home situations that throw a sensitive child off the track of normality. In the experience of the institute these range from alcoholic fathers to ambitious mothers who try to force their children too fast in school.[2]

Strange as it may seem, apparently no one at *Life* knew that Dr. Orton existed or that in 1929 he had already identified the cause of dyslexia among normal children: *the ideographic way of teaching reading*. In fact, it was Dr. Orton who had popularized the term dyslexia.

By 1954 it was clear to a lot of intelligent people what was causing the reading problem. *Collier's* magazine of November 26, 1954 explained it all in an article entitled "Why Don't They Teach My Child to Read?" by Howard Whitman. He wrote:

> The man next to me in the airport bus entering Pasco, Washington, said,"My six-year-old reads words at school and can't read the same words when I point them out at home in the newspaper. In school today the children aren't taught to read—they're taught to memorize."
>
> A man in the seat ahead chimed in, "Everything is pictures. My youngest is in the sixth grade. He'll still come across a word like *pasture* and he remembers a picture in his early reader and calls it *meadow."*
>
> Neither passenger knew I was making a national study of modern

education; they volunteered their remarks, sharing something they were concerned—and troubled—about. Like them, thousands of other American parents with first-grade children who are not catching on to reading as taught by the modernists, and those with upper-grade children handicapped by lack of a solid reading foundation, are concerned and troubled.

But most of all they are puzzled. Why is reading taught this way? A thousand times one hears the question, "Why don't they teach my child to read?" How can schools tolerate a method which turns out many children of eight, nine and older who stare helplessly at a word (not on their memory list) and cannot make a stab at reading it? What has happened to the method of teaching reading sound by sound, syllable by syllable, so that a child can at least make a reasonable attempt at reading any word?

Two basic teaching methods are in conflict here. One is the phonetic approach (known as phonics), the old-fashioned way in the view of modern educators. They are likely to call it the "spit and spatter" or "grunt and groan" method, satirizing the way youngsters try to sound out letters and syllables.

The other method, which the modernists have put into vogue, is the word-memory plan—also known as "sight reading," "total word configuration" or "word recognition." It has the more friendly nickname of "look and say," since the youngster is supposed simply to look at a word and say it right out. He memorizes the "shape" of the word, the configuration, and identifies it with pictures in his workbook. Often he is taught to recognize phrases or whole sentences in his picture book, or on flash (poster) cards, before he can independently sound out and pronounce such simple words as *cat* or *ball*.

The fundamental difference in approach in the two methods reaches deep into philosophy and scientific theory. Thinkers have wrangled for centuries over which comes first, the whole or its parts (an argument perhaps as endless as that over the priority of the "chicken or the egg"). The phonics advocates say the parts come first; the word-memory people say we start with the whole and the parts fall into place in due course.[3]

The article had made it quite clear that the cause of the children's reading problem was the teaching method. And Dr. Flesch's book, which appeared a year later, brought the same message to thousands of parents. And what was the reaction of the educators to this indictment of their methods? Typical was the following comment published in the July 1955 issue of *Nation's Schools*:

> How does one tell a gullible public that it is being exploited by a biased writer — as in the case with Rudolf Flesch and his book "Why Johnny Can't Read"? It will take time and patience for parents to learn that Mr. Flesch has mixed a few half-truths with prejudices to capitalize on two misconceptions. The first is his superficial notion as to what reading really is. The second is his misrepresentation as to how reading is taught.

Time magazine of January 9, 1956 summed up the educators' reaction to Flesch's book in these picturesque words: "American education closed ranks against Flesch, and when educators were not denouncing the 'Devil in the Flesch,' they were damning the 'Flesch peddlers.'"

And what did the professors of reading do after so much criticism and parental concern? They organized the International Reading Association, which has become the world's most powerful professional lobby for the advocacy of the look-say method. In the main, its presidents have been the authors of the leading look-say textbooks used in the schools. As professors of education they were also able to dictate how reading was to be taught in virtually every first-grade classroom in America. Rudolf Flesch described their monopolistic power without mincing words:

> It's a foolproof system all right. Every grade-school teacher in the country has to go to a teachers' college or school of education; every teachers' college gives at least one course on how to teach reading; every course on how to teach reading is based on a textbook; every one of those textbooks is written by one of the high priests of the word method. In the old days it was impossible to keep a good teacher from following her own common sense and practical knowledge; today the phonetic system of teaching reading is kept out of our schools as effectively as if we had a dictatorship with an all-powerful Ministry of Education.[4]

Flesch wrote that in 1955, but it is even more true today.

There is also the issue of deception. Have the educators been deceiving the parents all these years? They never asked the parents whether or not they wanted their children to be taught to read English as if it were Chinese. Have they deliberately foisted on the American people a defective teaching method which has caused enormous harm to millions of children, many of whom are now adults? Are not these educators responsible for our nation's precipitous decline in literacy?

In the early 1960s, Dr. Jeanne Chall, a respected member of the education establishment, obtained a grant from the Carnegie Corporation to do an in-depth study of the two conflicting reading instruction methods to find out which one was the more effective. The study was finally published in 1967 under the title *Learning to Read: The Great Debate.*[5] Dr. Chall's conclusion was that a phonics approach, that is, an initial emphasis on decoding, was the more effective method for teaching beginning reading.

Many thought that Dr. Chall had settled the issue once and for all and that phonics had won the great debate. But no such thing happened. True, for a time more phonics was included earlier in whole-word basal reading programs, but the basic ideographic approach remained unchanged. The professors of reading remained totally committed to their methodology. In fact, they invented a new term to describe it, "psycholinguistics."

Indeed, it was Professor Kenneth Goodman who formulated the new definition of reading which he articulated in the May 1967 *Journal of the Reading Specialist* as follows:

> Reading is a selective process. It involves partial use of available language cues selected from perceptual input on the basis of the reader's expectation. As this partial information is processed, tentative decisions are made to be confirmed, rejected or refined as reading progresses. More

simply stated, reading is a psycholinguistic guessing game.

That said it all. Moreover, it indicated that the professor made no distinction between an alphabetic writing system and an ideographic one. And that was the key to the deception. Some years later Goodman told a reporter from *The New York Times* (July 9, 1975) that it was perfectly all right if a child, when reading, substituted the word "pony" for "horse" because the child had gotten the meaning.[6]

A professor of reading who does not understand the difference between an alphabetic writing system and an ideographic one is like a mechanic who doesn't understand the difference between a horse-and-buggy and an automobile. The alphabet did for the ancient world what the computer is doing for the modern world. It made learning to read easy and speeded up the reading process enormously. It was a far more accurate and precise form of writing than ideographs. It permitted a tremendous growth in vocabulary, thereby expanding the use of language and the ability to think. It enhanced the exchange of information and knowledge. It helped produce better speech because language was now visible in the form of symbols representing speech sounds. And because it permitted man to do so much more with so much less, it is probably the single most significant invention of man.

To require children to give up all of the advantages of alphabetic writing in favor of an ideographic theory of reading makes no sense at all. What have we gained by it? Nothing. What have we lost by it? The literacy of a nation. The great debate should have been settled a long time ago. In fact, in 1983 Dr. Flesch reignited the debate with a new book, *Why Johnny Still Can't Read*.[7] But the educators just about ignored it.

But now, in the '90s, we are in a new phase of the debate—open warfare. This is the latest view of the situation as conveyed by

Education Week of March 21, 1990 in an article entitled, "From a 'Great Debate' to a Full-Scale War: Dispute Over Teaching Reading Heats Up." The article states:

> In 1967, one of the most prominent researchers in reading instruction, Jeanne S. Chall, analyzed the controversy that was then raging in the field in an influential book called *The Great Debate.*
>
> Today, nearly a quarter of a century later, the Harvard University scholar says the "debate" not only persists, but has, in fact, escalated to a full-scale war.
>
> The battle lines are drawn between advocates of phonics, who stress the importance of teaching the relationships between letters and sounds, and those of whole-language methodology, who believe children should be taught reading by reading whole texts.
>
> And so fierce have their arguments become that two recent attempts to find a common ground—a federally funded study and a proposal for the 1992 national assessment—have not only failed to quell the debate, but may have exacerbated it.
>
> "It's always been, in reading, that there was restraint with all our fighting," Ms. Chall says. "Now it's as if all restraints are gone."

And so, we are now in an educational war, dealing with the very same issues described by *Collier's* magazine in 1954 and Rudolf Flesch in 1955. In all this time, alphabetic phonics has remained the same, but the look-say, sight method has evolved from "psycholinguistics" into something called "whole language." Quite an interesting metamorphosis. What is whole language? It is more than just a new fad. It is the pedagogical expression of a radical, deconstructionist, socio-political movement, promoted by a network of radical, politicized educators whose ultimate goal is the transformation of American society. In the chapters that follow we shall demonstrate the accuracy and truth of that statement.

2. Whole Language, Linguistics and the Wittgenstein Connection

Anyone intimately involved in the ongoing battle being waged in primary reading instruction between the advocates of intensive, systematic phonics and those of whole language knows that an immense cultural and spiritual chasm lies between the two pedagogical philosophies. The best way to demonstrate the depth of this chasm is to simply juxtapose the definitions of reading as given by both sides of the conflict.

The traditional phonetic concept of reading is clearly given by Noah Webster in his American Dictionary of the English Language published in 1828. He writes:

> Read: to utter or pronounce written or printed words, letters or characters in the proper order; to repeat the names or utter the sounds customarily annexed to words, letters or characters.

Webster's definition is a straightforward description of what is done when a person "reads." It consists of uttering what is written

13

or printed in the proper order. This implies that an alphabetically written or printed message is an exact representation of its original spoken equivalent. It also implies that characters, such as numbers, represent specific, unambiguous words. It should be stated at this point that Webster was an orthodox Christian who believed that language was given to man by God at the time of man's creation. He writes:

> We read in the Scriptures, that God, when he had created man, "blessed them; and said unto them, Be fruitful and multiply, and replenish the earth, and subdue it: and have dominion over the fish of the sea," &c. God afterward planted a garden, and placed in it the man he had made, with a command to keep it, and to dress it; and he gave him a rule of moral conduct, in permitting him to eat the fruit of every tree in the garden, except one, the eating of which was prohibited. We further read, that God brought to Adam the fowls and beasts he had made, and that Adam gave them names; and that when his female companion was made, he gave her a name. After the eating of the forbidden fruit, it is stated that God addressed Adam and Eve, reproving them for their disobedience, and pronouncing the penalties which they had incurred. In the account of these transactions, it is further related that Adam and Eve both replied to their Maker, and excused their disobedience.
>
> If we admit, what is the literal and obvious interpretation of this narrative, that vocal sounds or words were used in these communications between God and the progenitors of the human race, it results that Adam was not only endowed with intellect for understanding his Maker, or the signification of words, but was furnished both with the faculty of speech and with speech itself, or the knowledge and use of words as signs of ideas, and this before the formation of woman. Hence we may infer that language was bestowed on Adam, in the same manner as all his other faculties and knowledge, by supernatural power; or, in other words, was of divine origin: for, supposing Adam to have had all the intellectual powers of any adult individual of the species who have since lived, we can not admit as probable, or even possible, that he should have invented and constructed even a barren language, as soon as he was created, without supernatural aid. It may indeed be doubted whether, without such aid, men would ever have learned the use of the organs of speech, so far as to form language. At any

rate, this invention of words and the construction of a language must have been by a slow process, and must have required a much longer time than that which passed between the creation of Adam and of Eve. It is, therefore, probable that language, as well as the faculty of speech, was the immediate gift of God. We are not, however, to suppose the language of our first parents in paradise to have been copious, like most modern languages; or the identical language they used, to be now in existence. Many of the primitive radical words may and probably do exist in various languages; but observation teaches that languages must improve and undergo great changes as knowledge increases, and be subject to continual alterations, from other causes incident to men in society.[1]

By giving Adam the power of speech, God gave man the ability to know objective reality, to know truth—which Webster defines as: "Conformity to fact or reality; exact accordance with that which is, or has been, or shall be." In fact, the first purpose of language for Adam was to enable him to know God, his Creator. That knowledge, in and of itself, established the basis for knowing the truth, the existence of God and the objective reality created by God. Thus, the believer speaks of the universe as God's creation.

According to Webster, Adam's initial vocabulary was given to him by God. Adam did not initially invent words which he then taught God. It had to be the other way around. But then God brings before Adam every living creature, "and whatsoever Adam called every living creature, that was the name thereof." And so Adam became an objective observer of the natural world around him, he became the world's first scientist and the world's first lexicographer.

As a believer and a linguist, Webster defined linguistics as "the science of languages, or of the origin, signification, and application of words." Modern linguists, however, begin with the premise that man is the product of evolution and that man, therefore, created language through a process of evolutionary development without the help of any supernatural deity. In other words, language is an arbitrary set of voice noises made by man to represent thought. Of course, even evolutionists can accept the notion that man developed and used language as a means of getting a grip on reality. Why else would language have been developed?

Curiously enough, Noam Chomsky, the world's leading linguist, believes that man is indeed the product of evolution but that his language faculty is not. He writes in *Language and Mind*:[2]

> [I]t is almost universally taken for granted that there exists a problem of explaining the "evolution" of human language from systems of animal communication.... [H]uman language appears to be a unique phenomenon, without significant analogue in the animal world. If this is so, it is quite senseless to raise the problem of explaining the evolution of human language from more primitive systems of communication that appear at lower levels of intellectual capacity. (p. 67)
>
> As far as we know, possession of human language is associated with a specific type of mental organization, not simply a higher degree of intelligence. There seems to be no substance to the view that human language is simply a more complex instance of something to be found elsewhere in the animal world. This poses a problem for the biologist, since, if true, it is an example of true "emergence"—the appearance of a qualitatively different phenomenon at a specific stage of complexity of organization. (p. 70)
>
> In fact, the processes by which the human mind achieved its present stage of complexity and its particular form of innate organization are a total mystery. (p. 97)

Furthermore, Chomsky believes that man's language faculty is biologically and genetically predetermined, that it is innate. In fact, his view is about as close to a Biblical creationist view as a humanist scientist can come to. He writes:

> The human mind appears to consist of different systems, each intricate and highly specialized, with interactions of a kind that are largely fixed by our biological endowment; in these respects it is like all other known biological systems, the physical organs of the body below the neck, for

example. One of these systems is the human language faculty. It is particularly interesting because it is a common property of humans, with little if any variation apart from quite serious impairment, and it appears to be unique to the human species; contrary to much mythology, other organisms appear to lack even the most rudimentary features of the human language faculty, a fact that has been shown quite dramatically in recent studies of apes. Thus human language appears to be a true "species property," and one that enters in a central way into our thought and understanding. (*The Reading Teacher*, Dec. 1994, p. 330)

As for his views on the teaching of reading, Chomsky says:

As a linguist, I have no particular qualifications or knowledge that enables or entitles me to prescribe methods of language instruction. (*Ibid*, p. 332)

Thus, Kenneth Goodman's claim, that his idea of reading being a "psycholinguistic guessing game" was suggested by something Chomsky said, may be a product of Goodman's strained imagination. From what Chomsky writes about a child's acquisition of language, it seems to be anything but a game. He writes:

The person who has mastered any human language has developed a system of knowledge that is rich and complex. This cognitive system provides specific and precise knowledge of many intricate and surprising facts. It seems that the mind carries out precise computational operations, using mental representations of a specific form, to arrive at precise conclusions about factual matters of no little complexity, without conscious thought or deliberation. The principles that determine the nature of the mental representations and the operations that apply to them form a central part of our biologically determined nature. They constitute the human language faculty, which one might regard as an "organ of the mind/brain." (*Language and Problems of Knowledge*, p. 131)[3]

But there are those among psycholinguists who believe that the evolutionary development of language was and still is a subjective psychological process with a rather loose connection to objective reality. The implication is that man, by creating language, creates reality out of his own head. Thus internal reality is considered more real than external reality which is interpreted subjectively. Consequently, "truth" is within, not without. Such an idea is anathema to adherents of the Bible who believe that God gave man language to enable him to *know* objective reality, not create it.

In other words, language divorced from God makes no sense to the believer, while for the atheist, cognitive psychologist or linguist, language derived from God is not only unbelievable but not even worthy of discussion. That is why, despite Chomsky, the chasm between evolutionists and creationists is so deep and so wide. That is why cognitive psychologist Jerome Bruner could complain in his memoir about "becoming the target of the ultra-right in America for espousing a curriculum that included a beautifully crafted account of human evolution. The hounds of creationism were set baying!" Thus, the chasm is political as well as philosophical.

And now we shall present a whole-language, psycholinguistic definition of reading as given by three whole-language professors in their book, *Whole Language: What's the Difference?* published in 1991:

> From a whole language perspective, reading (and language use in general) is a process of generating hypotheses in a meaning-making transaction in a sociohistorical context. As a transactional process (Rosenblatt 1978; Goodman 1984), reading is not a matter of "getting the meaning" from text, as if that meaning were *in* the text waiting to be decoded by the reader. Rather, reading is a matter of readers using the cues print provide and the knowledge they bring with them (of language subsystems, of the world) to construct a unique interpretation. Moreover, that interpretation is situated: readers' *creations* (not retrievals) of meaning with the text vary, depending on their purposes for reading and the expectations of others in the reading event. This view of reading implies that there is no single "correct" meaning for a given text, only plausible meanings. (p. 19)[4]

Obviously, when one compares this definition of reading to Webster's, one can see the stark difference between the two. Webster's is based on the premise that God endowed man with the power of speech so that man could know and deal with external as well as internal reality objectively. Webster defines the alphabet as "the series of letters which form the elements of speech." Thus, an alphabetic writing system represents spoken language, and that to read, as Webster explains, is "to utter or pronounce written or printed words, letters, or characters, in the proper order." In other words, one derives meaning—or the message—from text by decoding the text accurately. The author's message may be clear or unclear, but that judgment cannot be made until the message is accurately decoded and articulated in the form of speech.

The whole-language approach is quite different. It implies that it is the reader's subjective interpretation that determines what the author's message is, regardless of what the author intended to convey. Thus, in whole language the reader, not the author, creates the meaning, the reader, not the author, creates the message.

This view of reading naturally affects the way reading is taught in whole-language classrooms. The children are taught to develop a holistic reflex, that is, to automatically look at printed words as whole configurations, like Chinese characters, rather than to see the words alphabetically in their phonetic components. They are taught strategies rather than phonetic decoding, although some whole-language teachers will equate strategies with decoding. The children are taught to rely on configuration cues, picture cues, context cues, syntactic cues, and graphophonemic cues—some letter sounds, or phonemic cues—as one of the strategies to be used in reading. But this information becomes largely irrelevant phonetic knowledge in the child's head, knowledge which is rarely if ever used. Why? Because such use is discouraged by whole-language teachers who advocate taking risks, or guessing, and using word substitutions to arrive at meaning. Besides, when a child has developed a holistic reflex, it requires conscious effort to apply phonetic knowledge, effort which most children are reluctant to make because it slows down the reading process.

It is odd that a reading philosophy that puts so much emphasis on "meaning" should encourage guessing and word substitutions which make a mockery of accurate meaning. Indeed, we read in *Evaluation: Whole Language, Whole Child* by Jane Baskwill and Paulette Whitman (Scholastic, 1988):

> The way you interpret what the child does will reflect what you understand reading to be. For instance, if she reads the word *feather* for *father*, a phonics-oriented teacher might be pleased because she's come close to sounding the word out. However, if you believe reading is a meaning-seeking process, you may be concerned that she's overly dependent on phonics at the expense of meaning. You'd be happier with a miscue such as *daddy*, even though it doesn't look or sound anything like the word in the text. At least the meaning would be intact. (p. 19)[5]

The inference is that the phonics-oriented teacher who wants to help the child read the text accurately by helping her improve her decoding skills is somehow not interested in meaning. In whole language, readers are supposed to "create meaning" rather than derive it from the text. The concept of accuracy gets totally lost in the process. But we live in a high-tech civilization in which accuracy is exceedingly important, and to give a child the impresssion that it isn't is doing the child a tremendous disservice. Yet, whole-language advocate Julia Palmer, president of the American Reading Council, when questioned about word substitutions by a reporter from the *Washington Post* (11/29/86), replied: "Accuracy is not the name of the game."

How can a high-tech civilization advance with that kind of philosophy governing the education system?

The confusion is over the word "meaning" and how it is being used by whole-language educators. They define "reading" as "creating meaning." In fact, the Kentucky Department of Education describes its whole-language view of reading in its Outcome Based Education program as: "Students construct meaning from a variety of print materials for a variety of purposes through reading."

In phonics, children are taught to decode an author's message before they decide what it means. In other words, there is a difference between such questions as: "What does the message say?" and "What does the message mean?" Whole-language educators not only confuse the two but equate the two. And one can imagine the confusion this creates in the mind of the child.

The phonics-oriented teacher wants to make sure that the child can "read" or decode what "the author says," and in simple children's books the authors generally mean what they say, or what they say can be easily understood. What authors "mean" is what high school and college students might reflect on as they read works of greater complexity that challenge the intellect.

But where did this confusion about meaning, which seems to be at the heart of the psycholinguistic approach to reading, originate? Where did Kenneth Goodman get his idea of reading being "a psycholingusitic guessing game"? He says he got it from Chomsky who suggested "that readers make tentative decisions as they strive to make sense of text, and they remain ready to modify their tentative decisions as they continue reading." We can already see within this statement a confusion between the process of finding out what the author is saying, by decoding, and determining what he or she means, by interpretation or analysis. Obviously, not all texts require interpretation or analysis. But to use such a confusing concept as the basis for primary reading instruction can only lead to enormous confusion and frustration among children.

Perhaps we can best understand where all of this confusion

came from by seeking its philosophical source since so many whole-language advocates insist that whole language is a philosophy and not a method of instruction. The one name that stands out among many lesser lights is that of Ludwig Wittgenstein (1889-1951), the Austrian-born English philosopher who taught at Cambridge University from 1929 to 1947. His two chief works, *Tractatus Logico-Philosophicus* (1921) and *Philosophical Investigations*,[6] published posthumously in 1953, have profoundly influenced not only modern philosophy, but also psycholinguistics and cognitive psychology. Indeed, one finds references to Wittgenstein in the books of Chomsky, Jerome Bruner, and virtually every other author dealing with language. Indeed, it is quite possible that the term "whole language" itself is derived from a passage in *Philosophical Investigations*. Wittgenstein begins his treatise by quoting a passage from Augustine's *Confessions*[7] in which Augustine describes how he learned language by associating words with objects. Wittgenstein writes:

> In this picture of language we find the roots of the following idea: Every word has a meaning. This meaning is correlated with the word. It is the object for which the word stands. (p. 2)

Wittgenstein is simply stating the Biblical notion of language. But then he begins a very long tedious process of testing the limits of that idea. He writes:

> That philosophical concept of meaning has its place in a primitive idea of the way language functions. But one can also say that it is the idea of a language more primitive than ours. (p. 3)

Wittgenstein then presents us (in §2) with an example of a very primitive language of only four words based on the Augustinian concept. He writes:

> We could imagine that the language of §2 was the *whole* language of A and B; even the whole language of a tribe.... (p. 4)
>
> We can also think of the whole process of using words in (2) as one of those games by means of which children learn their native language. I will call these games "language games" and will sometimes speak of a primitive language as a language-game.... (p. 5)
>
> I shall also call the whole, consisting of language and the actions into which it is woven, the "language-game". (p. 5)

Is this where Kenneth Goodman got his idea for calling the whole-language concept of reading "a psycholinguistic guessing game"? In any case, Wittgenstein proceeds in his investigation of the Augustinian concept of words as names of objects. He writes:

> But what, for example, is the word "this" the name of in language-game (8) or the word "that" in the ostensive definition "that is called ...."?—If you do not want to produce confusion you will do best not to call these words names at all.... (p. 18)
>
> This queer conception springs from a tendency to sublime the logic of our language—as one might put it. The proper answer to it is: we call very different things "names"; the word "name" is used to characterize many different kinds of use of a word, related to one another in many different ways;—but the kind of use that "this" has is not among them.... (p. 18)
>
> This is connected with the conception of naming as, so to speak, an occult process. Naming appears as a *queer* connexion of a word with an object.—And you really get such a queer connexion when the philosopher tries to bring out *the* relation between name and thing by staring at an object in front of him and repeating a name or even the word "this" innumerable times. For philosophical problems arise when language *goes on holiday*. And *here* we may indeed fancy naming to be some remarkable act of mind, as it were a baptism of an object. And we can also say the word "this" *to* the object, as it were *address* the object as "this"—a queer use of this word, which doubtless only occurs in doing philosophy. (p. 19)

At this point, Wittgenstein begins speculating about the concept of "meaning." He writes:

> Let us first discuss *this* point of the argument: that a word has no meaning if nothing corresponds to it.—It is important to note that the word "meaning" is being used illicitly if it is used to signify the thing that 'corresponds' to the word. That is to confound the meaning of a name with the *bearer* of the name. . . . (p. 20)
>
> For a *large* class of cases—though not for all—in which we employ the word "meaning" it can be defined thus: the meaning of a word is its use in the language. (p. 20)

This concept is the beginning of a very dangerous process. By asserting that "the meaning of a word is its use in language" and not its attachment to an object, or the name of something in objective reality, we find ourselves at the threshold of a slippery slope leading to pure subjectivism.

Wittgenstein then quotes Socrates who says: "For the essence of speech is the composition of names." (p. 21) Once more, we are touching base with Augustine. But then Wittgenstein decides to wade into deeper philosophical water. Using the notion that the word "this" is not a name, he tries to use it to make distinctions between "simple constituent parts" and "composites," and between "names" and "descriptions." He writes:

> For naming and describing do not stand on the same level: naming is a preparation for description. Naming is so far not a move in the language-game—any more than putting a piece in its place on the board is a move in chess. We may say: *nothing* has so far been done, when a thing has been named. It has not even *got* a name except in the language-game. This was what Frege meant too, when he said that a word had meaning only as part of a sentence. (p. 24)

That concept strikes a familiar ring in whole language, where children are not taught to read words in isolation but only in sentences so that they can get the "meaning." The inference is that words only have "meaning" in context, that they cannot be considered objectively as names in isolation, that reading is a subjective process.

From this point on, Wittgenstein wanders off into endless philosophical speculation about the language-game. He seems to be saying that we are all locked in the language-game and that the philosopher is trying to find a way out but can't. He says:

> We are under the illusion that what is peculiar, profound, essential, in our investigation, resides in its trying to grasp the incomparable essence of language. That is, the order existing between the concepts of proposition, word, proof, truth, experience, and so on. This order is a *super*-order between—so to speak—*super*-concepts. Whereas, of course, if the words "language", "experience", "world", have a use, it must be as humble a one as that of the words "table", "lamp", "door". (p. 44)

> The question "What is a word really?" is analogous to "What is a piece in chess?" . . .
> Philosophy is a battle against the bewitchment of our intelligence by means of language. (p. 47)

> The results of philosophy are the uncovering of one or another piece of plain nonsense and of bumps that the understanding has got by running its head up against the limits of language. These bumps make us see the value of the discovery.
> When I talk about language (words, sentences, etc.) I must speak the language of every day. Is this language somehow too coarse and material for what we want to say? *Then how is another one to be constructed?*— And how strange that we should be able to do anything at all with the one we have! (p. 48)

And so, even though Wittgenstein sees language as a game, it is a game played on an Augustinian playing field. Nor would he approve of reading being defined as a "psycholinguistic guessing game." In investigating the word "reading," he writes:

First I need to remark that I am not counting the understanding of what is read as part of 'reading' for purposes of this investigation: reading is here the activity of rendering out loud what is written or printed; and also of writing from dictation, writing out something printed, playing from a score, and so on.

The use of this word in the ordinary circumstances of our life is of course extremely familiar to us. But the part the word plays in our life, and therewith the language-game in which we employ it, would be difficult to describe even in rough outline. . . .

Now what takes place when, say, [an adult] reads a newspaper?—His eye passes—as we say—along the printed words, he says them out loud— or only to himself; in particular he reads certain words by taking in their printed shapes as wholes; others when his eye has taken in the first syllables; others again he reads syllable by syllable, and an occasional one perhaps letter by letter. . . .

Now compare a beginner with this reader. The beginner reads the words by laboriously spelling them out.—Some however he guesses from the context, or perhaps he already partly knows the passage by heart. Then his teacher says that he is not really *reading* the words (and in certain cases that he is only pretending to read them).

If we think of *this* sort of reading, the reading of a beginner, and ask outselves what *reading* consists in, we shall be inclined to say: it is a special conscious activity of mind. . . .

The word "to read" is applied *differently* when we are speaking of the beginner and of the practised reader. . . . (pp. 61-62)

But when we think the matter over we are tempted to say: the one real criterion for anybody's *reading* is the conscious act of reading, the act of reading the sounds off from the letters. (p. 63)

And if I so much as look at a German printed word, there occurs a peculiar process, that of hearing the sound inwardly. (p. 67)

I feel that the letters are the *reason* why I read such-and-such. For if someone asks me "Why do you read such-and-such?"—I justify my reading by the letters which are there. (p. 68)

Obviously, Wittgenstein would be appalled by what whole-language people call "reading"! But Wittgenstein had no control over how future academics would interpret his philosophical ideas. He wrote:

> Language is a labyrinth of paths. You approach from *one* side and
> know your way about; you approach the same place from another side and
> no longer know your way about. (p. 82)
>
> What is your aim in philosophy?—To shew the fly the way out of the
> fly-bottle. (p. 103)
>
> My aim is: to teach you to pass from a piece of disguised nonsense to
> something that is patent nonsense. (p.133)

In a way, Wittgenstein brought philosophy to a dead end, by simply making us aware of the limits of language. But if we understand the functions of language in Biblical terms, then we understand that the primary purpose of language is to enable us to know truth.

It is no accident that we read in the Gospel According to St. John (1:1):

> In the beginning was the Word, and the Word was with God, and the
> Word was God.

God endowed man with what Chomsky calls our "language faculty" or our "species-specific human possession" so that man, made in God's image, would be able to know truth. The language that God gave man provides him with limitless capabilities to seek and know truth, to know what is, what exists. For the unbeliever, however, it isn't the limits of language that confine him, but the limits of truth, the limits of objective reality, the limits of what exists.

That is why for the believer, "the truth shall make you free" (John 8:32), but for the unbeliever the truth is an unspeakable prison.

3. What Is Whole Language?

Whole language is probably the most extreme form of look-say developed to date. It not only does not recognize any distinction between an alphabetic writing system and an ideographic one, it doesn't even recognize that alphabetic writing is a representation of speech. In a recently published book, *Whole Language: What's the Difference?*, the authors write:

> Oral language, written language, sign language — each of these is a system of linguistic convention for creating meanings. That means none is "the basis" for the other; none is a secondary representation of the other. (p. 9)[1]

These statements not only indicate a lack of understanding of what alphabetic writing is—a symbolic representation of oral language—but a lack of understanding of its benefits. Are these writers ignorant or are they deliberately misrepresenting the facts? If they are engaged in doing the latter, then the public has a right to know what their motive is. The authors of *Whole Language: What's the Difference?* give us an inkling that there is much more than meets the eye in their new reading theory when they write:

> Whole language is not only a good idea; it is also a threatening idea for those with a vested interest in the status quo. It threatens because it is *profoundly* different from predominant views about education. . . .[I]t has the potential not only for affecting learners and teachers in the classroom but for having widespread economic and political ramifications within the huge institution of education. (p. 3)[2]

In other words, whole language is more than just another way to teach reading. It is a revolutionary new approach to teaching basic skills. The authors elaborate:

> First and foremost, whole language is a *professional theory,* an explicit theory *in* practice. . . . [It is] the *deliberately* theory-driven practice — not simply the behaviors — that make a classroom whole language. (p. 7)

Thus, whole language methodology is based on a new "theory" of what reading is and how children learn to read. It is not based on the experience of three thousand years of teaching children to read an alphabetic writing system. The new theory is based on beliefs, not facts. For example, the authors write:

> A key whole language belief is that reading and writing are learned through really reading and writing (not through doing reading and writing exercises) and, therefore, that reading and writing should be what goes on in school (Edelsky & Draper 1989). Drills on isolated skills or language fragments are exercises, so they don't qualify as reading or writing; neither do entire stories exploited for the main purpose of teaching some skill rather than for a purpose appropriate to story. (p. 8)

In other words, their belief system, their faith, tells them that children do not learn to read by doing any sort of phonetic exercises. That, of course, is tantamount to believing that concert pianists don't learn to play piano by learning the notes and exercising the scales but merely by playing the piano.

Whole-language educators believe that children learn to read the same way they learned to speak — naturally. All you have to do is immerse the child in books, and through some miraculous process, the child will learn to read. Frank Smith, probably the world's leading whole-language theoretician, explains the process. He writes in *Understanding Reading*:

> Learning to read does not require the memorization of letter names, or phonic rules, or a large vocabulary . . . . Nor is learning to read a matter of application to all manner of exercises and drills . . . . [L]earning to read is not a matter of a child relying upon instruction, because the essential skills of reading — namely the efficient uses of nonvisual information — cannot be explicitly taught. (p. 198)[3]

If the essential skills of reading cannot be explicitly taught, then how does the child learn to read? Smith explains:

> It should not be a cause for dismay that we cannot say with exactitude what a child has to learn in order to read, or that a foolproof method of instruction cannot be found to direct a child's progress in learning to read. . . . But it is possible to specify the *conditions* under which a child will learn to read, and these are again the general conditions that are required for learning anything — the opportunity to generate and test hypotheses in a meaningful, collaborative context. . . . [T]he only way a child can do all this for reading is to read. If the question arises how children can be expected to learn to read by reading before they have learned to read, the answer is very simple. At the beginning — and at any other time when it is necessary — the reading has to be done for them. Before children acquire any competence in reading, everything will have to be read to them, but as their ability expands they just need help, the opportunity to engage in reading demonstrations. (p. 199)

Can a child become a good reader by way of this "natural" method? It all depends on how you define reading. If reading is defined as the ability to accurately decode the written text into its spoken equivalent, the whole-language method would not produce a good reader. In fact, whole-language teachers are not terribly concerned about accuracy. In an article entitled "Reading Method Lets Pupils Guess" in the *Washington Post* of Nov. 29, 1986, the reporter wrote:

> The most controversial aspect of whole language is the de-emphasis on accuracy. American Reading Council President Julia Palmer, an advocate of the approach, said it is acceptable if a young child reads the word house for home, or substitutes the word pony for horse. "It's not very serious because she understands the meaning," said Palmer. "Accuracy is not the name of the game."

If accuracy is not important, then how can one judge whether or not a child is a good reader? The answer may be found in the educators' new definition of reading, which is quite different from the one normal, everyday people use. The authors of *Whole Language: What's the Difference?* write:

> Whole language represents a major shift in thinking about the reading process. Rather than viewing reading as "getting the words," whole language educators view reading as essentially a process of creating meanings. (See the development of this view in the writings of Kenneth Goodman [Gollasch 1982] and Frank Smith [1971, 1986].) Meaning is created through a *transaction* with whole, meaningful texts (i.e., texts of any length that were written with the intent to communicate meaning). It is a transaction, not an extraction of the meaning *from* the print, in the sense that the *reader-created* meanings are a fusion of what the reader brings and what the text offers. . . . In a transactional model, words do not have static meanings. Rather, they have meaning *potentials* and the capacity to communicate multiple meanings. (p. 32)[4]

In other words, the reader can never be wrong because the transaction is totally subjective. One wonders how many writers would concur with this definition of reading. Writers generally take great pains to convey a particular message. The last thing they want is for the reader to "create" a meaning which is not there. If the reader, not the writer, creates the meaning, what's the point in reading what others write? Why not simply stare at the page and say anything you want? Or why stare at the page at all?

Rudolf Flesch asserted in 1955 that if you teach a child to read English as if it were Chinese, that child would develop a reading problem. Yet, Frank Smith writes:

> My present assertion is that any written language is read as Chinese is read, directly for meaning. The fact that some written languages are also more or less related to the sound system of a spoken language is quite coincidental as far as the reader is concerned. As I suggested earlier, the alphabet could have originated purely for the convenience of writers. Certainly, there is no evidence that fluent readers identify letters in order to identify familiar words, and English spelling is, at best, an inadequate guide to the identification of words that are unfamiliar. (p. 153)[5]

One of the errors Smith constantly makes in his writings is confusing beginning reading with fluent, experienced reading. Of course, the experienced reader does not have to identify the letters in familiar words. But he certainly has to look closely at the letters and syllables in unfamiliar, multisyllablic words, such as the many new pharmaceutical terms.

Nowhere is Smith's ignorance more demonstrable than when he asserts "that any written language is read as Chinese is read, directly for meaning." Apparently Smith is unaware that written Chinese is not a purely ideographic writing system. Its present characters are the result of a lengthy and complex evolution from early pictographs. But many of these characters have come to represent sounds. In fact, these phonograms make up about three quarters of all Chinese characters. (See *The Nature of the Chinese Character* by Barbara Aria, Simon & Schuster, 1991, p. 12.) If these phonograms were read "directly for meaning," they would be nonsensical.[6]

Another important aspect of the Chinese character that adds to its distinction and difference from our writing is its form and beauty. In other words, Chinese characters have an aesthetic dimension lacking in our alphabetically written words. The English printed word "love" is not intrinsically beautiful. It is our association of the written word with its spoken equivalent that gives it its beauty. In English, the aesthetic dimension is in the sound of the word not the way it looks in print. Of course, a good calligrapher can make any English word look beautiful, but its articulated equivalent might repel the reader.

Also, the great advantage alphabetic English has over Chinese is in the number of symbols that must be learned. Once an English-speaking child learns the sounds of our 26 letters, the various spelling forms of our 44 sounds, and how to blend the sounds, that child will be able to read anything. On the other hand, the Chinese child must memorize several thousand Chinese characters — including the phonograms — in order to learn to read. A far more tedious and difficult task than learning to read English. The fact that a Chinese typewriter has 1,000 keys is an indication of the greater difficulty involved in learning the Chinese writing system.

Therefore, the notion that one can read alphabetical writing as one reads Chinese ideographic symbols is wholly untenable since three quarters of the latter are used as sound symbols. An individual learns to read an alphabetic writing system by developing a phonetic reflex, an automatic association between letters and sounds and syllables and sounds. Once that association is established, one becomes a phonetic reader. Phonetic readers can sometimes read so quickly and fluently that it may appear that they are looking at the words as ideographs. But it is instantaneous decoding that is taking place, for in alphabetic reading it is the spoken word, the subvocalized word, that conveys the meaning to the brain. Thus, alphabetic reading combines both sight and sound in one process, thereby creating a continuous link between the written language and the spoken word.

Let me add to this chapter a short dissertation on how Chinese children learn to read Chinese. It is taken from an article written by John Edgar Johnson and published in 1873 in *The Biblioteca Sacra and Theological Eclectic* (Vol. 30, pp. 62-76) entitled "The Chinese Language."[7] Mr. Johnson writes:

> The Chinese is a language by itself, perfectly unique. It is the only specimen of a purely primitive tongue that now remains to us, and for this reason, if for no other, possesses great interest for the student of philology. It is just such a language as two persons would probably devise if thrown together in a desert, neither ever having seen a human being before.... We shall never be able to understand the Chinese, until we know more of their language. . . .
>
> A good many of its characters are ideographic; their meaning is suggested by their form or sound. There is no alphabet, and each object or idea is represented by a distinct sign. Of course, there is really no end to the language; it is infinite. Some writers have estimated the number of words as high as two hundred and sixty thousand, eight hundred and ninety-nine (Montucci); but the total of really different symbols in use among good writers will not exceed twenty-five thousand. Ten thousand signs, however, will enable one to read any book; while three thousand is sufficient for all ordinary purposes. The origin of these characters, like that of the alphabet among Western nations, is lost in tradition. Chinese writers ascribe it to Hwangti, an early emperor, or to Tsang-Lieh, a celebrated statesman, both of whom are said to have lived about 2700 B.C. The first characters were derived from a study of nature, and were imitations of its forms. . . .
>
> The first characters, we have said, were rude outlines of natural objects. A crescent, for instance, was recognized as representing the moon. A circle with a dot in the center, stood for the sun. The word *sin,* heart, was represented by a figure which resembled that organ. It is evident that the number of such signs that could be invented was comparatively limited, and so it became necessary, quite early, to combine those symbols, already

understood, for the purpose of conveying new ideas. . . .

Perhaps seven eighths of all the characters in Chinese have been formed from the union of about two thousand symbols. We may suppose that the mode of procedure was something as follows. The spoken language was already well understood. Hwangti, or Tsang-Kieh, instead of adopting arbitrary signs to represent sounds, as has been done in other languages, depicted the object and applied to it the name which it had in the colloquial language. There was nothing about the character itself that gave one the least idea as to its sound; that had to be learned arbitrarily. Just, in fact, as is the case with the letters of the alphabet. But it will be seen that this method had its limits. When about two thousand signs had been devised, human ingenuity was well-nigh exhausted and the symbols were getting to be very complex. But meanwhile nearly every sound of which the vocal organs were capable having been represented, the emperor or the statesman, whichever it was, hit upon the plan of combining these original characters to form new ones.

These compounds or derivatives which constitute, as we have said, the large mass of all the words in the Chinese language, were formed in this manner. The symbol on the left was to indicate, though oftentimes remotely, the meaning of the new sign; the symbol on the right was purely phonetic, lost its signification, but gave to the compound its name. For instance, in the spoken language, *ma no* meant a cornelian or agate. It was impossible to make an ideograph which would distinguish this stone from others, and hence recourse was had to the syllabic method. The symbol which signifies *gem* or *stone* was taken, and to this were joined two other characters which together had the sound of *ma no*. In this manner it will be seen that in a short time there came to be a great many words of widely different meaning but pronounced in the same way. *Ting,* which is an ancient hieroglyphic for a sting, or nail, gives its name to at least thirty-six combinations. And hence a native of China would not understand, oftentimes, one of his own countrymen when reading aloud. Suppose the former hears the word *ting* pronounced; how can he tell, except from the context, which one of the thirty-six compounds is meant? He must look on the book. There is a difference in the written character, but none in the spoken word.

The range of pronunciation in Chinese, however, is much greater than in any other language. The different cadences which they are able to give a word lie quite beyond the descriptive powers of a European. Some words, and especially foreign ones, are formed by the union of signs which sound like the new word when pronounced. There is no root, which gives meaning, and the reader is frequently cautioned against falling into error on this account by placing the sign for "mouth" beside the new compound to show that all of the component words are merely phonetic. This is, in fact, the syllabic method of writing. Thus, at Canton, where the Chinese come in contact with foreigners, it was found necessary to have some symbol to represent Mister; so they took the character *mi*, "beautiful," and *sz*, "scholar," not because there was anything in the meaning of these words to suggest the object; far from it, but simply because when pronounced together they sounded like Mister.

So too coffee is written *ka fi; ka* means "frame," and *fi* means "not," and of course they do not indicate the idea. An inhabitant of Canton who should meet these words would pronounce them mentally, and immediately detect their meaning. But a man back in the country, who knew nothing about foreigners, and never heard them named, would puzzle over them, seeking to discover their signification from the meaning of their parts. Good scholars are very careful how they employ purely phonetic words, and their use is therefore quite limited. . . .

There are several methods by which the characters of the language have been arranged for the purpose of reference. The one adopted by the dictionary called Kanghi Tsz' Tien is in general use. Two hundred and fourteen familar symbols, which enter into nearly all the derivatives, are taken as clefs, or radicals. These are arranged according to the number of strokes of which they are composed. First, those of one stroke, etc., down to those formed by seventeen strokes. Then again, the derivatives under each radical are arranged in the same manner. So that if you wish to look out a word in the dictionary, notice first its radical part, distinguish that. Most usually it is written, as has been said, at the left of the compound; but sometimes it is placed above, below, or so as to enclose the rest of the symbol. Having discovered the radical, which, on account of variations, is not always an easy task, count the number of strokes of which it is composed. . . .

Our first piece of advice, then, to a person who thought of taking up the study of Chinese, would be this: Forget everything you know about the genius of language. Your present ideas will be a positive damage to you. Get rid of them at any cost. Begin over again. First, commit to memory the two hundred and fourteen radicals; they are all familiar words, and the time thus expended will not be thrown away. Then, learn the names and meaning of all the common phonetics or primitives, which are rather more than a thousand in number. With this alphabet you will be prepared to enter upon the acquisition of the derivative forms, which, after all, constitute at least seven eighths of the language.

An author whose name is now forgotten recommends the student, after he is pretty well advanced, to commit to memory the four books and the five classics. This is the method pursued by the Chinese youth. Or rather, they begin by committing to memory sentences, pages, and then whole books, before they are instructed in the meaning of a single character that they have learned. A dozen sit in one room, and repeat aloud the words which they wish to fix in their minds. Of course, it makes a noise. But the quick ear of the pedagogue detects the slightest inaccuracy of tone, and, reaching over with a long bamboo, he somewhat forcibly calls the attention of his pupil to the fact.

As we can see from the above, a child learning to read English has a far easier time of it if he or she is taught by intensive, systematic phonics. The child first learns to recognize the 26 letters of the alphabet, and then learns the sounds the letters stand for. The child is then drilled in consonant-vowel combinations in order to develop an automatic association between letters and sounds and syllables and sounds. By developing this phonetic reflex, the child is then able to become an accurate, proficient reader of written English. While there is nothing in the Chinese character that gives one the least idea as to how it is pronounced, the written English word is composed of letters and spelling forms that give the reader an exact idea of how it is pronounced. What a tremendous improvement over the Chinese system.

The Chinese student must memorize 214 radicals and a thousand primitives before he can begin to read. And then he must memorize four books and five classics. Not an easy task. Yet, Professor Smith would have American children learn to read English as if it were Chinese, depriving the child of all the advantages of our alphabetic system. And, no doubt, he calls that progress! What a diabolical way to produce an illiterate America at the expense of the taxpayer.

While Prof. Smith tends to belittle the invention of the alphabet, Dr. Robert K. Logan, a professor of physics and computer expert at the University of Toronto, has written a fascinating book that shows the importance of the alphabet to our civilization. In the book, *The Alphabet Effect: The Impact of the Phonetic Alphabet on the Development of Western Civilization* (Morrow, 1986),[8] Dr. Logan writes:

> It is not just the concrete nature of Chinese ideograms but the difficulty in classifying them that makes them less conducive to abstract scientific thinking than an alphabetic script. . . . (p. 55)
>
> The linking together of standardized repeatable elements to form words also enables the alphabet to serve as a paradigm for deductive logic in which ideas or statements are linked together to form arguments. This is not the case with Chinese writing and might partially explain why the Chinese never developed Western-style logic. Their thinkers favored dialectical forms rather than deductive ones, and their reasoning tends to be inductive rather than deductive. It is not logical but rather analogical, much as Chinese characters are analogs of the words they represent.
>
> The linear, sequential mode of building a system that the alphabet encouraged and Chinese characters discouraged also influenced industrial development in the East and the West. Despite their technological progress, the Chinese never linked their inventions together to create the assembly-line production characteristic of the Western Industrial Revolution. (p. 57)[9]

In other words, there is much more involved in the differences between alphabetic writing and ideographic writing than Frank Smith would have us believe. That being the case, how could anyone seriously think that it is possible to teach American children to read English as if it were Chinese? Yet, that is what our educators are doing with whole language.

4. The Alphabetic Method

Nobody knows exactly when or where the alphabet was invented. Scholars think it was invented by the Phoenicians around 2000 B.C. Prior to the invention of the alphabet human beings at first used pictographs which later evolved into ideographs.

A pictograph is a graphic symbol that looks like the thing it represents. You don't have to go to school to learn to read pictographs. We use them today on road signs and in airports. Everyone is familiar with the little figures on restroom doors. One figure wears a skirt, the other wears pants. But now that so many women wear pants, it can be confusing. In other words, even simple pictographs can be ambiguous, if not ambivalent. However, pictographs are particularly useful in international airports where travelers may not speak the local language and must rely on simple pictorial symbols for directions.

As civilization became more complex, the scribes had to depict things that did not lend themselves to depiction. It's easy enough to draw a picture of a tree or an animal. But how do you draw pictures of abstract ideas? How do you draw pictures of good and evil, right and wrong, never and forever, guilt and innocence? You can't. So the scribes drew little symbols that did not look like the ideas they represented. We call these symbols ideographs. And now you did have to go to school to learn what all of these symbols stood for. And because ideographic writing was so difficult to master, literacy was restricted to a small group of scribes, scholars and priests who spent years learning the system.

Modern Chinese has evolved from a purely pictographic writing system into one that uses characters to stand for words and speech sounds as well. It's a terribly complex system to learn, particularly for westerners.

However, somewhere around 2000 B.C. someone made a remarkable discovery. Someone discovered that all of human language is composed of a small number of irreducible speech sounds. And that person decided that instead of using a writing system composed of thousands and thousands of symbols, none of which looked like the things they represented and took years to learn and were easily forgotten, why not create a set of symbols to represent only the irreducible speech sounds of the language and we would have a very simple writing system that required memorizing a very small number of symbols that stood for sounds. And so the first alphabet was invented.

The beauty of the alphabet is that it permitted the writer to convey his thoughts with precision and accuracy because the written words were a direct representation of spoken language. This was not the case with ideographs which represented ideas that could be expressed in many different ways. For example, a commonly seen ideograph these days is the cigarette in a circle with a diagonal line across the circle. The ideograph can be interpreted or articulated in many different ways: *smoking not allowed, smoking not permitted, smoking prohibited, nicht rauchen, defense de fumer, no fumar*, etc. In other words, the spoken language is used to interpret the ideograph, but the ideograph itself does not represent any precise wording. However, the sign that reads "No Smoking" is an alphabetic representation of two English words. It is a precise transcription of the spoken language, and you must be able to understand English or read it in order to know what it says.

It is obvious that ideographs are useful, but quite limited in their usefulness. The advantages of alphabetic writing were immediately understood by the ancients. Since human beings use language as their means of communication and thought, a method whereby speech could be accurately put down on paper provided the ancients with a means whereby abstract thought could be captured, concretized and thereby further worked over, refined, and expanded. Accuracy became the name of the game as shades of meaning could be developed as never before. As John Taylor Gatto writes in *The Exhausted School*:

> There are more synonyms for the concept of deceit in the English language than for any other single idea: . . . intimidate, deceive, contrive, fake, sham, pretend, flimflam, misrepresent, dupe, hype, trick, humbug, bluff, gammon, rook, cozen, gull, and so on.[1]

Which illustrates the power, scope, and inexhaustible possibilities of alphabetic writing — the fact that all of these subtle differences of meaning can be written down, articulated and understood.

The new alphabetic writing system replaced all of the ideographic systems being used in the West and became the greatest boon to intellectual and spiritual advancement that civilization has ever known. It was so simple that even children could learn to read. In fact, we have an excellent record of how reading was taught in ancient Rome. In a little book entitled *The Education of Children at Rome* by George Clarke, published in 1896,[2] we read:

In the elementary school . . . instruction was confined to reading, writing, and arithmetic. . . . The general term for the instruction given in the elementary school was litterae. For the methods employed in teaching reading and writing we are dependent chiefly on Quintilian, who treats the subject at considerable length and with his usual good judgment, in the first chapter of his book.

In teaching to read the first step was to obtain familiarity with the forms and sounds of the letters. It was a practice in Quintilian's time, of which he did not approve, to teach the names and order of the letters before their forms. The senses of sight and hearing ought to work side by side. The method of learning the names and order first, in Quintilian's opinion, prevents the pupil from recognizing a letter when he sees it, as he does not give attention to its shape, but depends on his memory of the sequence. For this reason, he says, when teachers think the letters have been sufficiently imprinted on the mind in their usual sequence, they reverse the order and pick the letters out promiscuously until the pupil recognizes them from their shape and not from their position. "Moreover," he adds, "I do not disapprove of the familiar practice of seeking to stimulate children to learn by giving them ivory letters to play with, or if anything else can be invented in which they will take more pleasure, and which it will delight them to handle, look at, and call by its name." Tiles, on which alphabets or verses were scratched before baking, were used in the youngest classes. Horace speaks of children being coaxed to learn their letters by tid-bits of pastry. . . .

Apparently, children were taught to recite the alphabet by heart before they actually saw the letters and could identify them by name. Ancient Rome did not have cereal boxes, milk cartons, newspapers and magazines which children could see all around them. Nevertheless, Quintilian recommended that the children look at the letters as they were learning the alphabet. Today, we call that kind of learning "multisensory," sight and sound working together. Mr. Clarke continues:

The letters having been thoroughly learned, the next step was to master their various combinations into syllables. From Quintilian's remark that the custom of learning the sounds before the forms, which was injurious in the case of letters, was not so in the case of syllables, it would seem that it was usual to give pupils successive combinations such as *ba, be, bi*, etc., *ca, ce, ci*, etc., to spell and repeat until they had memorized them, and then to proceed to more difficult ones. Every possible combination had to be thoroughly mastered (syllabis nullum compendium est, perdiscendae omnes) before the child was permitted to read words. "It is a bad plan, though a common one, to let him postpone the most difficult syllables, so that when he has to write words he will be at a loss. Much trust must not too readily be placed in the first act of memorizing; constant and long-continued repetition will be necessary. In reading there must not be too much haste about connecting syllables into words, or about reading fast, until the pupil can form the combinations of letters in syllables without stumbling or hesitation, or at any rate without having to stop to think about it. Then he may begin to form words from syllables and continuous sentences from words. It is incredible how much delay is caused in reading by undue haste. It gives rise to hesitation, interruptions, and repetitions when pupils attempt more than they are equal to, and when, going wrong, they lose confidence even in what they already know. Reading should first of all be sure, then continuous; it must for a long time be slow, until by practice speed and accuracy are acquired."

The same author suggests that at this stage pupils should have their memories trained by learning by heart the sayings of wise men and chosen passages from the poets (the latter being more agreeable to children), by way of amusement. The memory, he says, is almost the only faculty in children of this age (when they are incapable of originating anything) which can be improved by the teacher's care. He recommends as a means for rendering the organs of speech more perfect and the pronunciation more distinct, that pupils should be required to repeat as rapidly as possble words and verses of intentional difficulty, composed of many syllables harshly combined together. Without such practice as this he thinks that faults of pronunciation will become hardened and incurable. In reading poetry due attention was paid to metre and accent.

The characteristic feature of the Roman method of teaching to read, as above described, was a painstaking diligence, and a determination to lay once and for all a solid foundation for the educational superstructure. A thorough knowledge of the phonetic value of each letter and of each simple combination of letters was insisted on before reading was attempted; so that the pupil might be able without difficulty to read even words which he had never seen or heard before.

The texts used for reading lessons were generally the works of the poets. "The poets," says Horace, "shape the tender stammering lips of childhood." . . . The favourite poets were Livius Andronicus, whose translation of Homer was commonly used as a school text-book, and in later times Vergil and Horace. The works of Terence, Cato the Elder, and the "sentences" of Publilius Syrus were also used, and passages were chosen from them to be learned by heart.

Thus, the Romans used intensive, systematic phonics to teach children to read. The method was characterized by "painstaking diligence" in which "a thorough knowledge of the phonetic value of each letter and of each simple combination of letters was insisted on before reading was attempted." This was the method used throughout the Western world to achieve the highest literacy of any civilization in history, and this is the method which is now virtually banned in the government schools of the English-speaking world.

The Romans understood that "constant and long-continued repetition" was necessary so that the child would develop an automatic association between letters and sounds and not have "to stop to think about it." The goal was to lay a solid foundation of reading skill on which the educational superstructure could be built. "Reading should first of all be sure, then continuous; it must for a long time be slow, until by practice speed and accuracy are acquired." Our whole-language advocates tell us that "accuracy is not the name of the game." Guessing is. The foundation they are providing the children is one of sand.

5. The Origin of Look-Say

The look-say method — also known as the sight or whole-word method — was invented back in the 1830s by the Rev. Thomas H. Gallaudet, the director of the American Asylum at Hartford for the Education of the Deaf and Dumb. He had been using a sight, or whole-word method in teaching the deaf to read, by juxtaposing a word, such as *cat,* with the picture of a cat. And because the deaf were able to identify many simple words in this way, Gallaudet thought that the method could be adapted for use by normal children.

Gallaudet, who believed that education was a science and could be improved by scientific experimentation, gave a detailed description of his new method in the *American Annals of Education* of August 1830. It consisted of teaching the child to recognize a total of fifty sight words written on cards "without any reference to the individual letters which compose the word." After the child had memorized the words on the basis of their configurations alone, the letters of each word were taught. The final step was to teach the letters in alphabetical order.

In 1836 Gallaudet published *The Mother's Primer*, based on his look-say methodology. Its first line was: "Frank had a dog; his name was Spot." In 1837 the primer was adopted by the Boston Primary School Committee. Horace Mann was then Secretary of the Board of Education of Massachusetts, and he favored the new method. The educational reformers of the time were against anything that smacked of old orthodox practices, and they considered intensive, systematic phonics to be one of them. The *American Annals of Education,* representing the progressive views of the time, provided a ready platform for the critics of the alphabetic-phonics method. One could find such opinions as the following in its pages:

> He [the child] should read his lessons as if the words were Chinese symbols, without paying any attention to the individual letters, but with special regard to the meaning.... This method needs neither recommendation nor defense, with those who have tried it: and were it adopted, we should soon get rid of the stupid and uninteresting mode now prevalent. (Oct. 1832, p. 479)

> If it is true, that so long as we cling with intense fondness to the deformities of our orthography — with a fondness like the mother's love to her offspring, enhanced by deformity — much time is, and must be, wasted over the elementary books of reading and spelling. It becomes the friends of education to examine the facts, and act with energy, as men living in an age of reform. (Apr. 1832, p. 173)

> The ABC is our initiative tormentor, requiring much time and herculean effort, altogether thrown away. (Nov. 1833, p. 512)

Such was the climate of the time. Gallaudet's primer was imitated by other textbook writers, and the children of Boston were taught to read by this new sight method. By 1844 the defects of the new method were so apparent to the Boston schoolmasters, that they issued a blistering attack against it entitled "Modes of Teaching

Children to Read," and urged a return to intensive, systematic phonics.[1] They were particularly careful in explaining to the public the difference between an alphabetic writing system and an ideographic one and why the former was superior to the latter. They wrote:

> The grand and distinctive feature of this invention [the alphabet] is, that it establishes a connection between the written and the audible signs of our ideas. It throws, as it were, a bridge across the otherwise impassable gulf which must ever have separated the one from the other. The hieroglyphics and symbols of the ancients, performed but one function. To those who, by a purely arbitrary association, were able to pass from the sign to the thing signified, they were representatives of ideas — and ideas *merely;* hence they are called ideographic characters, and that mode of writing has been denominated the *symbolic,* and is exemplified in the Chinese language. (p. 322)
>
> On the other hand, words written with alphabetic characters perform two functions. Taken as whole pictures, they, like Chinese characters, represent ideas; but taken as composed of alphabetic elements which represent simple sounds, they conduct us directly to the audible sign which, in the case of common words, we have from childhood been accustomed to associate with the thing signified. Owing to the last office which these words perform, namely, that of representing sounds, this mode of writing is called the *phonetic.* It has been said with truth, that "the art of writing, especially when reduced to simple phonetic alphabets like ours, has, perhaps, done more than any other invention for the improvement of the human race." If any one wishes still further to be convinced of the difference between the two, let him compare the figure 5 , which is purely a symbol, with the written word five; the one gives no idea whatever of the spoken word, whereas the other conducts us directly to it. Here the contrast is too striking to be misapprehended. A person may read Chinese, without knowing a single sound of the language, simply because Chinese characters never were intended to represent sounds.
>
> The new system of teaching reading, abandons entirely this distinctive feature of the phonetic mode of writing, and our words are treated as though they were capable of performing but one function, that of representing ideas. The language, although written with alphabetic characters, becomes, to all intents and purposes, a symbolic language. Now we say, as ours is

designedly a phonetic language, no system of teaching ought to meet with public favor, that strips it of its principal power. (p. 323)

The Boston schoolmasters also explained how and why imposing an ideographic teaching technique on an alphabetic writing system created learning problems, and they listed them as follows (pp. 334-335):

1st. — Teaching whole words according to the new plan, to any extent whatever, gives the child no facility for learning new ones. Every word must be taken upon authority, until the alphabet is learned.

2d. — Since the alphabet must, at some period, be acquired, with all its imperfections, it is but a poor relief, to compel a child, at first, to associate seven hundred different, arbitrary forms with the ideas they represent, and then to learn the alphabet itself. . . .

3d. — Another objection to converting our language into Chinese, arises from the change which must inevitably take place in the modes of associating the printed word with the idea which it represents, when the child is taught to regard words as composed of elements. Children, at first, learn to recognise the word, by the new method, as a single picture, not as composed of parts; and for aught we know, they begin in the middle of it and examine each way. It is not probable that they proceed invariably from left to right, as in the old mode. However that may be, an entire change must take place when they begin to learn words, as composed of letters. . . . It is of this change we complain. All will acknowledge the importance of forming in the child, correct habits of association, such as will not need revolutionizing at a subsequent period in life. . . . In pursuing any study or art, it is of the greatest importance to have the first movements, whether of the eye, the hand, or the tongue, right. The end will be soonest obtained to submit to any delay that exactness may require.

4th.—The new system fails to accomplish the object which it proposes. The main design of this mode of teaching seems to be, to escape the ambiguity arising from the variety of sounds which attach to some of the letters, as well as from the variety of forms by which the same sounds may be represented. The defenders of this system seem to forget, since these anomalies are elementary, that they must be carried into the formation of words. . . .

5th. — It introduces confusion into the different grades of schools.

The elements must be taught somewhere. If neglected in the primary schools, they must be taught in the grammar schools. And thus the order of things is reversed, and disarrangement introduced into the whole school system. . . .

     6th. — It cherishes and perpetuates a defective enunciation. Children so universallly come to the school-room, especially from uneducated families, with habits of incorrect articulation, that the efforts of the teacher, at an early period, should be directed towards the correction of these habits. The only sure way to accomplish this, is to drill the pupils on the elements of sound. . . . A defect in the enunciation of the elements, is a radical one, and the new system is directly calculated to perpetuate it. If there was no other argument against the system, this, of itself, would be sufficient to show its utter futility.

All of the arguments given by the Boston schoomasters in 1844 are just as relevant today. Of course, the whole-language advocates will argue that that was then and that things are different now. Kids *enjoy* whole language, and that's what really counts! But the schoolmasters of 1844 even had an answer for that. They wrote:

The grand mistake lies in the rank assigned to pleasure. To gratify the child, should not be the teacher's aim, but rather to lay a permanent foundation, on which to rear a noble and well-proportioned superstructure. If, while doing this, the teacher is successful in rendering mental exertion agreeable, and in leading the child from one conquest to another, till achievement itself affords delight, it is well; such pleasure stimulates to greater exertion. But if, to cultivate pleasure-seeking is his aim, he had better, at once, abandon his profession, and obtain an employment in which he will not endanger the welfare, both of individuals and society, by sending forth a sickly race, palsied in every limb, through idleness, and a vain attempt to gratify a morbid thirst for pleasure. . . . (p. 339)

     Nothing has been more productive of mischief, or more subversive of real happiness, than mistaking what may afford the child present gratification, for that which will secure for him lasting good. (p. 338)

It is interesting to note that both the ancient Romans and the Boston schoolmasters of 1844 understood the purpose of primary education: to the provide the child with a sound foundation on which to build the intellectual superstructure.

The experiment with the whole-word method was short-lived in Boston, but the methodology itself was preserved in the newly created state-owned normal schools where future teachers were to be trained for the public schools. Although the look-say method was used here and there, phonics remained the preferred means of teaching children to read until the turn of the century when the Progressives came on the scene with their new ideas.

Who were the Progressives? They were a new breed of educator, members of the Protestant academic elite, who no longer believed in the religion of their fathers. They rejected the Bible and put their new faith in science, evolution and psychology. Science provided the means to know the material world. Evolution explained the origin of man, thus relegating the story of Genesis to mythology, and psychology institutionalized the scientific study of human nature and provided the scientific means to control human behavior.

Many of these progressives studied in Leipzig, Germany, under Prof. Wilhelm Wundt, the father of experimental psychology. Among the most noteworthy were G. Stanley Hall, John Dewey's future teacher at Johns Hopkins who later became president of Clark University; James McKeen Cattell, whose response-time experiments formed the "scientific" basis for the revival of the look-say method;[2] Charles Judd, who became head of the University of Chicago's school of education, where his protégé, William Scott Gray, developed the Dick and Jane look-say basal reading program; and James Earl Russell, who became president of Teachers College, Columbia University.

These men brought back to America Wundt's teachings and methodology and set up psych labs of their own in American universities. In these labs man was to be studied scientifically as one would study any other animal. But since human beings could not be experimented on in labs, the psychologists used animals. In 1928, Prof. Edward L. Thorndike, head of educational psychology at Teachers College, wrote: ". . . experiments on learning in the lower animals have probably contributed more to knowledge of education, per hour or per unit of intellect spent, than experiments on children." [3] He also wrote: "The best way with children may often be, in the pompous words of an animal trainer, 'to arrange everything in connection with the trick so that the animal will be compelled by the laws of his own nature to perform it.'" [4]

Out of this methodology emerged behavioral psychology. In distinguishing behaviorism from earlier introspective psychologies, John B. Watson wrote that the behavioral psychologist "must describe the behavior of man in no other terms than those you would use in describing the behavior of the ox you slaughter." [5]

Thus, the behavioral psychologist studies only what can be seen and measured in human behavior. Watson wrote: "Behaviorism claims that consciousness is neither a definite nor a usable concept. The behaviorist . . . holds, further, that belief in the existence of consciousness goes back to the ancient days of superstition and magic."

The new teaching techniques of the progressive-behaviorist curriculum were based on the principles of animal training. For example, in the field of reading instruction, Prof. Walter Dearborn, a protégé of James McKeen Cattell, who later joined Harvard University, described the look-say method of teaching reading as follows (*School & Society,* 10/19/40):

> The principle which we have used to explain the acquisition of a sight vocabulary is, of course, the one suggested by Pavlov's well-known experiments on the conditioned response. This is as it should be. The basic process involved in conditioning and in learning to read is the same. [6]

The progressives were also socialists. Why? Because, as

atheists, they were convinced that socialism offered the only salvation from evil. To them, the causes of evil were societal: ignorance, poverty, and social injustice. As evolutionists they rejected such Biblical concepts as sin, innate depravity, or the fall of man. They attributed the causes of social injustice to capitalism, individualism and religion and were determined to replace them with socialism, collectivism and atheism, or humanism. They were motivated by the need to prove to themselves and the world that they were right and the Bible was wrong. They were convinced that once socialism had been achieved, crime would disappear and the natural goodness of man would flourish, bringing about the utopian society they were certain could be attained.

6. The Role of John Dewey

Undoubtedly, the one man most responsible for the revival of the look-say method was none other than John Dewey, the leading philosopher of the progressive education movement. Unlike many of his colleagues, Dewey did not study at Leipzig. He was introduced to the new psychology by G. Stanley Hall, his professor at Johns Hopkins University. From there, in 1884, Dewey went to the University of Michigan where he became an instructor in the philosophy department.

In 1887, Dewey published his textbook, *Psychology,* in which he advocated the use of psychological techniques in the classroom. He believed that: ". . . education is growth under favorable conditions; the school is the place where those conditions should be regulated scientifically." [1]

In 1894, Dewey joined the faculty at the University of Chicago as Chairman of the Department of Philosophy, Psychology, and Pedagogy. The university, endowed by John D. Rockefeller, had been founded in 1890. It was as head of the department of pedagogy that Dewey began to concentrate on education as the means of bringing about socialism in America. Dewey and his progressive colleagues knew that Americans were not about to give up their private property, the free-enterprise system, their individuality, or their religion for a new socialist society. They realized that if socialism was to be achieved, it would have to be through the education of the young who would reject the values of individualism and religion and create a socialist, collectivist utopia.

But what kind of curriculum would do the job? The situation at Chicago afforded Dewey the opportunity to put his educational ideas into practice by creating an experimental school. The school would serve as a laboratory for psychology and pedagogy in the same manner that labs were used for experiments in the physical sciences. In fact, it came to be known as the Laboratory School.

The purpose of the school was to find out what kind of curriculum was needed to produce the socialized individual who would turn America into a socialist society. The question for the radical educator was how to socialize children so that they would become the kind of selfless egalitarians who would eagerly serve "humanity" as represented by the socialist state.

Dewey decided that the best way to achieve this new collectivist personality was to turn the classroom into a place where these desirable social traits could be developed. We read in *The Dewey School*:

> Since the integration of the individual and the social is impossible except when the individual lives in close association with others in the constant free give and take of experiences, it seemed that education could prepare the young for the future social life only when the school was itself a cooperative society on a small scale.[2]

What kind of curriculum would fit the school that was a mini-cooperative society? Dewey's recommendation was indeed radical: build the curriculum not around academic subjects but around occupational activities which provided maximum opportunities for peer interaction and socialization. Since the beginning of Western civilization, the school curriculum had been centered around the development of academic skills, the intellectual faculties, and high literacy. Dewey wanted to change all of that. Why? Because high literacy produced that abominable form of independent intelligence which was basically, as Dewey believed, anti-social.

Thus, from Dewey's point of view, the school's primary commitment to literacy was indeed the key to the whole problem. In 1898, Dewey wrote an essay, "The Primary-Education Fetich," in which he explained exactly what he meant:

> There is . . . a false educational god whose idolators are legion, and whose cult influences the entire educational system. This is language study — the study not of foreign language, but of English; not in higher, but in primary education. It is almost an unquestioned assumption, of educational theory and practice both, that the first three years of a child's school-life shall be mainly taken up with learning to read and write his own language. If we add to this the learning of a certain amount of numerical combinations, we have the pivot about which primary education swings. . . .
>
> It does not follow, however, that because this course was once wise it is so any longer. . . . My proposition is, that conditions — social, industrial, and intellectual — have undergone such a radical change, that the time has come for a thoroughgoing examination of the emphasis put upon linguistic work in elementary instruction. . . .
>
> The plea for the predominance of learning to read in early school life because of the great importance attaching to literature seems to me a perversion.[3]

Dewey then argued how important it was for the child to experience life through classroom activities, projects and social interaction before learning to read about them. And the reading materials themselves had to be relevant to the child's needs. He wrote:

Every respectable authority insists that the period of childhood, lying between the years of four and eight or nine, is the plastic period in sense and emotional life. What are we doing to shape these capacities? What are we doing to feed this hunger? If one compares the powers and needs of the child in these directions with what is actually supplied in the regimen of the three R's, the contrast is pitiful and tragic.... No one can clearly set before himself the vivacity and persistency of the child's motor instincts at this period, and then call to mind the continued grind of reading and writing, without feeling that the justification of our present curriculum is psychologically impossible. It is simply superstition: it is a remnant of an outgrown period of history.

Finally, Dewey, the master strategist, set forth what must be done:

Change must come gradually. To force it unduly would compromise its final success by favoring a violent reaction. What is needed in the first place, is that there should be a full and frank statement of conviction with regard to the matter from physiologists and psychologists and from those school administrators who are conscious of the evils of the present *régime*. ... There are already in existence a considerable number of educational "experiment stations," which represent the outposts of educational progress. If these schools can be adequately supported for a number of years they will perform a great vicarious service. After such schools have worked out carefully and definitely the subject-matter of a new curriculum, — finding the right place for language-studies and placing them in their right perspective, — the problem of the more general educational reform will be immensely simplified and facilitated.

Here was, indeed, a master plan, involving the entire progressive education community, to create a new socialist curriculum for the schools of America, a plan, based on the new psychology, that was indeed carried out and implemented. It was a plan that denigrated the intellect of the child in favor of his motor development. And this became the typical bias of the behavioral psychologist who denied consciousness in favor of what could be seen and measured.

Yet, what is the most obvious and breathtaking development in every child? It is his or her ability to learn to speak, the distinctive characteristic which made the human child different from the offspring of other species. Every child is, by virtue of his nature as a human being, a dynamo of language learning, and the traditional primary curriculum took advantage of that language-learning energy in favor of literacy. Psychologists like Edward L. Thorndike, who thought they could learn more about how children learned by studying animals than human children, were quick to agree with Dewey on emphasizing the motor instincts of children over their verbal instincts.

In 1899, Dewey published *The School and Society,* his blueprint for socialism via education based on his experiments at the Laboratory School.[4] It clearly established him as the leader of progressive education. In 1904 he left Chicago and joined the faculty at Columbia University and Teachers College in New York. There, working with James McKeen Cattell, Edward L. Thorndike, and James Earl Russell, he grew in stature as the moral interpreter of American progressivism.

And finally it should be noted that Dewey did not get his notion of socialism from Karl Marx. He got it from an American, Edward Bellamy, a Unitarian journalist, who wrote a book entitled *Looking Backward,* a futuristic fantasy about a socialist America in the year 2000.[5] Bellamy's book was published in 1888 and is considered one of the most socially influential books in American history.

7. Who Was Huey?

One of the key recommendations made by Dewey to help promote primary curriculum reform was "a full and frank statement of conviction with regard to the matter from physiologists and psychologists" that would give the reform movement a scientific sanction and authority. This was necessary if teachers and principals were to be convinced that what was being asked of them was educationally sound. Only a book advocating a radical change in reading instruction by a bona-fide psychologist would carry the weight of scientific authority. Such a book was indeed written and published in 1908 with the title, *The Psychology and Pedagogy of Reading*.[1] The author was a psychologist by the name of Edmund Burke Huey.

Who was Huey? He was born in Curllsville, Pennsylvania, in 1870, got an A.B. at Lafayette College, Cattell's alma mater, then went to Clark University where he studied psychology with G. Stanley Hall and did his Ph.D. dissertation on the psychology and physiology of reading. In 1899 he took a position as professor of psychology at the State Normal School in Moorhead, Minnesota, but left there to spend the years 1901 and 1902 in Europe where he visited psychologists in Germany and France.

On his return from Europe, Huey taught genetic psychology for a year at a Normal School in Miami, Ohio, spent another year at Clark as an assistant and honorary fellow in psychology and, in 1904, took a position as professor of psychology at the University of Western Pennsyslvania. There, he set up a psych lab, continued his experimental studies in the psychology of reading and wrote his now famous book which was published in 1908.

The significance of the book is that it signalled the takeover of the primary school curriculum by the psychologists who then proceeded to "scientifically" analyze the three R's and reshape them in accordance with psychological beliefs. Even though these beliefs contradicted hundreds of years of teaching experience, the psychologists were convinced that their experimental methods made all of that experience obsolete.

Huey's book did everything that Dewey believed was necessary to get the educators to accept psychology's authority as the arbiter of what was to be taught in the primary schools and how it was to be taught. Huey was very much aware of his important task. In fact, he wrote (p. 301):

> A survey of the views of some of our foremost and soundest educators reveals the fact that the men of our time who are most competent to judge are profoundly dissatisfied with reading as it is now carried on in the elementary school. . . .The immense amount of *time* given to the purely formal use of printed and written English has been a prime source of irritation. It seems a great waste to devote, as at present, the main part of a number of school years to the mere mechanics of reading and spelling.

The task was to shift the emphasis in primary education from the teaching of basic academic skills to having the children develop motor skills in socially agreeable activities. Huey continued (p. 303):

Besides, as child nature is being systematically studied, the feeling grows that these golden years of childhood, like the Golden Age of our race, belong naturally to quite other subjects and performances than reading, and to quite other objects than books; and that reading is a "Fetich of Primary Education" which only holds its place by the power of tradition and the stifling of questions asked concerning it. It is believed that much that is now strenuously struggled for and methodized over in these early years of primary reading will come of themselves with *growth*, and when the child's sense organs and nervous system are stronger; and that in the meantime he should be acquiring own experiences and developing wants that will in time make reading a natural demand and a meaningful process, with form and book always secondary to own thought.

Such views take form in assertions that reading, except at least as an exercise entirely incidental to other activities and interests, should usually be deferred until the age of eight, or as some put it, until the age of nine or ten. Such expression have been made by many representative educators and scientists, among whom I may mention especially President Hall and Professor Burnham of Clark University, Professor Dewey of Columbia University, Professor Patrick of the University of Iowa, and Professor Mosso, the world's greatest specialist on Fatigue. . . .

In an article on "The Primary Education Fetich" in the *Forum,* Vol. XXV, [Dewey] gives his reasons for such a conclusion. While the fetich of Greek is passing, there remains, he says, the fetich of English, that the first three years of school are to be given largely to reading and a little number work. This traditional place was given to reading in an early century, when the child had not the present environment of art gallery, music, and industrial development, but when reading was the main means of rising and was the only key to culture. Reading has maintained this traditional place in the face of changed social, industrial, and intellectual conditions which make the problem wholly different.

Huey's reference to the "Golden Age of the race," the preliterate period in human evolution, can hardly be called golden. The idea that prehistoric man lived in a kind of idyllic, preliterate paradise is based on fantasy alone. Also, the use of the word "fetich" by Dewey in regard to the emphasis on reading in primary education indicates a deeper understanding of the connection between literacy and religion. Judaism and Christianity, both of which are based on the Bible, require high literacy.

There is a very close connection between the invention of the alphabet and the appearance of the Holy Scripture. Man had to wait until the alphabet was invented before the prophets could transcribe the word of God accurately and precisely on paper. In fact, in the Gospel according to St. John, we read: "In the beginning was the Word, and the Word was with God, and the Word was God." Thus, Christian civilization required a sense of precision and accuracy in reading if Christianity were to be passed from one generation to the next.

The dictionary definition of "fetich" (also spelled "fetish") is: "an object selected temporarily for worship, as a tree, stone, etc.; any object believed by superstitious people to have magical power; any thing or activity to which one is irrationally devoted."

Dewey and his colleagues had rejected the religion of their fathers and had become humanists, putting their faith in science, evolution and psychology. To them the Bible was mythology and religion was superstition. Obviously, Huey shared their views. He continued (p. 305):

> Against using the period from six to eight years for learning to read and write, Professor Dewey accepts the opinion of physiologists that the sense-organs and nervous system are not adapted then to such confining work, that such work violates the principle of exercising the fundamental before the accessory, that the cramped positions leave their mark, that writing to ruled line forms is wrong, etc. Besides, he finds that a certain mental enfeeblement comes from too early an appeal to interest in the abstractions of reading.
>
> Again, Professor Dewey believes that the prevalent methods of teaching reading are such as cultivate wrong habits and attitudes concerning books. One can pick out the children who learned to read at home. They read naturally. One cannot read naturally when he reads for reading's sake.

The argument that children of six are too young or immature to learn to read not only contradicts experience but contradicts psychology itself. Between the ages of two and eight the child is a marvel at language learning. His mind is developing at a rate that will never be duplicated in later years. His ability to deal with abstract symbols is attested to by his ability to handle language itself, which is nothing but a highly organized system of sound symbols. In addition, this writer, author of a phonics-based reading program, knows from personal experience that children of that age, and even younger, are quite capable of learning to read and enjoying it, provided they are taught in the proper manner.

As far as we know, neither Dewey nor Huey had ever taught a child to read. But Huey's recommendation that children be taught to read at home before going to school is laudable, provided, of course, that the parents use the proper methods. Huey continued (p. 306):

> Reading must be postponed. The child is motor at the period when we teach him to read, and must not do this passive thing so much. . . . However, Professor Dewey thinks that suddenly "throwing out" the language work from the early grades would be a mistake. Present educational ways must be a compromise. The schools generally cannot completely change until experiment schools, now on the frontier, work out best ways. The hope of the educational world is for such work from experiment schools.

Dewey had warned that "change must come gradually," or else the public would react violently against such radical reforms. Huey also strongly advocated using a whole-word methodology in beginning reading. He wrote (p. 337):

> The child has not at this stage developed the logical and ideational habits that most printed language demands, any more than had primitive man when he used pictographs and gestures. Let the child linger then in the oral stage, and let him use the primitive means of expression and communication as he likes to do; this at least until we have developed a body of genuine child-reading matter. . . .

The history of the languages in which picture-writing was long the main means of written communication has here a wealth of suggestion for the framers of the new primary course. It is not from mere perversity that the boy chalks or carves his records on book and desk and walls and school fences, nor from chance that a picture-book is of all-absorbing interest. There is here a correspondence with, if not a direct recapitulation of, the life of the race; and we owe it to the child to encourage his living through the best there is in this pictograph stage as a means both of expression and impression, before we pass on to the race's later acquirements of written speech and phonic analysis. (pp. 338-39)

What an absurd argument for teaching children to read English words as if they were pictographs. We don't have young adults first learn to drive a Roman chariot before they learn to drive a car! Huey also argued: (pp. 348-49)

It is not indeed necessary that the child should be able to pronounce correctly or pronounce at all, at first, the new words that appear in his reading, any more than that he should spell or write all the new words that he hears spoken. If he grasps, approximately, the total meaning of the sentence in which the new word stands, he has read the sentence. Usually this total meaning will suggest what to call the new word, and the word's current articulation will usually have been learned in conversation, if the proper amount of oral practice shall have preceded reading. And even if the child substitutes words of his own for some that are on the page, provided that these express the meaning, it is an encouraging sign that the reading has been real, and recognition of details will come as it is needed. The shock that such a statement will give to many a practical teacher of reading is but an accurate measure of the hold that a false ideal has taken of us, viz., that to read is to say just what is upon the page, instead of to *think*, each in his own way, the meaning that the page suggests....

Until the insidious thought of reading as word-pronouncing is well worked out of our heads, it is well to place the emphasis strongly where it belongs, on reading as *thought-getting* independently of expression. (p. 350)

Who can deny that our present-day whole-language educators

are doing exactly as Huey prescribed back in 1908? But Huey had no idea how all of this would turn out. He died in 1913 at the age of 43, not living long enough to see what enormous harm these teaching methods would cause in the decades ahead. Nevertheless, his book became the enduring authority on reading pedagogy even though he himself, as far as we know, had never taught a child to read.

8. Did They Know It Didn't Work?

One of the most important educators of the time was G. Stanley Hall — the first of the new breed of psycho-educator. Hall, born on a farm in Massachusetts in 1846, graduated from Williams College in 1867, attended the Union Theological Seminary, then spent the years 1868 and '69 in Germany studying physiology and psychology. Hall returned to the U.S. in 1871, taught at Antioch College, then at Harvard. In 1876 he returned to Germany where he studied under Wilhelm Wundt in Leipzig. Wundt, of course, was the father of experimental psychology, and his laboratory was the first of its kind ever set up. Concerning his experience in Germany, Hall later wrote in his autobiography:

> Germany almost remade me. . . . I came home feeling that I had also attained maturity in my religious consciousness, where most suffer such dwarfing arrest. I had felt the charm of pantheism . . . , of agnosticism; of even materialism; had wrestled with Karl Marx and half accepted what I understood of him; thought Comte and the Positivists had pretty much made out their case. . . . But the only whole-hearted scheme of things which I had accepted with ardor and abandon was that of an evolution which applied no whit less to the soul than the body of man. This was bedrock.

> Darwin, Haeckel, and especially Herbert Spencer seemed then to me to represent the most advanced stage of human thought. . . . It is no wonder that this was the period of my life when the youthful spirit of revolt was most intense. The narrow, inflexible orthodoxy, the settled lifeless mores, the Puritan eviction of the joy that comes from amusements from life . . . . I fairly loathed and hated so much that I saw about me that I now realize more clearly than ever how possible it would have been for me to have drifted into some, perhaps almost any, camp of radicals. . . . It was most fortunate that these deeply stirred instincts of revolt were never openly expressed and my rank heresies and socialistic leanings unknown.[1]

Hall returned to Harvard in 1878 where he studied for his Ph.D. in psychology under William James. But when he finally got his Ph.D. he wasn't quite sure what to do with it. He wrote in his autobiography, "I finally decided that neither psychology nor philosophy would ever make bread and that the most promising line of work would be to study the applications of psychology to education."

In 1882 Hall established America's first experimental psych lab at Johns Hopkins University. Among his students were John Dewey and James McKeen Cattell who were to join him in later years in applying psychology to education. Hall was also the father of the Child Study movement in which psychology was applied to child development. In 1889 Hall became president of the newly created Clark University in Worcester, Massachusetts, where, in 1899, Edmund Burke Huey got his Ph.D. in the psychology of reading. Concerning Huey's book and the teaching of reading, Hall wrote:

> The best pedagogues are now drifting surely, if slowly, toward the conclusion that instead of taking half the time of the first year or two of school to teach reading, little attention should be paid to it before the beginning of the third year, that nature study, language work, and other things should take the great time and energy now given to this subject. . . . We can agree with Huey that the home is the natural place for a child's

learning to read, and intelligent children of intelligent parents, will almost do so of themselves sooner or later. Primary reading should no longer be made a fetich.[2]

The Dewey essay of 1898 had certainly made its impact on Hall! As for teaching methods, Hall was inclined to rely on the findings of his colleagues in their psych labs. He himself had never taught a child to read. He wrote:

> This is not the place to analyse in detail the many psycho-physic processes involved in the act of reading, which in recent years has been made the subject of manifold and fruitful investigations, but we must briefly résumé the pedagogical results of this work, which have established a number of approximate norms and given such a wealth of educational suggestions despite the fact that but relatively few of these studies have been made upon children. . . .
>
> Nearly all reading methods now start from the word and sentence rather than from the letter, and these are more often chosen for their form value than for their thought value. Becker shows that words are first recognized as wholes from their gross forms rather than from the letters that compose them, and Messmer showed that in the tachistoscope long words may be recognized as rapidly as short ones, but that they tend to be analysed into small groups of letters. Cattell and Sanford showed that certain letters and combinations in ordinary small type are recognized far easier than others, and there are many indications that the consonants are more important than vowels for recognition.

These experiments in word recognition by Cattell and others are often cited as the "scientific" basis for the whole-word method. If readers can recognize whole words as quickly as they recognize individual letters, why not teach children to read by showing them whole words only and having them memorize them by their configurations alone? But what the experimenters failed to understand is that there is a big difference between how experienced adult readers look at words and how children, learning to read, look at words.

The first study on how children actually learn a "sight vocabulary" was conducted in 1912 by a teacher at the elementary school at the University of Chicago. Walter F. Dearborn, a pupil of Cattell's who later became head of educational psychology at Harvard, wrote about the study in a paper commemorating Cattell's work.[3] He wrote:

> In the first study ["Learning to Read," Josephine Horton Bowden, *Elem. Sch. Teacher*, Vol. 12] the pupils, who had had no instruction in reading, were taught by a word method without the use of phonics and the problem was to determine by what means the children actually recognized and differentiated words when left to their own devices. The following quotation indicates the methods employed by the experimenter: "First, incidents; for example, one day when the child was given the cards to read from, it was observed that she read with equal ease whether the card was right side up or upside down. This incident suggested a test which was later given. Second, comments of the child; for example, when she was asked to find in the context the word 'shoes,' she said that 'dress' looked so much like 'shoes' that she was afraid she would make a mistake. Third, questioning; for example, she had trouble to distinguish between 'sing' and 'song.' When she had mastered the words she was asked how she knew which was which. Her reply was, 'by the looks.' When questioned further she put her finger on the 'i' and the 'o.' These three types of evidence correspond to introspection with the adult. The fourth type of evidence is a comparison of the words learned with the words not learned as to the parts of speech, geometric form, internal form, and length. Fifth, misreadings; for example, 'dogs' was read 'twigs,' and 'feathers,' 'fur.' Sixth, mutilations; for example, 'dogs' was printed 'digs,' 'lilac' was written 'lalci.'"
>
> Some of the conclusions may be cited, first as regards the kind of words most easily learned on the basis of word forms. Four out of six children learned more "linear" words, i.e., words like "acorns," "saw," in which there are no high letters, than of any other group. In but one case were the "superlinear" words more easily recognized. This is contrary to the finding of Messmer on adults; the latter considered that the "linear" words are less easily recognized because the contour is unbroken.
>
> Misreadings or the mistaking of one word for another occurred most frequently in these early stages, first when the words were of the same

length (which again controverts Messmer's findings); secondly, when words had common letters, the "g" and "o" of "igloo" caused it to be read as "dogs"; thirdly, when the initial letters of words were the same; and fourthly, when the final letters were the same. Words were recognized upside down nearly as easily as right side up, but two children noticing any difference. The word seems to be recognized as a whole, and as the author notes, recognized upside down just as the child would recognize a toy upside down.

The general conclusions of the study may be quoted:

"The comments and the questions, as well as the misreadings, seem to show that children learn to read words by the trial and error method. It may be the length of the word, the initial letter, the final letter, a characteristic letter, the position of the word in the sentence, or even the blackness of the type that serves as the cue. There were surprisingly few instances of learning by imitation. The first occurred in the fifth week, when one child pointed out the word 'the' and two other children pointed out other 'the's,' though similar opportunities had been presented before. Suggestion, which is a noticeable element in the reading of young children, also played a minor part. There is no evidence in any of the cases studied that the child works out a system by which he learns to recognize the words. That he does not work out phonics for himself comes out quite clearly in the transposition test. Furthermore, only once did a child divide a word even into its syllables. There is some evidence that the child is conscious of the letter though there is none that he analyzes the word letter by letter, except in the case of "E," who so analyzed the word "six." Sometimes, when the child seemed to have made a letter analysis, he failed to recognize the word a second time, and in some cases did not learn it at all.

"Under the methods of instruction employed with this class as outlined above, it appears that these beginners in reading have after two months or more of instruction secured a sufficient concept of the general appearance of a very limited number of words to recognize them as wholes, that in doing this they made use of only very general cues or points of differentiation between words and have not noticed the finer points of distinction between words and parts of words. It appeared very doubtful to the experimenter whether, under this method of teaching words as visual wholes, the pupils would, of themselves, have come to make this latter necessary analysis with much success. Without some foregoing analysis and subsequent synthesis, the differences between words are not great enough to be recognized merely from the total visual appearance. The early introduction of phonics may supply, in some measure, this analysis. There is an undoubted advantage in having words presented at the start as units and wholes, as contrasted with the discarded teaching by letters. But that a word method can be used very long without some detailed analysis of the structure and parts of the words is altogether too common a notion in the theory if not in the practise of teaching."

Thus, even a teacher committed to the whole-word method had to admit that the method had serious shortcomings and that "the early introduction of phonics" was needed to provide the child with more than just configuration cues.

The significance of the study was in the fact that it revealed the inadequacies of the method which the progressives wanted to put in the schools. They were torn by their desire to de-emphasize literacy in the primary grades and their knowledge that phonics would still be needed, in spite of their new methods. G. Stanley Hall lashed out against phonics when he wrote in 1911:

Learning to read and write, however we look at it, is thus an almost purely mechanical product of drill, with almost nothing rational or even educational about it. Teaching it is a breaking-in process. Save historically (which is a far cry for children) there is no reason why one letter should represent a given sound any more than any other. A Morse code, numbers, pictures of the hand in making the deaf mute alphabet, or any other form of letter e.g., Arabic, a cypher would be no more and no less reasonable. Hence most time spent in explaining is lost and in fact usually worse than lost, for it is farfetched and adds to the confusion in the child's mind. *Per se*, too, it is anti-educational because it does not develop but constrains both sense and mentation. But for the content to be got at or imparted by mastering the process, the necessity of read-writing would be an almost unmitigated curse to the human race. It is a psycho-physiological absurdity.[4]

Hall even believed that illiteracy wasn't all that bad. He wrote:

Very many men have lived and died and been great, even the leaders of their age, without any acquaintance with letters. The knowledge which illiterates acquire is probably on the whole more personal, direct, environmental and probably a much larger proportion of it practical. Moreover, they escape much eye-strain and mental excitement, and, other things being equal, are probably more active and less sedentary. It is possible, despite the stigma our bepedagogued age puts upon this disability, for those who are under it not only to lead a useful, happy, virtuous life, but to be really well educated in many other ways. Illiterates escape certain temptations, such as vacuous and vicious reading. Perhaps we are prone to put too high a value both upon the ability required to attain this art and the discipline involved in doing so, as well as the culture value that comes to the citizen with his average of only six grades of schooling by the acquisition of this art.

This is the kind of thinking among the progressive leaders that set the stage for the curriculum reform that was to come in the years ahead. As the leader of the child-study movement, Hall's views were taken quite seriously. Yet, perhaps the key to the error the psychologists had made in their response-time experiments can be found in an observation Cattell made in his journal on February 13, 1885, while carrying out his experiments in Wundt's laboratory:

> I have found some interesting things — for example you can see the picture of a hat in less time than you can see the printed word "hat," *but it takes much longer to name the picture than the word.*" [5] [Our emphasis.]

Therein lies the key as to why the look-say, whole-word method is inferior to the phonetic method. Why? Because the printed word is the unambiguous representation of a specific spoken word, while the picture of the hat, very much like an ideograph, did not convey precisely how the hat was to be described. Should the response be "derby," "cap," "homburg," "beret," "Borsalino," "top hat," "turban," etc.? After all, there is no generic, universal hat in existence, only different kinds of hats. But the word "hat" is a generalization which the reader can immediately and unambiguously read if he or she has an automatic ability to decode letters into their spoken equivalents. But the child who substitutes "pony" for "horse" and is told by a whole-language teacher that this sort of inaccurate reading is okay is going to be very confused and frustrated in later life when faced with a situation in which accuracy in reading is imperative.

9. The Making of Whole-Language Ideology

Although the whole-word method has dominated primary reading instruction in America since the 1940s, the whole-language variety seems to be the more recent work of several reading establishment gurus who have developed the new methodology into a belief system approaching that of a religion. A guru, of course, in Hindu culture, is a personal spiritual leader and teacher whose every word is slavishly and uncritically absorbed by his followers. As a kind of religious dogma, whole language relieves teachers of the burden of having to think for themselves.

Yetta Goodman, wife of chief guru Kenneth Goodman, contributed a history of whole language to *The Whole Language Catalog,* a compendium of the ideology's wisdom and practice published in 1991.[1] She writes:

> Those of us who have been close to the present use of the term *whole language* are unsure of its origins. . . . In 1978 Dorothy Watson and others in Columbia, Missouri, formed the first teacher support group called Teachers Applying Whole Language (TAWL). Ken Goodman and I wrote

a paper in 1979 called "A Whole Language Comprehension-centered Reading Program." . . .

Some of the beginings of whole language come from research in the 1960s on the reading process, especially the work of Kenneth Goodman and Frank Smith (1971), and from the subsequent move to apply the research findings to reading instruction. Working from different perspectives they established the notion of a unified single reading process as an interaction between the reader, the text, and language. (p. 386)

Among the major psychologists whose teachings have shaped the minds of whole-language believers are, as Yetta Goodman cites: John Dewey (1859-1952), radical socialist philosopher of progressive education; Jean Piaget (1896-1980), Swiss psychologist whose theories of child development greatly influenced Western educators; Lev Vygotsky (1896-1934), Soviet psychologist who worked on the social formation of the mind. Mrs. Goodman writes:

Whole language is a new response to an old argument. John Dewey said of the movement variously called *the new education* or *progressive schools* that it was a "product of discontent with traditional education. In effect it is a criticism of the latter." Dewey expressed this discontent: "The traditional scheme is, in essence, one of imposition from above and from outside. It imposes adult standards, subject matter and methods upon those who are only growing slowly toward maturity." . . .

Influences on whole language include the traditions of humanism and science. We take from humanism a respect for all learners regardless of their ages, abilities, or backgrounds. We take from science the latest discoveries in psychology, linguistics, psycholinguistics, and sociolinguistics. (p. 387)

Kenneth Goodman writes:

Whole language picks up where the progressives left off. . . . It is this combination of science and humanistic educational and social philosophy that forms the foundation for whole language curriculum. The curriculum in reading and writing starts with pupils reading and being read whole, meaningful, relevant texts. It starts with pupils inventing the writing

system and discovering the conventions of writing as they use writing ....
We involve learners from the beginning in predictable and meaningful
print in a wide range of contexts ....

We read to our pupils at all ages ....

We use the psychological concepts of Piaget and Vygotsky to
underscore Dewey's concept of learning as transaction: pupils making
sense of their world and being changed themselves in the transactions. (p. 281)

It is interesting that the Goodmans' veneration of the past only
goes back to the 1890s and the work of John Dewey. To them
several thousand years of educational experience in which children
were taught to read effectively and proficiently are brushed aside in
favor of the "latest" researches by psychosociolinguists.

Thus, the major theoreticians and originators of the whole-
language ideology are really only three people: Kenneth and Yetta
Goodman and Frank Smith. The rest are key disciples, followers,
elaborators of the work of the masters, colorful practitioners, and
writers of whole-language textbooks.

Thus, if you want to know what whole language is all about, you
simply have to know what is in the heads of Ken and Yetta
Goodman and Frank Smith. Their heads are full of John Dewey,
Lev Vygotsky, Noam Chomsky and other socialist, humanist
thinkers. What is also interesting is that the rise of whole language
coincides with the rise of deconstructionist philosophy in the 1970s
throughout the academic world. Is there a relationship between the
two? What the two certainly have in common is their preoccupation
with language and text. But we shall deal with that in a later chapter.

At this point we simply want to know more about Ken and Yetta
Goodman and Frank Smith. Who are these professors of education
who are so systematically destroying the literacy of American
children?

The Goodmans are probably the best-known reading-instruction
specialists in the English-speaking world. Ken Goodman got his

A.B. degree at U.C.L.A. in 1949, his M.A. at Los Angeles State College in 1953, and his Ed.D. at U.C.L.A. in 1963. He taught public school in Los Angeles from 1949 to '53 and from 1958 to '60. He was also employed as a social worker from 1953 to '58. He taught as a professor of elementary education at Wayne State University (Detroit, Mich.) from 1962 to 1975. In 1976 he was co-author of Scott, Foresman's successor to Dick and Jane, Reading Unlimited. From 1975 to the present he has been at the University of Arizona (Tucson) as a professor of education specializing in language, reading and culture.

Thus, Goodman has spent his entire professional career working his way up in the reading establishment. In 1982 he served as president of the International Reading Association, the reading establishment's citadel in which the look-say method was enshrined by its founder, William Scott Gray, creator of Dick and Jane.

It was Ken Goodman's proposition that reading is "a psycholinguistic guessing game" that brought him considerable notoriety in reading circles and dubbed him the father of the "psycholinguistic" method of teaching reading. For all intents and purposes, it was the beginning of the development of the whole-language ideology which then developed into the whole-language movement.

It all started at the 1967 meeting of the American Educational Research Association in Chicago at which Goodman presented a paper in which he called reading a psycholinguistic guessing game. The paper was immediately published by *The Journal of the Reading Specialist*. Since then it has been widely reprinted, quoted and even translated into several foreign languages. Goodman writes (p. 98):[2]

> Though the concept grew out of my miscue research, I have some quite diverse people to thank for my ideas coming together in that paper.

Goodman then relates how in 1965 it was Jeanne Chall who recommended him to Cornell psychologist Harry Levin, who in turn invited him to spend a month that summer at Ithaca. There he interacted with several other psychologists and linguists.

But the highpoint of the month were the three days that Noam Chomsky was there. Goodman writes:

> Noam Chomsky used a term that struck a responsive chord with me: *tentative information processing*. He suggested that readers make tentative decisions as they strive to make sense of text, and they remain ready to modify their tentative decisions as they continue reading.
>
> That idea fit very well with what I was learning from my miscue research. It helped explain why people made miscues (which I had defined as *deviations from expected responses to the print in oral reading*) and why they did or didn't correct them as they continued reading.

Having made that great discovery, Goodman goes on to state:

> The most common view of reading up to that time was that it consisted of successive accurate identifications of the words in the text. Few had considered that getting to sense in reading might not involve accurate identification of every word and might involve information not in the words on the page at all.

How about the possibility of accurately identifying every word as well as using information not in the words on the page! That should certainly give sense to the text. Besides, it is not clear whether Chomsky was describing adult readers confronting a difficult text or a child of six just learning to read. Nowhere in my reading of Chomsky is there any indication that he endorsed or approved of the whole-language method of teaching reading. Whole-language teachers constantly confuse reading by an experienced adult with reading by a beginner. But be that as it may, Goodman's aim is to pretend that there is nothing wrong with a reading-instruction method that makes it virtually impossible for the learner to become an accurate reader. He writes:

> And as I put that idea [tentative information processing] into my own developing view it meant that reading was a *psycholinguistic guessing game*. In my research I found readers anticipating what was coming. They predicted grammatical patterns; they reworded the text; they inserted, omitted, substituted, and changed the word sequence. Sometimes they lost themselves in the process, but often they produced sensible text readings that differed in remarkable ways from an expected reading.

What Goodman describes so graphically are the errors that a disabled reader makes in trying to decipher the text. Had the reader been taught to read by way of intensive, systematic phonics, instead of by an ideographic method, he would not be making those errors. He would not reword the text, or insert words that weren't there, omit words that were there, and substitute words, for he would be able to instantaneously decode the words on the basis of his automatic knowledge of the letter sounds and their easily recognizable consonant-vowel syllabic combinations.

Reading is not a guessing game to an alphabetic-phonetic reader. It is an easy and accurate decoding of what is on the page. Goodman continues:

> In the reading guessing game we use strategies to make sense of print. We sample or select from the print — it would be too slow and distracting to use it all. We predict what will be coming ahead from what we already know. We make inferences and merge them with what we explicitly know so that we can't tell when we're done what we took from the text and what we put into it. And we have strategies for correcting when we lose meaning.

And so, at the heart of the whole-language belief system is the ludicrous dogma that reading is a psycholinguistic guessing game. The fact that for millions of people reading is not a guessing game — psycholinguistic or otherwise — makes no difference to whole-language believers. To them, you must read like a disabled reader or else you are not really reading. You are merely word calling. To Goodman, reading is:

> a selective process. It involves partial use of available language cues selected from perceptual input on the basis of the reader's expectation. As this partial information is processed, tentative decisions are made to be confirmed, rejected or refined as reading progresses. More simply stated, reading is a psycholinguistic guessing game.

Frank Smith, who, in his book *Insult to Intelligence,* describes Ken Goodman as "a leader of literacy teachers in the drive for humanity and intelligence in education," which in itself is an insult to intelligence, writes:

> The influence of a few individuals can be enormous. For twenty years Yetta and Kenneth Goodman have been the center of a growing movement among classroom teachers to resist the incursion of programs and tests in reading and language education.... Back in 1972, Kenneth Goodman and I published an article called "The Psycholinguistic Method of Teaching Reading." The title was intended to be satirical. Our argument was that such a method of teaching reading could never exist, because the essence of the psycholinguistic point of view was that children learned to read from people, not from programs.... The latest term for the philosophy that most antiprogram educators share is "whole language." (p. 188)[3]

And so, look-say begat psycholinguistics, which begat whole language.

All of this is quite interesting from a chronological point of view. Jeanne Chall, who recommended Goodman to Harry Levin, may be having regrets these days. In 1965 she had just completed her study of reading which appeared in 1967 as a book entitled *Learning to Read: The Great Debate.* In that book Chall established once and for all that alphabetic phonics used in beginning reading instruction produces better readers than the sight or look-say method. Naturally her book upset a lot of professors of reading. Meanwhile, Goodman had continued on his road of discovery. Today, the views of Chall and Goodman are so divergent that *Education Week* of March 21, 1990, called it a "full-scale war." And as in any war, there are casualties. In this war the casualties are the children!

Goodman also mentions how deeply he was influenced by Noam Chomsky, the M.I.T. linguist. Chomsky is also known as a radical leftist who spends as much time damning America as he does working on linguistics. Since Goodman met Chomsky during the escalating days of the Vietnam war, we can assume that there was much political discussion during the seminar at Cornell.

Frank Smith also was greatly influenced by Noam Chomsky. Smith tells us that back in the 1960s, while working as a newspaper editor in Perth, Australia, he became interested in the ideas of Chomsky who had come up with some new theories linking linguistics with psychology. Chomsky had acquired considerable notoriety in the academic world by publishing a blistering review of B. F. Skinner's book, *Verbal Behavior*. Chomsky and former behaviorist George A. Miller then established a new field of study, psycholinguistics.

In 1960, Miller and humanist psychologist Jerome Bruner, with the help of a grant from the Carnegie Corporation of New York, founded the Center for Cognitive Studies at Harvard University. Smith writes:

> With Chomsky playing an active role in its affairs, the center became a mecca for scholars, researchers, and a few fortunate graduate students, from all over the world. When I received an unexpected invitation to leave the newspaper world of Perth to enroll in a doctoral program at the Center for Cognitive Studies, I could not resist the opportunity. (p. 24)

And so, Smith came to Harvard where he spent "three

exhilarating years exploring the nature of learning, especially as it is exhibited by the fresh clear minds of infants." His doctoral dissertation was "on a narrow area of visual perception, selected as a specialized and abstract topic that could be disposed of expeditiously. I knew nothing of teaching at any level."

Thus, it is quite possible, and probably quite common, to become a doctor of education without knowing anything about teaching. Smith then worked on something called Project Literacy at Cornell University and then spent a year at the federally funded Southwest Regional Laboratory (SWRL) where, at taxpayer expense, a very poorly conceived linguistics-oriented primary reading program was produced. Smith didn't like it because, in his view, it had too much phonics. Actually, it was a product of the so-called eclectic approach in which the repetition of sight words was augmented by a linguistically oriented choice of vocabulary and a simultaneous introduction to some letter sounds.

It didn't work because it set up conflicting learning habits. The whole-word and phonetic methods are mutually exclusive. They cannot work together because they produce a cognitive conflict. If you are taught to read by intensive phonics you do not need to memorize printed words as whole configurations. But if you are taught primarily to memorize words by their configurations, and no effort is made to develop an automatic association between letters and sounds, the child may then develop a permanent blockage against phonetic learning. In other words, such a method of instruction can cripple a child for life.

The SWRL program was not a success. It displeased sight fanatics like Smith and did not provide phonics advocates with the kind of program they wanted. Actually, as a response to *Why Johnny Can't Read,* two very good phonics programs were put on the market in 1963: *Open Court Basic Readers* published by Open Court, and *Basic Reading* published by Lippincott. The latter program, written by two experts in phonics instruction, Glenn McCracken and Charles C. Walcutt, is no longer in print even though it was enormously successful as a reading program.

Which brings us to the Philadelphia story. In 1975, the Federal Reserve Bank of Philadelphia wanted to find out why so many young people were coming out of that city's schools without employable skills. They wanted to find out what was needed to improve the system's performance. And so a team of researchers from the bank and the school district spent 28 months investigating every aspect of the system. In trying to determine why some schools did better than others, they discovered that it was the school's reading program that was the determining factor.

Although the schools were using a variety of basal reading programs, including several popular sight, meaning-oriented programs, it turned out that the schools that used the Lippincott phonics-oriented program produced the better readers and the better test scores.[4]

In other words, the Philadelphia study merely confirmed what Flesch had written in 1955 and Chall had written in 1965. But don't expect the whole-language fanatics to be impressed. Smith has nothing but contempt for phonics and its advocates. He writes:

> The self-appointed leader of the phonics movement is Rudolph [sic] Flesch, who thirty years ago published a popular book entitled *Why Johnny Can't Read*. His patent-medicine prescription was that every child could be taught to read provided that all parents and teachers employed scrupulously the method outlined in his book, which was drilling children in the sounds of the letters. Twenty-five years later he concluded that since many children were still not learning to read, it must be because his good advice and generous offer had been ignored. (p. 108)

Smith's snide putdown of Rudolf Flesch is typical of this smug, arrogant attitude so prevalent among whole-language charlatans. Just to set the record straight, Flesch never considered himself the leader of anything. Those of us who had the privilege of knowing him considered him to be a kind, self-effacing, and very private human being whose only desire was to help parents understand why their bright, perfectly normal children weren't learning to read in school and to offer them a simple and effective method of teaching reading at home, which many parents used quite successfully.

Intensive, systematic phonics is no patent-medicine prescription. Its success as a method of teaching reading is as old as alphabetic writing itself, and its track record is without equal. The fact that the reading establishment spent the next twenty-five years resisting a return to intensive phonics is the reason why Flesch felt compelled to write *Why Johnny* Still *Can't Read* in 1981. But Smith and his ilk are busily spreading the canard that phonics is responsible for the reading problem. He writes:

> In fact, in recent years more parents and teachers have been trying to teach children the Flesch way than in any other period of history, urged and supported by the federal government, abetted by the regional research and development laboratories, encouraged by the publishers of elaborate commercial tests and programs, and browbeaten by politicians and administrators. What has failed is phonics. (p. 108)

Blaming phonics for the reading problem is like blaming lemons for scurvy when lemons are the cure. It's hard to believe that Smith can be that ignorant. He's too smart to be that dumb.

Having been a member of the Reading Reform Foundation since its founding in 1961 by Watson Washburn, I can attest to the difficulty we had in getting schools and superintendents to even consider using intensive phonics in beginning reading instruction. Whatever successes we achieved were usually undone a year or two later by the whole-word mafia.

It is true that something called "phonics" — or what we in the Reading Reform Foundation call "phony phonics" — has always been taught in the schools. Even today, whole-language teachers insist that they teach phonics — or "graphophonemic cues" as they like to call it. But that sort of incidental, piecemeal, fragmentary phonics is taught as phonetic cues, just one cue among many which the child is to use in his psycholinguistic guessing game. Those of us who have been in this battle for the last thirty years are quite familiar with all of the tricks and falsehoods the reading-for-meaning charlatans have used to bamboozle the public. Smith writes:

> Loathe to blame himself and his method, Flesch instead constructed a false enemy, the "look-and-say" method of teaching reading .... (p. 109)

More lies. Flesch no more constructed a false enemy than did Orton in 1929, the Boston schoolmasters in 1844, and a host of other researchers and scholars who have dealt with this problem. Flesch's book was addressed to the mother of a child with a reading problem whom he proceeded to tutor quite successfully using the method Smith denigrates.

Having had the same experience as a tutor, I can state without equivocation that intensive, systematic phonics is the only way to guarantee that a child will learn to read with fluency and proficiency and without miscues.

The idea that Flesch was "loathe to blame himself and his method" is so preposterous as to question Smith's basic understanding of what reading is all about. In the first place, Flesch was not in the primary reading instruction business. He only got involved because there was a problem which a mother had brought to him. And thanks to his research and investigations we found out what was causing the problem. Others before him had identified the problem and its cause, but he was the first to write a book about it that the public could understand and act on. And thanks to his book some things did change for the better, many children were saved from lives as functional illiterates, and many teachers learned the proper way to teach children to read. But the establishment was simply too powerful to be beaten by one man with one book because there were too many Frank Smiths and Ken Goodmans and dozens of books and professional publications promoting the other side.

A more recent book, however, seems to have annoyed the promoters of whole language no end. It is Marilyn Jager Adams's *Beginning to Read: Thinking and Learning about Print,* published in 1990.[5] The book was considered so controversial that *The Reading Teacher* of February 1991 devoted virtually its entire issue to "a critique by literacy professionals" with a response by Adams. *The Reading Teacher,* of course, is an official publication of the International Reading Association which favorably promotes whole language and rarely gives advocates of intensive, systematic phonics space in its publications. Prof. Patrick Groff of San Diego State University states in a preface to Michael Brunner's *Retarding America: The Imprisonment of Potential:*

> The data from experimental research notwithstanding, [whole language] dominates journals, conferences, inservice workshops, course offerings, and even design and marketing strategies related to reading development materials. Oddly, education periodicals tend not to accept manuscripts that criticize WL, thereby rejecting years of scientific research. For example, in the past five years, the official organ of the International Reading Association, *Reading Teacher,* published 118 complimentary articles on WL. Only one record of a debate on the issue interrupted the journal's longstanding lovefest with WL. It has been even longer since the National Council of Teachers of English allowed any open discussion of WL on the pages of its periodical, *Language Arts.* (p. xvi)[6]

Adams's book was written as a result of a Department of Education grant given to the Center for the Study of Reading. The late Senator Zorinsky of Nebraska, greatly concerned about declining literacy in America, was able to attach an amendment to the 1986

Human Services Reauthorization Act, which required a study of primary reading instruction in American public schools and the role of phonics in such instruction. Adams, a psychologist, was given the job because of her reputation for objectivity and her previous research in the field. A *Summary* of the book was also prepared for those unable or unwilling to read the entire book itself. Adams writes:

> I freely admit that I did not welcome this assignment. The debate over beginning reading instruction had long since admitted polemic and propaganda alongside well-founded research and responsible argumentation. People told me that I would lose old friends and make new enemies. People told me I would be shot. (p. 371)[7]

Even though Adams concluded that "both sides of the debate were right," and that the phonics and whole language methods were "necessary complements, effective and realizable only in complex interdependency with one another," she was severely criticized by whole language advocates. Those of us who have witnessed the suffering and frustration of the victims of whole-word, whole language instruction found no solace in Adams's attempt to create harmony where conflicting, mutually exclusive reflexes are at the psychological heart of the reading-methods debate. Such conflicts, as Pavlov discovered, do not create harmony, but dysfunction and disorganization of behavior.

Probably the harshest of Adams's critics was Yetta Goodman, who wrote:

> In normal circumstances, those who have conflicting belief systems can simply set the book aside and decide that there is nothing to learn from it. Because of the political nature of Adams's book and the *Summary,* however, it is necessary to go beyond the authors' goals and raise issues that have been ignored or misinterpreted. . . .[8]
>
> In focusing on words and the unexamined assumption that oral

language simplistically maps onto written language, Adams explores the nature of English writing. The discussion is organized as if alphabetic systems are the only ones that count in the world today. It is ethnocentric to believe that the alphabet is "the most important invention in the social history of the world" (p. 18), although the invention of writing may have been. Both China and Japan have high literacy rates. There are many arguments among literacy scholars concerning writing systems and how and why each evolved. Many political and socio-cultural issues influence their development and use. Adams indicates that "writing systems cannot be perfectly categorized" (p. 15), yet she continues to treat the alphabetic writing system of English as one that can be learned best through direct instruction on letter/sound correspondence.[9]

If nothing else proves the imbecility of Yetta Goodman, it is her ridiculous criticism of Adams for paying the alphabet its due. The invention of the alphabet did for the ancient world what the computer is doing for the modern world, only moreso. The alphabet made learning to read easy, it speeded up communication, it permitted an incredible expansion of vocabulary and therefore an expansion of knowledge.

Robert K. Logan, in his fascinating book, *The Alphabet Effect: The Impact of the Phonetic Alphabet on the Development of Western Civilization*,[10] writes:

> The magic of the phonetic alphabet is that it is more than a writing system; it is also a system of organizing information. Of all mankind's inventions, with the possible exception of language itself, nothing has proved more useful or led to more innovations than the alphabet .... It has influenced the development of our thought patterns, our social institutions, and our very sense of ourselves. The alphabet...has contributed to the development of codified law, monotheism, abstract science, deductive logic, and individualism, each a unique contribution to Western thought. Through the printing press it has reinforced or encouraged many of the key historical events of modern Europe including the Renaissance, the Reformation, the industrial Revolution, and the rise of democracy, mass education, nationalism, and capitalism. (p.17)

We use the letters of the alphabet to order the words in our dictionaries, the articles in our encyclopedias, and the books in our libraries. These systematic approaches to coordinating information based on the medium of the alphabet have suggested other forms of classification and codification that are part and parcel of Western science, law, engineering, and social organization.... It has provided us with a conceptual framework for analysis and has restructured our perceptions of reality. (p. 18)

The alphabet effect is a subliminal phenomenon. There is more to using the alphabet than just learning how to read and write. Using the alphabet ... also entails the ability to: 1) code and decode, 2) convert auditory signals or sounds into visual signs, 3) think deductively, 4) classify information, and 5) order words through the process of alphabetization....

What [children] learn are the intellectual by-products of the alphabet, such as abstraction, analysis, rationality, and classification, which form the essence of the alphabet effect and the basis of Western abstract scientific and logical thinking. The use of the phonetic alphabet helps explain why Western and Chinese thinking are so different (abstract and theoretical for the West versus concrete and practical for the East). (p. 21)

Modern Chinese and Japanese have slowly evolved into complex phonetic systems which still retain many cumbersome ideographic features. But even the Chinese and Japanese acknowledge the superiority of alphabetic writing. That's why they want to learn English. But, apparently, Mrs. Goodman is determined to spend the rest of her life proving that children can learn to read very well without phonics. As for her bias against phonics, she writes:

Both the *Summary* and complete book assert that phonics teaching is downplayed in elementary classrooms. They support a myth that there has been a lack of focus on phonics teaching since the 1930s. I taught for 10 years in the Los Angeles area in the 1950s and was a substitute teacher for some of that time. In primary classrooms, I had to follow lesson plans from Dick and Jane basals that focused on the explicit teaching of initial, medial, and final consonants, moving to long vowels and then to short vowels and on to blends, etc.[11]

The phonics taught in Dick and Jane was incidental to the whole-word methodology on which Dick and Jane was based. The teaching of a sight vocabulary was basic to the Dick and Jane method, which taught children to develop a holistic reflex—to view words automatically as whole configurations. The phonics which was taught later simply provided the reader with some phonetic clues to use along with picture, configuration and context clues. Children who were not able to develop a phonetic reflex—an automatic ability to associate letters and sounds—were condemned to be crippled readers for the rest of their lives. Mrs. Goodman writes:

> As I write this critique, I am reading Mike Rose's (1989) *Lives on the Boundary*.... The research cited by the Adams book is in direct opposition to the kind of evidence that Rose provides.... In the Rose work, the people marginalized by good reader/poor reader studies, by sensationalized percentages about illiteracy are given voice. We discover people who are affected by racism, poverty, rigid schooling and by cultural views that vary greatly between their worlds and the worlds of academia. They are not illiterate; rather their literacy does not appropriately fit the values of particular status groups in society. The teaching of intensive direct phonics will not improve the status of those maginalized by society. There are other more powerful issues at stake.[12]

Again, Mrs. Goodman is dead wrong. Intensive direct phonics will indeed improve the status of those marginalized by society. It will give them the means to get out of their poverty by providing them with the standard literacy required to make it in our economy. That's how generations of immigrants in the past were able to move from the slums into the middle and upper classes. As for the final word, Marilyn Adams had this to say:

> In response to Goodman, I point out that—unless they have learned to read or write an alphabetic script—Chinese adults and even eminent scholars are found to flunk the sorts of segmentation tests that are widely

given to kindergartners in our country. In contrast, having studied a script that is principally alphabetic, those who are successful readers invariably have phonemic awareness while those who lack phonemic awareness are invariably unsuccessful.

To my mind, the discovery and documentation of the importance of phonemic awareness, owed so much to the late Isabelle Liberman, is the single most powerful advance in the science and pedagogy of reading this century. . . .

Finally, I do argue strongly that fluent reading ultimately pivots on deep and thorough overlearning of letters, of spelling patterns (where that includes the sequenced order of letters within them), and of spelling-sound correspondences.[13]

Amen!

10. Psychology's Best Kept Secrets

It is more than a little curious that in a nation where so much research has been done by psychologists on the nature of human cognition — how children learn — that these same psychologists have shown virtually no interest in the greatest learning problem plaguing American education: the teaching of reading. It is true that there is much interest in diagnosing reading disability and exploring "dyslexia," but no interest in the instructional cause of reading disability, despite the fact that Dr. Samuel T. Orton first drew attention to the problem back in 1929.

Which brings us to the Center for Cognitive Studies where Frank Smith allegedly absorbed the wisdom of Noam Chomsky *et al.* The chief architect of the Center was Jerome Bruner who tells us in his autobiography, *In Search of Mind,* that cognitive psychology was born in 1956 at a symposium on the cognitive sciences held at the Massachusetts Institute of Technology. Two of the key persons who participated in that symposium were Harvard behavioral psychologist George Miller and linguist Noam Chomsky.[1]

It was that symposium that convinced Miller to leave B.F.

Skinner's behaviorist camp at Harvard and join Jerome Bruner in developing cognitive psychology. Miller writes:

> I went away from the Symposium with a strong conviction, more intuitive than rational, that experimental psychology, theoretical linguistics, and the computer simulation of cognitive processes were all pieces from a larger whole, and that the future would see a progressive elaboration and coordination of their shared concerns. (Bruner p. 122)[2]

Three years later, in 1959, Chomsky was to give the coup de grace to the behaviorist theory about language by a devastating review of B. F. Skinner's book, *Verbal Behavior* (1957). Skinner had sought to explain language development in humans as a form of conditioned stimulus-response behavior similar to the way that animals in psych labs could be trained through conditioning techniques. Pavlov's famous experiments on dogs in Russia were the best known example of such experiments, the results of which were to permit psychologists to devise techniques that could be applied in changing and molding human behavior.

J. B. Watson, the father of American behaviorism, had written in 1924:

> Behaviorism . . . holds that the subject matter of human psychology is the behavior of the human being. Behaviorism claims that consciousness is neither a definite nor a usable concept. . . .(p. 2)
>
> The behaviorist asks: Why don't we make what we can observe the real field of psychology? Let us limit ourselves to things that can be observed and formulate laws concerning only those things. Now what can we observe? We can observe behavior — what the organism does or says. And let us point out at once: that saying is doing — that is, behaving. (p. 6)[3]

Chomsky demonstrated that the behaviorists' attempts to explain language in the limited terms of stimulus-response behavior were fundamentally flawed. He argued that "our interpretation of the world is based on representational systems that derive from the structure of the mind itself and do not mirror in any direct way the form of the external world." In other words, the human child is born with a brain that already contains a certain innate faculty that permits the child to learn language rapidly, without direct instruction from anyone. But the mystery is that the structure of the mind does indeed mirror the form of the external world, for the function of language is to name the external world. The child's ability to master the phonological structure of the language, the abstractions of sound symbols, as well as syntax and grammar so rapidly and effortlessly suggested to Chomsky that man's genetic makeup provided him with a highly developed language learning capability.

In 1960 Miller and Bruner got an unrestricted grant of a quarter-million dollars from the Carnegie Corporation of New York to set up their Center for Cognitive Studies at Harvard. Miller brought ideas about communication theory, computation, and linguistics to the Center whereas Bruner brought ideas about social psychology, developmental psychology, and anthropology to the mix. It was obvious that the new interest in the mind had been spurred by the new computer technology. For, as Bruner writes, "You cannot properly conceive of managing a complex world of information without a workable concept of mind." The result is that the Center brought together the ideas and theories of scholars and scientists working in many associated fields and drew graduate students from M.I.T., Harvard, and elsewhere.

Bruner concentrated on early childhood mental development which brought him into contact with the work of the Swiss psychologist Jean Piaget whose pioneering work in the field had contributed greatly to an understaning of how the child's mind grows. Piaget saw the child as an egocentric individual, gradually modifying his egocentrism as he adapted himself to the reality of others.

But Bruner, a socialist, was not entirely satisfied with the

Piagetian view which seemed to favor the development of individualism. "Piaget's children," writes Bruner, "are little intellectuals, detached from the hurly-burly of the human condition." He was far more attracted to the work of Lev Semyonovich Vygotsky (1896-1934), the Soviet cognitive psychologist. Bruner writes:

> Vygotsky's world was an utterly different place, almost the world of a great Russian novel.... Growing up in it is full of achieving consciousness and voluntary control, of learning to speak and then finding out what it means, of clumsily taking over the forms and tools of the culture and learning how to use them appropriately. (p. 138) . . .
>
> Vygotsky published little, and virtually nothing that appeared in English before 1960; indeed, until the late 1950s, most of what he wrote in Russian was suppressed and had been banned after the 1936 purge. Sickly and brilliant, he died of turberculosis in his thirties. . . . He was a Russian and a Jew, deeply interested in the arts and in language. . . . His objective was to explore how human society provided instruments to empower the individual mind. He was a serious intellectual Marxist, when Marxism was a starchy and dogmatic subject. This was his undoing at the time of the Stalinist purges. . . . Though I knew Piaget and never knew Vygotsky, I feel I know Vygotsky better as a person. (p. 137)[4]

The man who introduced Bruner to Vygotsky was Alexander Luria, the Soviet psychologist whose book, *The Nature of Human Conflicts,* had been translated into English and published in the United States in 1932. Luria wrote in his preface:

> The researches described here are the results of the experimental psychological investigations carried on at the State Institute of Experimental Psychology, Moscow, during the period of 1923-1930. The chief problems of the author were an objective and materialistic description of the mechanisms lying at the basis of the disorganisation of human behaviour and an experimental approach to the laws of its regulation. . . .To accomplish this it was necessary to create artificially affects and models of experimental neuroses which made possible an analysis of the laws lying

at the basis of the disintegration of behaviour. (p. xi)[5]

Pavlov himself, Luria's mentor, had proudly summed up the results of his famous experiments in a book, *Twenty Years of Objective Study,* published in 1935. These experiments on animals had enormous implications for experiments on human beings. Pavlov wrote:

> The power of our knowledge over the nervous system will, of course, appear to much greater advantage if we learn not only to injure the nervous system but also to restore it at will. It will then have been really proved that we have mastered the processes and are controlling them. Indeed, this is so. In many cases we are not only causing disease, but are eliminating it with great exactitude, one might say, to order. (p. 690)[6]

Thus, Pavlov had already done considerable experimentation on the causes of behavioral disorganization. Luria writes:

> Pavlov obtained very definite affective "breaks," an acute disorganisation of behaviour, each time that the conditioned reflexes collided, when the animal was unable to react to two mutually exclusive tendencies, or was incapable of adequately responding to any imperative problem. (p. 12)

Apparently, there were many psychologists at that time working on the same problem. Luria writes:

> We are not the first of those who have artificially created disorganisations of human behaviour. A large number of facts pertaining to this problem has been contributed by contemporary physiologists, as well as by psychologists.
>
> I. P. Pavlov was the first investigator who, with the help of exceedingly bold workers, succeeded experimentally in creating neuroses with experimental animals. Working with conditioned reflexes in dogs, Pavlov came to the conclusion that every time an elaborated reflex came into conflict with the unconditioned reflex, the behavior of the dog markedly

changed. . . .

Although, in the experiments with the collision of the conditioned reflexes in animals, it is fairly easy to obtain acute forms of artificial affect, it is much more difficult to get those results in human experiments. . . .

K. Lewin, in our opinion, has been one of the most prominent psychologists to elucidate this question of the artificial production of affect and of the experimental disorganisation of behaviour. The method of his procedure — the introduction of an emotional setting into the experience of a human, the interest of the subject in the experiment — helped him to obtain an artificial disruption of the affect of considerable strength. . . . Here the fundamental conception of Lewin is very close to ours. (pp. 206-7)[7]

Who was K. Lewin? Why he was the very same Kurt Lewin who came to the United States in 1933, founded the Research Center for Group Dynamics at M.I.T. (which later moved to the University of Michigan), and invented "sensitivity training." Shortly before his death in 1947, Lewin founded the National Training Laboratory which established its campus at Bethel, Maine, under the sponsorship of the National Education Association. There teachers were instructed in the techniques of sensitivity training and how to become effective change agents.

After Lewin's death, his colleagues continued to develop his sensitive-training sessions which became known as t-groups (t for training). The t-group became the basis of the encounter movement in which participants get in touch with their feelings.

Carl Rogers, one of the chief practitioners of the t-group, considered sensitivity training to be "perhaps the most significant social invention of this century."[8] All of this spurred the development of humanist "Third Force" psychology by Rogers, Abraham Maslow and others, which has had an enormous influence on the affective curriculum of public education.

Lewin had started his career as a social psychologist in Berlin where he organized a "collective" in which he and his students pursued the experiments which Luria later recognized as highly effective. Some of Lewin's students were Russians who studied under him in the early 1920s and returned to the Soviet Union to teach and continue their researches at the University of Moscow. In 1929 Lewin attended the Ninth International Congress of Psychologists at Yale where, according to Harvard psychologist Gordon Allport, his work "was decisive in forcing some American psychologists to revise their own theories of the nature of intelligent behavior and of learning."

In 1932, Lewis M. Terman, head of the psychology department at Stanford, invited Lewin to spend six months as a visiting professor at Stanford. Lewin had been recommended by Edwin G. Boring, director of the Psych Lab at Harvard, who had been greatly impressed with Lewin at the Yale conference. After the stint at Stanford, Lewin decided to return to Germany via the Pacific and the Trans-Siberian railroad. In Moscow he was able to confer with his fellow psychologists, including Luria. Hitler had just come to power in Germany, and in August 1933, Lewin left Germany for good.

The importance of Lewin in this story is that he represented the collectivist mentality in the psychological community which had its own socio-political agenda. Certainly, the psychologists who were experimenting with artificially induced behavioral disorganization in their laboratories in Germany, the Soviet Union, and the United States had a reason for their experiments. And Lewin was considered highly skilled in such experimentation with human beings which greatly interested American psychologists. Lewin's biographer, Alfred J. Marrow, writes:

> Students of progressive education also saw the need for studies of group behavior. This was stimulated by the educational philosophy of John Dewey. To carry out Dewey's theory of "learning by doing," teachers organized such group projects as student self-government and hobby-club activities. This called for the development of leadership skills and

collective setting of group goals. . . . Lewin's pioneering research in group behavior thus drew upon the experience of educators in deciding upon and developing topics for research and in establishing a strong interest among social psychologists and teachers. (p. 167)[9]

One of Lewin's most significant experiments was aimed at determining the behavioral effects of frustration on children and how these effects are produced. Marrow writes:

> The experiment indicated that in frustration the children tended to regress to a surprising degree. They tended to become babyish. Intellectually, children of four and a half years tended toward the behavior of a three-year-old. The degree of intellectual regression varied directly with the strength of the frustration. Change in emotional behavior was also recorded. There was less smiling and singing and more thumbsucking, noisiness, and restless actions. Aggressiveness also increased and some children went so far as to hit, kick, and break objects. There was a 30 per cent rise in the number of hostile actions toward the experimenter and a 34 per cent decrease in friendly approaches. . . .
>
> The authors summarized their main findings as follows: "Frustration as it operated in these experiments resulted in an average regression in the level of intellectual functioning, in increased unhappiness, restlessness, and destructiveness, in increased ultra-group unity, and in increased out-group aggression. The amounts of increase in negative emotionality were positively related to strength of frustration." (p. 122)

In other words, Lewin and his colleagues had proven beyond a shadow of a doubt that frustration could cause the same symptoms of behavioral disorganization in children that Pavlov, Luria and associates had produced in their laboratories with animals. On the matter of teaching reading, Lewin favored the look-say, whole-word method. Marrow writes:

> Lewin's students had unusually wide latitude in choosing their particular fields of study. Sara Forrer, for example, decided to investigate Ovid Decroly's method of teaching retarded children to read. . . . The

Belgian teacher had postulated that children retain sentences more easily than single words and words more readily than single letters. Lewin stated, in referring to Forrer's experiment, that "the findings confirm the marked advantage of the 'global' method of reading and writing. To a child taking no joy in learning to write an alphabet, a change of valence (attractiveness) occurs more quickly when he is allowed as soon as possible to write meaningful communications in sentence form." (p. 258)[10]

What is interesting in all of this is that Clara Schmitt in 1914 (see chap. 13) had shown in her analysis of the errors made by mentally defective and normal children that the mentally defective had problems learning to read phonetically. And even when they were taught to read phonetically, they made the kinds of errors that normal children make when taught to read by the look-say method. Decroly was obviously confirming that the "global," or whole language method, was easier for retarded children than the more abstract alphabetic system. But to assume that the global (i.e. whole language) method was also better for normal children was either a serious error on Lewin's part, or a deliberate effort to promote look-say. He must have known that the Central Committee of the Communist Party in the Soviet Union had rejected the whole-word method in 1932 mainly through the work of his colleagues, Luria and Vygotsky.

Lewin obviously believed in the Marxist doctrine that the end justifies the means. In his book, *Resolving Social Conflicts,* published in 1948, he wrote:

> In regard to a change toward democracy this paradox of democratic leadership is still more pointed. In an experimental change, for instance, from individualistic freedom (laissez faire) to democracy, the incoming democratic leader could not tell the group members exactly what they should do because that would lead to autocracy. Still some manipulations of the situation have to be made to lead the group into the direction of democracy. . . .
> To instigate change toward democracy a situation has to be created for

a certain period where the leader is sufficiently in control to rule out influence he does not want and to manipulate the situation to a sufficient degree. The goal of the democtratic leader in this transition period will have to be the same as that of any good teacher, namely, to make himself superfluous, to be replaced by indigenous leaders from the group. (p. 39)[11]

In other words, during the transition period from individualism to "democracy" (i.e., collectivism) the end can justify the means, because the "end" is the greater good. The look-say method may be needed during the transition period in order to make Americans less literate and thereby less independent as individuals. This would indeed be a necessary strategy for moving the nation toward a socialist, collectivist society. And, of course, it was in keeping with Dewey's own views on reading instruction given in his essay, "The Primary School Fetich," published in 1898.

Vygotsky died in 1934 and Lewin died in 1947, but Luria, who knew them both, continued his work. During World War II he did painstaking research on brain-injured people, discovering many facets of how the brain works. He had worked closely with Vygotsky from 1924 to 1934, the period in which they had worked on early childhood development and the artificial means of creating behavioral disorganization. During that period Vygotsky also worked on the problems of Soviet education, applying psychology to the problems of massive illiteracy which, according to James Wertsch, "has been almost completely overcome today."

How were the Soviets able to achieve this? By using an alphabetic-phonics method of teaching reading!

The Bruner-Luria connection was a very close one. Bruner attended psychological conferences in Moscow, and, in 1960, Luria visited the Center for Cognitive Studies. Bruner writes:

Luria and I became fast friends almost immediately. We were compatible tempermentally and very much in agreement about psychological matters. . . . (p. 145)

> In the fifteen or so years that I knew him well, I do not think that two months ever went by without a letter from him, a new book or translation of his.... He was the czar of Russian psychology, but a more benign czar would be hard to imagine! (p. 144)

Why were they so compatible? Well, as a student Bruner not only sympathized with communism, but in his senior year at Duke, he became a member of the Communist Party. He writes:

> That last year at Duke was 1938, the bitter winding down of the Spanish Civil War. My roommate, Irv Dunston, and I were invited to become members of a Marxist "study group" held at the home of a gifted young mathematics professor. Each week we would prepare by reading something of Marx or Lenin. I liked the slogans — that production was for use not for profit, to each according to his effort, and so on — but the turgid arguments of Marxist "thinkers" repelled me....
>
> My fondness for the slogans must have been enough, for we were asked eventually to join a "cell" of the Communist Party in Durham, "with real working-class people." After a late-into-the-night discussion, we decided that this was our duty....
>
> The cell meetings, in that dingy apartment near the railroad station in Durham, were the intrinsic, the conspiratorial appeal — our code names included.... My "duties" were to take an active part on campus in the American Student Union, to put the "right" candidates into office....
>
> The year ended; I departed Durham. I never even had to resign from the Party. I was given no names or contacts, but told simply that I would soon know who and how. I guess I didn't make it. (pp. 29-30)[12]

Thus ended Bruner's formal relationship with the Communist Party. But nowhere in his autobiography does Bruner indicate any loss of belief in socialism or Marxism. The fact that he felt so compatible with Luria and preferred Vygotsky to Piaget would lead one to believe that Bruner has remained sympathetic to communism throughout his professional life. He and his fellow psychologists thought nothing of attending psychological conferences in Moscow during the height of the Cold War while American soldiers were dying in Vietnam fighting communism.

On matters of education, Bruner was instrumental in creating in 1965 the famous — or infamous, depending on your point of view — social studies curriculum for ten-year-olds, *Man: A Course of Study*, better known as MACOS. Bruner writes:

> [A]fter a year or two of very favorable notices . . . and widespread adoptions, the course came under attack from the extreme-right-wing John Birch Society in league with the newly emerging "creationists," opposed to the teaching of evolution. Between them they mounted the now familiar right-wing harassment of any school district proposing to use the course. . . . Governor Reagan of California, whose state sheltered the core of the John Birch, came out squarely against the course . . . . And so symbolic had the course become for the extreme Right that they managed to pass on their "literature" about it to a right-wing group in Australia, then in opposition to the widespread adoption of the course there. (p. 194)[13]

One would have to conclude from the above that the Center for Cognitive Studies was not exactly a hotbed of conservative, anti-communist thinking. And it is interesting to note that when Frank Smith left the Center with his newly acquired Ph.D., he embarked on his career as a phonics-basher par excellence and was soon catapulted into the position of "expert" on reading and literacy by the look-say establishment.

11. The Political Agenda in Whole Language

In the previous chapters we noted the influence of socialists John Dewey, Noam Chomsky, and Lev Vygotsky in the whole-language belief system. Dewey contributed humanism and progressivism to the whole-language movement; Chomsky contributed his linguistic theories; and Vygotsky contributed a collectivist educational psychology to the mix. A fourth Marxist who has deeply influenced whole-language theory and practice is Paulo Freire, the Brazilian educator who developed ways of using literacy programs to promote revolution. His book, *The Pedagogy of the Oppressed,* is a key work among left-wing radical educators. However, let's start with Vygotsky.

In the introduction to James Wertsch's biographical study, *Vygotsky and the Social Formation of Mind,* we read:

> Vygotsky was a staunch advocate of dialectical and historical materialism. He was one of the creators of Marxist psychology. For Vygotsky, Marxist philosophy was not a dogma or a doctrine in which one could find answers to concrete questions in psychology. Rather, in

mastering Marxism he assumed that a psychologist could assimilate a general method of scientific research, which could then be applied to concrete problems. (p. ix)[1]

The big problem Vygotsky was concerned with was discovering the principles of socialization so that they could be applied in rearing and educating Soviet children into becoming good communists. He studied the external and internal aspects of the socialization process focussing on the development of speech, thinking and the higher mental functions. Wertsch writes:

> People such as Vygotsky and his followers devoted every hour of their lives to making certain that the new socialist state, the first grand experiment based on Marxist-Leninist principles, would succeed. When one appreciates the life-giving energy provided by this environment and by the commitment of intellectuals to the creation of a new society, Vygotsky's work and influence become easier to understand.... According to Luria, "Vygotsky was ... the leading Marxist theoretician among us ... in [his] hands, Marx's methods of analysis did serve a vital role in shaping our course." (pp. 10-11)[2]

In his zeal to preserve the revolution, Vygotsky concentrated his efforts on finding the most effective and scientific way to produce the new Soviet man who would consolidate and expand the new collectivist society. His mission required examining human nature scientifically in order to determine what was genetic and what was susceptible to social engineering. Whole-language educators have latched onto several of Vygotsky's key concepts. One of them is the "zone of proximal development."

Ken Goodman, a great admirer of Vygotsky, writes in *The Whole Language Catalog* (p. 207):

> Effective teachers have always realized that they must know their pupils well. . . . They are kidwatchers: They are always observing their pupils, watching for learning and growth and signs of need and potential.

Vygotsky (1978) talked about "zones of proximal development," naturally occurring points in children's development where they can learn easily if they get a little help. Whole language teachers understand that they must observe their pupils carefully, through informal and formal means to know them well. ... These teachers know how to create conditions that will cause learners to exhibit and make the most of their zones of proximal development.[3]

Another important concept of Vygotsky's is that of mediation. Goodman writes:

In defining themselves as mediators whole language teachers understand that less can be more. They realize that helping a learner solve a problem is better than giving him or her an algorithm or a solution. In reading and writing teachers interfere as little as possible between the text and the reader. Teachers mediate by asking a question, offering a useful hint there, directing attention to an anomaly, calling attention to overlooked information, or suggesting a strategy.

Goodman is also enamored of Paulo Freire who sees the teacher as liberator. Goodman writes:

Liberating pedagogy sees learners in a power relationship to society. The learners must own the process of their learning. They must see learning, including literacy and language development, as part of a process of liberation.[4]

Liberation from what, one might ask. Liberation from parents, from family, from religion, from capitalism, from tradition, from the Bible. On the matter of classroom practice, Goodman writes:

Freeing pupils to take risks is a major concern of whole language classrooms. . . . Whole language classrooms liberate pupils to try new things, to invent spellings, to experiment with a new genre, to guess at meanings in their reading, or to read and write imperfectly.

Our research on reading and writing has strongly supported the importance of error in language development. Miscues represent the tension between invention and convention in reading ... In whole language classrooms risk-taking is not simply tolerated. It is celebrated. Learners have always been free to fail.

When whole-language educators deny that whole language is just another reading instruction program, they are quite correct. Whole language is basically a political program, not an academic one. The authors of *Whole Language, What's the Difference?* (p. 67) write:

> The whole language theoretical premise underlying which topics are pursued and how they are treated is *All knowledge is socially constructed.* Therefore all knowing is political. In an effort to promote critical literacy ... teachers who work with theme cycles try — no matter whether the topic is overtly "political" or not — to show how the topic is related to other more general questions. They try to demystify social institutions by helping children investigate connections between surface facts and underlying social structures, between lived experience and structural features of class, gender, and race. . . .
> ... Whole language is gaining momentum when disparities between economic classes are widening, when the number of homeless people are increasing, when freedom to criticize is threatened by right-wing groups such as Accuracy in Media and Accuracy in Academia.[5]

It is obvious that the so-called right wing poses the greatest threat to the success of the whole-language movement. In an article written by whole-language advocates in *Education Week* of February 27, 1985, we read:

> The accumulating evidence clearly indicates that a New Right philosophy of education has emerged in this country. . . .[B]y limiting reading instruction to systematic phonics instruction, sound-symbol decoding, and literal comprehension; and by aiming its criticism at reading books' story lines in an effort to influence content, the New Right's philosophy runs counter to the research findings and theoretical perspectives of most noted reading authorities.

> If this limited view of reading (and, implicitly, of thinking) continues to gain influence . . . the New Right will have successfully impeded the progress of democratic governance founded on the ideal of an educated — and critically thinking — electorate.[6]

The idea that systematic phonics, or literal comprehension of a text, or sound-symbol decoding pose a threat to "the progress of democratic governance" sounds so ridiculous as to question the intelligence if not the sanity of those who make such assertions. In case the authors of that article don't know, the New Right's philosophy of education is the very same philosophy espoused by the Founding Fathers of our limited form of government as outlined in the United States Constitution, no doubt viewed by whole-language political thinkers as a right-wing document.

In those early days of the republic, education was considered primarily a parental and local concern. In fact, home-schooling was widely practiced, and children were often taught to read and write at home or at a Dame's School before they went on to any form of formal education. And since there was a strong Biblical component in education, it was implicitly assumed that the purpose of education was to pass on to the future generation the knowledge, wisdom and moral values of the previous generation.

That, of course, is no longer the case. When the progressives took over American education at the turn of the century, their goal was to use the schools as the means of changing America from a capitalist, individualistic, religious nation into a socialist, collectivist, atheist or humanist nation. Their vision of a socialist America was to be found in the futuristic novel by Edward Bellamy, *Looking Backward,* published in 1888. In that novel Bellamy projected the fantasy of a socialist America in the year 2000. It was that vision that motivated John Dewey and his colleagues to educate young Americans in a manner which would lead them to turn America into the kind of egalitarian, collectivist society Bellamy envisaged.

John Dewey often used the word "democracy" as a euphemism for socialism, and as we know, communist countries often referred to themselves as democracies. Remember the late, unlamented German *Democratic* Republic of the Eric Honaker era? An article in *The Reading Teacher* of November 1987 states:

> Whole Language views the learner as profoundly social. Thus practice congruent with Whole Language includes participating in a community of readers during small group literature study, peer writing workshops, group social studies projects with built in plans for collaborative learning.[7]

It is obvious that whole-language teachers are attempting to "socialize" reading, to make it a collective experience, in complete contradiction to how people actually read in their private lives. In reality, a "community of readers" is really a community of believers all believing the same thing. The same article speaks of a "political vision woven through Whole Language beliefs. . . . Its goal is empowerment of learners and teachers."

What does learning to read have to do with political power? Why should a child in primary school, struggling to master the three R's, be concerned with "empowerment"? Is that the reason why parents send their children to school? An article by Frank Smith in *Phi Delta Kappan* of Jan. 1989 is quite instructive. He writes:

> Literacy is power. Literacy can do more than transform thought; it can transform the world. Literacy can raise social consciousness and provide a means for the expression and fulfillment of this consciousness.
>
> ... Paulo Freire's pedagogic technique raises social consciousness not as a way of using literacy but as a means of acquiring it.[8]

Smith's reference to Paulo Freire is quite revealing, for Freire has used adult literacy in the third world to foment Marxist revolution. Freire used a form of "critical consciousness," which he called "conscientization," to awaken critical thinking in the minds of the "oppressed." Phillip Berryman, in his book, *Liberation Theology,* writes:

> Implicit in the "Freire method" is a political agenda that can be called revolutionary, although Freire and his followers are highly critical of all attempts to organize in a top-down manner. . . . They believe that through a *concientizacion* (conscientization) process "the people" themselves must decide what sort of organizational approach they will take. Freire himself has worked with socialist and revolutionary governments in Tanzania, Guinea-Bissau, and Angola. (p.37)[9]

Freire is considered a "master dialectician" by his progressive American admirers and colleagues who revere him as a sort of Brazilian incarnation of John Dewey, whose socialist spirit still hovers over the education establishment. Incidentally, the word "dialectician" has nothing to do with learning to speak foreign dialects. It refers to the Marxist process by which history is supposed to advance. It was the German philosopher F. W. Hegel who conceived of history as advancing by way of a process of continual conflict which he called the dialectic. The conflict took place between the thesis, or present state of affairs, and the antithesis, the pressures for future change. This intense and protracted conflict was theoretically resolved by the creation of a synthesis, which in turn became the new thesis which then created the new basis for conflict. In other words, history advances by way of this dialectical conflict.

Communists believed that Marx had formulated the scientific principles by way of which this conflict could be guided by an organized revolutionary elite, the Communist Party. The methodology was called "dialectical materialism" and its most potent weapon was in exacerbating the contradictions within a society. Freire had mastered the dialectical technique. In the introduction to his 1987 book, *Literacy: Reading the Word, and the World,* written with radical professor Donaldo Macedo of the University of Massachusetts, Freire writes:

> The illiteracy crisis world over, if not combatted, will further exacerbate already feeble democratic institutions and the unjust, asymmetrical power relations that characterize the contradictory nature of contemporary democracies. The inherent contradiction in the actual usage of the term "democracy" is eloquently captured by Noam Chomsky, *On Power and Ideology* (1987), in his analysis of the United States society.
>
> "'Democracy,' in the United States rhetoric refers to a system of governance in which elite elements based in the business community control the state by virtue of their dominance of the private society, while the population observes quietly. So understood, democracy is a system of elite decision and public ratification, as in the United States itself. Correspondingly, popular involvement in the formation of public policy is considered a serious threat. It is not a step towards democracy; rather, it constitutes a 'crisis of democracy' that must be overcome."
>
> In order to overcome, at least partly, this "crisis of democracy," a critical literacy campaign must be instituted. It must be a literacy campaign that transcends the current debate over the literacy crisis which tends to recyle old assumptions and values concerning the meaning and usefulness of literacy, that is the notion that literacy is simply a mechanical process which overemphasizes the technical acquisition of reading and writing skills.
>
> ...[W]e call for a view of literacy as a form of cultural politics. In our analysis, literacy becomes a meaningful construct to the degree that it is viewed as a set of practices that functions to either empower or disempower people. In the larger sense, literacy is analyzed according to whether it serves to reproduce existing social formation or serves as a set of cultural practices that promotes democratic and emancipatory change.... [L]iteracy cannot be reduced to the treatment of letters and words as purely mechanical domain. We need to go beyond this rigid comprehension of literacy and begin to view it as the relationship of learners to the world, mediated by the transforming practice of this world taking place in the very general milieu in which learners travel. (p.vii)[10]

Freire has thankfully supplied us with about as good and clear a description of whole-language theory and practice as one is likely to find anywhere. In Freire's view, reading as a mechanical skill — that is, mastering the sound-symbol system and reading with accuracy and precision — is rejected in favor of a new consciousness-raising critical literacy to be used ultimately to change our political system. Thus, the political agenda is the central motivating force behind the whole-language movement, and that's why the theme of "empowerment" is constantly evoked by its promoters. Frank Smith writes:

> Of course, there is no way that students will be empowered until teachers themselves are empowered. And this will not happen until teachers are autonomous in their classrooms. Teachers can be held accountable by the community outside for raising literacy, but not told by external authorities precisely how literacy is to be achieved.
>
> The basic question is, Who is to be in charge of classrooms — teachers or outsiders? All the prescribed programs, all the pre-specified and detailed objectives, and all the mandated assessments are impositions from the outside. They interfere not only with the autonomy of teachers but with the ability of teachers and students to act together in pursuit of learning....
>
> I see but one solution for all these problems. Teachers must become more professional; they must regain control of classrooms, assert themselves politically, and demand that all outside interference in educational practice be halted....
>
> How are teachers to achieve this autonomy? The answer involves professional and political issues and demands professional commitment and political clout.[11]

And so the teaching of reading has been turned into a political struggle for control of the minds and hearts of American children who hold the key to America's future. Smith's insistence that teachers achieve full autonomy in the classroom, assert themselves politically, and act together with the students "in pursuit of learning," implies that parents, as outsiders, are to be excluded from the process and to have no say or influence over what or how their children are to be taught. The indoctrination of the students is to be exclusively the domain of their autonomous, nonaccountable teachers.

That such indoctrination should include political content was made clear in an article in *Young Children* (January 1989) entitled "Children's Political Knowledge and Attitudes," coauthored by three professors. They write:

> There is a clear rationale for early childhood educators to explore and promote political socialization in young children, and to play an important role in it. Children have and express political knowledge and attitudes. . . . Early childhood educators have an important role in helping children understand their social and political environment. Teachers can choose to model positive citizenship, practice a consensus decision-making process, and foster feelings of altruism and benevolence, all the while providing language opportunities to help children learn politically oriented vocabulary.[12]

In other words, elementary school teachers will include political indoctrination by way of vocabulary development, which is very much in line with the methods of Freire and Vygotsky. Concerning empowerment, William T. Fagan, in an article entitled "Empowered students; empowered teachers" (*The Reading Teacher,* April 1989), writes:

> Teachers have power over how reading and writing are taught, over how children experience reading and writing within the school text. . . . Teachers who impose a narrow view of reading or writing (word sounding, precision in spelling) may confuse children so that they began to feel powerless in the school context.[13]

That's another one of these nutty statements that fall so easily and abundantly from the lips of these professional ignoramuses. The idea that teaching a child to read by intensive phonics or to spell correctly will make him or her feel powerless is like saying that teaching a child how to make change correctly will deprive the child of the exhilarating power of throwing money away!

The putting down of phonics — "word sounding and precision in spelling" — is a constant theme among whole-language ideologues. Ken Goodman, in *What's Whole in Whole Language,* writes:

> Phonics methods of teaching reading and writing reduce both to matching letters with sounds. It is a flat-earth view of the world, since it rejects modern science about reading and writing and how they develop. (p.37)[14]

Apart from Prof. Goodman's atrocious writing style, his arguments can be exposed for the sham they are. If anything represents a flat-earth view of the world, it is ideographic writing that went out of style in the West some three or four thousand years ago but which Goodman and his cohorts are trying to restore as the wave of the future. Not all educational researchers share Prof. Goodman's strange cognitive aberrations. But unfortunately, too many do, and they are anything but true scientists. Their "experiments" are often conducted to produce pre-conceived outcomes. Even the results of Goodman's own "research" has been challenged by other educational researchers.[15] But whole-language "experts" simply ignore what they cannot answer, or issue more distortions of the truth.

That was certainly the case in November 1988, when *Phi Delta Kappan* published an attack on phonics written by Marie Carbo, a whole-language promoter, entitled "Debunking the Great Phonics Myth."[16] What Carbo tried to debunk was Jeanne Chall's influential book, *Teaching to Read: The Great Debate.* Carbo's attack was very detailed, very technical, with 88 footnotes taking up four pages.

It was assumed by the cheerleaders of the whole-language

movement that phonics had met its nemesis. But Prof. Chall was not about to play dead. She responded in March 1989 with a blistering article of her own in which she demolished Carbo's "research" point by point and chided the *Kappan* for publishing such an "irresponsible and possibly harmful" article. In closing, she wrote:

> One must conclude that the efforts of Marie Carbo to "debunk" the "great phonics myth" have failed. The many claims she makes regarding the shortcomings of the research on the phonics issue seem to be more characteristic of her own analyses than of those of the researchers she criticizes.
>
> Many scholarly publications guard against such misrepresentations by employing qualified readers as peer reviewers to critique articles before they are published, particularly in areas of controversy and of social importance. Such cautions are necessary to protect children — and the educational community that serves them.
>
> Thus, although Marie Carbo tried to show that the value of teaching phonics is a myth, the research evidence from 1910 to 1988 shows that the *real* "myth" is that children can learn to read English text without knowing or learning anything about phonics or letter-sound correspondences. Marie Carbo seems to believe strongly in such a myth. But, of course, she is wrong.[17]

It is obvious that it is the political twist of the whole-language movement that motivates its leaders to distort the teaching of reading into something it was never meant to be. And the distortion started with John Dewey whose political agenda was no secret. He wrote in *Democracy and Education* in 1916:

> The notion that the "essentials" of elementary education are the three R's mechanically treated, is based upon ignorance of the essentials needed for realization of democratic ideals. (p. 192)[18]

Isn't it odd that the three R's, "mechanically treated," produced our highly literate Founding Fathers who could write an eloquent, history-making Declaration of Independence and create a free society where literacy became virtually universal without the help of professors of education?

Dewey's socialism was so extreme that he even denied the individual's ownership of his own mind. He wrote:

> When knowledge is regarded as originating and developing within an individual, the ties which bind the mental life of one to that of his fellows are ignored and denied.
>
> When the social quality of individualized operations is denied, it becomes a problem to find connections which will unite an individual with his fellows. Moral individualism is set up by the conscious separation of different centers of life. It has its roots in the notion that the consciousness of each person is wholly private, a self-inclosed continent, intrinsically independent of the ideas, wishes, purposes of everybody else. (p. 297)[19]

In *The School and Society* Dewey wrote:

> Earlier psychology regarded mind as a purely individual affair in direct and naked contact with an external world. The only question was of the ways in which the world and mind acted upon each other. The entire process recognized would have been in theory exactly the same if there were one mind living alone in the universe.
>
> At present the tendency is to conceive individual mind as a function of social life — as not capable of operating or developing by itself, but as requiring continual stimulus from social agencies, and finding its nutrition in social supplies. The idea of heredity has made familiar the notion that the equipment of the individual, mental as well as physical, is an inheritance from the race: a capital inherited by the individual from the past and held in trust by him for the future. The idea of evolution has made familiar the notion that mind cannot be regarded as an individual, monopolistic possession, but represents the outworkings of the endeavor and thought of humanity; that it is developed in an environment which is social as well as physical, and that social needs and aims have been most potent in shaping it — and the chief difference between savagery and civilization is not the naked nature which each faces, but the social heredity and social medium. (pp. 90-91)[20]

Is it not interesting that Dewey speaks of the individual inheriting the knowledge of the past and "held in trust by him for the future," and yet he advocates abandoning hundreds of years of past experience in teaching in favor of some new untried methodology? The socialist revolutionaries were making a mockery of their inheritance. What they wanted was a brave new collectivist world built on the ashes of the old.

Freire echoes Dewey's views on individualism when he writes:

> [T]he individualistic ideology ends up negating social interests or it subsumes social interests with individualistic interests....[T]he individualistic position works against the comprehension of the real role of human agency. (p. 59)[21]

Freire also puts down the teaching of the "mechanics" of reading. He writes:

> I always saw teaching adults to read and write as a political act, an act of knowledge, and therefore a creative act. I would find it impossible to be engaged in a work of mechanically memorizing vowel sounds, as in the exercise "ba-be-bi-bo-bu, la-le-li-lo-lu." Nor could I reduce learning to read and write merely to learning words, syllables, or letters, a process of teaching in which the teacher fills the supposedly empty head of learners with his or her words. (p.34)[22]

But at the heart of Freire's philosophy is the notion that education and politics are inseparable. He writes:

> From the critical point of view, it is impossible to deny the political nature of the educational process as it is to deny the educational character of the political act. . . . But it is in this sense, as much for the educational process as for the political act, that one of the fundamental questions arises: in favor of whom and what (and thus against whom and what) do we promote education? And in favor of whom and what do we develop political activity? The more we gain this clarity of understanding through practice, the more we perceive the impossibility of separating the inseparable:

the education of politics. We can understand, then, that it is impossible to even think about education without considering the question of power. (p.38)

What we educators have to do, then, is to clarify the fact that education is political, and to be consistent with it in practice. (p.39)[23]

Perhaps the political agenda of the whole-language movement is best summed up by an article in *The Whole Language Catalog* entitled "The Politics of Whole Language" written by Bess Altwerger and Barbara Flores. They write:

> The traditional approach to teaching reading works effectively as this sorting mechanism, virtually assuring that one group of children — usually the poor and minorities — don't win or earn that admission ticket. Whole language teaching is subversive, in the best sense of the word, because it seeks to restore equality and democracy to our schools, to our children, and in essence, to our society. . . .
>
> Whole language puts power for learning, decision-making, and problem-solving back into the hands of teachers and students. It creates active learners; it empowers all of us to act upon and transform our environments and society in general. We are not just asking for a change in the teaching of reading, but a radical change in the social and political structure of schooling and society. (p. 418)[24]

How do you *restore* equality and democracy to a system that supposedly never had them? How do you "put back" into the hands of teachers and students powers they never had? Actually, the real purpose of the whole-language movement is simply to destroy every last vestige of traditional values the public schools still have. And there isn't much left.

12. The Hypocrisy of Whole Language

Although the advocates of whole language profess to be guided by the research of Soviet educational psychologist Lev Vygotsky, they have conveniently overlooked the fact that Vygotsky favored a phonics method of teaching reading. No doubt, he would have been appalled at the methods being used by whole-language teachers today, for they had been tried in the Soviet Union and they were found to be inadequate.

The article on primers in the *Great Soviet Encyclopedia* (Vol. 4, p. 423) is an interesting source of information. It reads:

> PRIMER, a textbook designed to teach reading and writing; a primary handbook for developing language and logical thinking in children.
>
> Illustrated primers are also among the initial means of aesthetic education. The teaching of reading and writing is accomplished by various methods (the syllabic method, the phonetic method, the "whole-words method," and so on); the corresponding primers are written for each method. The phonetic, analytic-synthetic method, which is the basis on which modern Soviet primers are compiled, is the most feasible method of teaching reading and writing.[1]

That's a pretty clear, unequivocal endorsement of intensive, systematic phonics as the "most feasible method of teaching reading and writing." Note also that primers are used to teach "logical thinking" to children, not critical thinking as is done in whole language. The article goes on to give a short history of Russian primers, which is worth reading:

> The first Slavic-Russian primers were the alphabet-grammar of Ivan Fedorov (L'vov, 1574), the primer of Lavrentii Zizanii (Vil'no, 1596), and the similar primer of V. Burtsov (Moscow, 1634). In the 17th century the best primer was the illustrated one by Karion Istomin (1694); it contained drawings of the objects in each lesson. In the 16th to 18th centuries, primers were composed according to the letter-by-letter method. In the mid-19th century primers composed according to the syllabic method and then the phonetic method (F. Studitskii, 1846; V. Zolotov, 1860) appeared. In 1864, K. D. Ushinskii created the first Russian primer constructed according to the analytic-synthetic sound method. The *New Alphabet* by L. N. Tolstoi, compiled according to the so-called aural method, appeared in 1875. The successors of Ushinskii . . . made a number of improvements in the analytic-synthetic sound method and in primers themselves.[2]

The final paragraph provides the crucial information:

> The first Soviet primers, compiled according to the so-called whole-words method, were replaced in 1932 by primers in which the analytic-synthetic sound method was revived (P. O. Afanas'ev and N. A. Kostin). Since then all primers have been compiled according to this method.

There you have it. The Soviets discarded the whole-word method in favor of intensive phonics. But why was the whole-word method adopted in the first place, since the history of teaching reading in Russia indicates that they had used a phonetic method prior to the revolution?

It appears that John Dewey and his colleagues, who visited Soviet Russia in the early days of the communist regime, were able to persuade Lenin's wife Krupskaya, who was in charge of education, to adopt the new progressive curriculum, which included the whole-word method, for Soviet primary schools.

And so the new reading instruction method was put into Soviet schools before it was even ready for American schools. In fact the Soviet schools served as full-fledged experimental labs where American progressive education ideas could be tested. And they were.

In 1922, Anna Louise Strong, a graduate of the University of Chicago, went to Russia where she investigated the new Soviet education. In February 1924, in an article published in *Survey Graphic,* she wrote:

> Their idea is modeled more on the Dewey ideas of education than anything else we know in America. Every new book by Dewey is grabbed and translated into Russian for consultation. Then they make their own additions.
>
> The purpose of Soviet education was, in the words of a Soviet teacher, "to teach the child collective action. We are trying to fit him to build a socialist state. We have our self-governed school community, in which teachers, children and janitors all have equal voice. It decides everything, what shall be planted in the school garden, what shall be taught. If the children decide against some necessary object, it is the teacher's job to show them through their play and life together that the subject is needed." (*School and Society*, 3/1/24)[3]

However, the Dewey-Soviet experiment came to an abrupt end in August 1932 when the Central Committee of the Communist Party abandoned the laboratory method and ordered a structured curriculum. The reaction of American progressives to the news was predictable. Dr. Lucy L. W. Wilson, a principal of a Philadelphia high school who had visited Russia, wrote the following report in *School and Society* (1/28/33):

> The consternation in the camps of educational progressives in this

country caused by the decree of the Central Committee of the Communist Party of the Soviet Union . . . was far greater than was any joy among the stalwarts. Probably few of the latter cared to understand the Soviet educational experiments, and fewer still sympathized with their aims and ideals or even believed in their existence. But the believers in progressive education . . . have been rejoicing to see in the Russian educational program an attempt to give the masses in its state-supported public schools the kind of education that some private schools in this country and in Europe have been striving earnestly to give to the relatively few who come to them. Hence their present disappointment.

It is true that the masterful teachers in the Soviet schools have been remarkably successful in developing healthy and strong boys and girls, active, courageous, independent in thought and in action, struggling valiantly for the interests of the working class — as they saw them. But sometimes — not always — these same children have been a bit weak in reading, writing and arithmetic as well as in definite factual knowledge in physics, in chemistry, in mathematics, in geography and in history — subjects now included in the three Rs of the "fully literate" in newest Russia.

These healthy, strong, courageous, independent boys and girls with scrapping and uneven funds of information and an imperfect grasp of mathematics and physics have not developed into the fully competent engineers, technicians and managers demanded by Five Year Plans, old and new. . . .

More than a year ago the Central Committee of the Communist Party, in its educational resolution sounded the warning:

"The basic defects at the present moment is that instruction in the schools does not give a sufficient amount of general educational subjects and does not satisfactorily solve the problem of preparing for the higher schools fully literate people well acquainted with the basic subjects of study."[4]

And so, the Dewey experiment was scrapped, and the Russians went back to teaching their children to read by the phonics method. American critics of progressive education hoped that its failure in the Soviet Union would cause its advocates in the U.S. to see the folly of their ways. One such opponent, Prof. William C. Bagley of Columbia University, made his views known in *School and Society* (1/14/33). He wrote:

> I have before me a translation of the decree . . . . This document states categorically that while the committee had decreed in September, 1931, that "no one method should be accepted as fundamental," the "laboratory" method has been so regarded in many schools and with unfortunate results.
>
> The decree directs the commissariats of education in the several republics of the Union "to liquidate these perversions of the laboratory method." . . . Hereafter the "accepted form of teaching in both the elementary and secondary schools must be classroom recitation based on a strict schedule and designed for a definite group of pupils." The decree sweeps "psychological" organization into the discard and enthrones hard-boiled "logical" organization. The teacher is to present his subject "in a systematic and sequential way, the pupils to be trained in the use of text-books." . . .
>
> Now if all this does not constitute as nearly complete an "about face" as modern education records, our American educational pilgrims to the land of the Soviets have been giving us false reports. Ever since this organization of the Soviet schools, Russia has been the Mecca of the advocates of the Progressive theories, which emphasize pupil-freedom, pupil-initiatives, pupil-experiences, pupil-activities and the breaking down of subject-matter boundaries. These were reflected in Soviet school practice more faithfully and on a wider scale than anywhere else in the world.
>
> Russia has been indeed the most favorable field for the exploitation of the Progressive doctrines, for the new school system, starting so to speak from "scratch," was emphatically free from the "stranglehold of tradition" which, the progressives have assured us, is the great obstacle encountered by their doctrines in other countries. . . .
>
> The official rejection of progressivism and the acceptance of the ideals of system, order and discipline is an event of outstanding significance. The Soviets' stake in an efficient school system is plain. Staring them in the face is the imperative need for a generation of men and women who will have the strength and the competence essential to the realization of the successive Soviet "plans." An educational theory that is inherently weak as a theory and inevitably enfeebling in its results can not produce such a generation. Apparently the leaders have found this out and have proceeded to jettison

the theory in order to save the ship. . . .

In our country, the need for strength and competence is probably just as great, but it is not so clearly discernible. A great plan is not at stake — for we have no plan. And in addition to this, our profession and a goodly segment of the public have been so thoroughly hypnotized by the appealing features of progressive education that they are quite insensitive to its fundamental weaknesses. The very terms used in our professional discussions load the dice in its favor — calling it "new," for example, and contrasting it with what has been increasingly referred to as the "traditional."...

American educational theory has too long been committed by a limited psychology and an essentially opportunistic philosophy to a debilitating hedonism. It would be difficult to conceive of a more unfortunate educational basis for the critical years that so clearly lie ahead.[5]

If it didn't work in the Soviet Union, why did our progressive educators believe that it would work in the U.S.? Probably because the Soviet Union was already a communist dictatorship and no longer needed a debilitating, hedonistic philosophy of education. What they needed were engineers and scientists who would be able to build the greatest war machine on earth.

But America was still a capitalist country, with no possibility whatever of becoming a communist dictatorship via a revolution. The only way that America could become a communist society was if future generations, trained and indoctrinated in socialist ideology in school, would eventually change America to become like the Soviet Union.

And so, our progressive educators, instead of abandoning their plans, pushed them forward with greater vigor. They were particularly keen on getting their methods into the primary schools where the new whole-word reading programs (i.e. Dick and Jane) were being adopted. *Even though they knew that these methods had produced appalling results in the Soviet Union, they were determined to inflict them on American children.*

The results, of course, were predictable. Complaints about the new teaching methods were numerous but conveniently ignored by the progressives who stuck to their agenda. One such complaint by Robert P. Carroll of Pennsylvania State College was published in *School and Society* (1/1/38). Although written in 1938, it could have been written last week:

> During the last few years it seems that interest in the teaching of reading has increased tremendously throughout the country in general. Various books and articles have been written about the matter, but a number of points have not yet been made clear. Both clarity and logic seem to be lacking especially in the teaching of beginners.
>
> Some have condemned the old method of teaching the letters and phonics, but assume that pupils should get them somehow along the way. They are also opposed to the use of the flash card, maintaining that pupils should learn words from the context. The idea is that we should surround pupils with a lot of interesting books and let them "read and read." The mystery is, how are pupils who do not know words, phonics nor letters going to take up a book and get anything whatever out of the context? How could a group of American adults take up a lot of interesting books in Chinese and learn right away to read without any previous knowledge of the words or characters?
>
> No one would think of asking a man to build a house if he knew nothing about the materials to be used, the tools, and the like. Why not be equally sound in the teaching of reading? Learning to read certainly is a matter of building, of developing, of acquiring more and more. If a child does not have the tools with which to build, he simply can not build. . . .
>
> It has been stated by many educational leaders that to teach children their letters would interfere with their "earmarking" words; that it would cause them to break up the word into letters instead of seeing the word as a whole. If a child learns a word by sight and later learns his letters and learns to spell the word, he then has to break it up. In considering the potency of recent reactions, will not this "delayed" breaking up of the word interfere more with his reading than if he put the word together at first and remembered it as he made it? In other words, if the breaking up has to come some time, why is it not better to do the breaking at the beginning or else to build in the beginning and never have any more emphasis on the parts

of the word?...

In the October, 1936, issue of the *Journal* of the National Education Association, page 205, Dr. Arthur I. Gates refers to the fact that "At the end of grade three, at least 40 percent of all pupils fall below the norms . . . shown to be the minimum required for handling the fourth grade reading curriculum without handicap."

If present methods are producing such poor results it seems that we should begin to try something different. The great trouble is that the foundation work is poor. There are too many things that pupils know only vaguely. They are greatly confused and know little about how to help themselves out of the maze. If they recognize a group of letters they do not know what sound or word the group makes. Another handicap coming from not learning the alphabet and the order of the letters is that pupils have difficulty in using a dictionary in the higher grades. . . .

Furthermore, the "sight method" may be partly the cause of some pupils being poor spellers, the first impression of a word being casual and giving the wrong idea about the sequence of the letters.

Uncertainty, haziness and vagueness are great handicaps to the most capable adults. It seems logical to assume that they are greater handicaps to children. In order to avoid these factors in the education of the child it would seem that we should begin with the most elementary things and teach them thoroughly; that we should teach thoroughly the tools for learning. This would include the alphabet, phonics, spelling and writing.[6]

As we said, this letter could have been written last week about "whole language." As much as whole language educators like to promote their ideas and methods as being "new," they certainly are not. And the basic defects of their methodology were exposed in 1844 by the Boston schoolmasters, in 1929 by Dr. Orton, in 1932 by Russian educators, in 1933 by Prof. Bagley, in 1938 by Robert Carroll, in 1954 by Howard Whitman, in 1955 by Rudolf Flesch, in 1965 by Prof. Chall (although she did not address the psychological damage caused by the sight method), in 1973 by this writer in *The New Illiterates*, in 1981 by Dr. Flesch. And yet, the "educators" persist in their flagrant error.

What is even more telling are the psychological reasons why

the Russians threw out look-say and returned to a phonetic method of teaching reading. It has a lot to do with the experiments that Soviet psychologists were conducting in their laboratories in the 1920s and '30s.

It is well known that Soviet psychologists had experimented with methods of artificially inducing behavioral disorganization in human beings. In fact, the major experimental work in that field was conducted by Soviet psychologist Aleksandr R. Luria, whose book, *The Nature of Human Conflicts,* was translated into English and published in the United States in 1932. The translator was Dr. W. Horsley Gantt of Johns Hopkins University who himself had spent the years 1922 to 1929 in the Soviet Union working for five of those years in the laboratories of Prof. Pavlov on the physiology of the brain. In 1930 Gantt established the Pavlovian Laboratory at the Phipps Psychiatric Clinic at Johns Hopkins University. He also founded the Pavlovian Society for Research and was editor-in-chief of the *Pavlovian Journal of Biological Psychiatry.* Thus, by the 1930s, very cordial and intimate relations existed among Soviet and American psychologists and psychiatrists.

In Chapter One of his book, Luria writes:

> Pavlov obtained very definite affective "breaks," an acute disorganization of behavior, each time that the conditioned reflexes collided, when the animal was unable to react to two mutually exclusive tendencies, or was incapable of adequately responding to any imperative problem. (p. 12)[7]

We now know beyond a shadow of a doubt that by imposing whole-word teaching techniques on an alphabetic writing system, one can artificially induce dyslexia, thereby creating a learning block or reading neurosis. Reading disability is a form of behavioral disorganization induced by the whole-word, look-say method, because look-say sets up two mutually exclusive tendencies: the tendency to look at written English as an ideographic system, like Chinese, and the tendency to look at written English as a phonetic system because it is alphabetic.

The alphabetic system is in harmony with the spoken language because it is based on it. But the ideographic look-say system is in opposition to the spoken language because it is an entirely separate system of graphic symbols with no direct relation to any specific spoken language. Arabic numbers are a perfect example of such a system, because they can be read in any language. But numbers, when spelled out alphabetically in a particular language, can only be read in that language. In look-say, the written word is treated as a picture that can be interpreted by the reader in any way he or she wishes. As Prof. Goodman has said, it doesn't matter if the child reads the written word "horse" as "pony" — or, for that matter, "five" as "fifty" — for he's getting the meaning!

Now Luria, who is considered one of the most prominent neuropsychologists of the twentieth century, was a close colleague of Vygotsky. He has said, "All of my work has been no more than the working out of the psychological theory which [Vygotsky] constructed. . . . I divide my career into two periods: the small and insignificant period before my meeting with Vygotsky and the more important and essential one after the meeting." [8] (Wertsch, p. 9)

Believe it or not, it was Luria and Vygotsky who were chiefly responsible for getting rid of the look-say method in the Soviet schools. Confirmation of this comes to us indirectly through an article which appeared in the *Journal of Reading* of December 1981, a special issue devoted to education and literacy in communist Cuba. In an article entitled "Teaching reading in the Cuban primary schools," we are told that in the 1970s, Cuban "teams of curriculum experts" were given the job of "developing a unified methodology" for Cuban schools. The authors write:

After reviewing the relevant research, these curriculum specialists chose the Phonic/Analytic/Synthetic method of teaching reading which was originally developed and researched in the Soviet Union and is still in use there. This method and curriculum materials which evolved from it now constitute the official approach to the teaching of reading in the Cuban primary schools, and are used throughout the public education system.[9]

The article then goes on to tell us that the "psychological roots" of the Soviet method "can be traced to the work of Lev Vygotsky, Alexander Luria (one of Vygotsky's students), and their associates." Since whole language educators are so familiar with the work of Vygotsky, it's hard to believe that they are not aware of Vygotsky's views on the teaching of reading. The article tells us:

Following Vygotsky, Luria characterizes reading and writing as an integrated process developmentally progressing through various stages. He recognizes that the reading process differs with different languages. For example, largely nonphonetic writing systems like Chinese are not dependent on auditory decoding as are phonetic codes. The conventional symbols of Chinese do not record the phonetic composition of words, but rather ideas and concepts. In such a writing system, the visual modality is primary and, therefore, most developed. But, for languages that have alphabet writing systems (such as Spanish or English), Luria believes that reading should be approached primarily through the auditory channel.

. . . Consequently, methodologies for teaching reading should be based on the principle that comprehension of written, as well as oral, language is fundamentally related to the sound structure of the word and this is so whether the written word is perceived as a whole, in syllables, or as separate letters. . . .

While many children learn to read by the "sight" approach, they usually do not develop the "phonematic hearing" which results from the auditory analysis and synthesis of word sounds. Thus, they are hampered in their development of the other language skills of spelling, writing, and speech articulation. To bypass such auditory training is to deprive the child of an important key to language. From this perspective, the methodology used in the teaching of reading assumes unexpected importance.

Are there any reading instruction programs in America based on the same principles as the Soviet teaching methods endorsed by Luria and Vygotsky? The article informs us:

> In the United States, the approach closest to the Phonic/Analytic/ Synthetic Method was developed in the late 1930s by Anna Gillingham, an educator, in collaboration with Samuel Orton, a neurologist interested in dyslexia. Orton decried the use of the "sight" method in the schools and emphasized the importance of the auditory blending process.
>
> A number of methods adapted to classroom use qualify to be termed as "Orton" approach, such as those of Spalding and Spalding (1957), Traub (1977), Slingerland (1967) and Pollack (1979). What is characteristic of all of them is ... they are intensive phonic approaches moving from sound/ symbol relationships to words, phrases, sentences and then on to extended connected discourse.
>
> The Orton approach is known to be particularly effective in teaching dyslexic students because of their great difficulty with the sequence of sounds in words.[10]

Orton, as we have pointed out in an earlier chapter, was the neuropathologist who first sounded the alarm back in 1929, pointing out the negative learning and emotional effects of the look-say, whole-word method. The teaching methods he helped develop with Anna Gillingham were used not only to retrain the thousands of children who had become reading disabled because of look-say, but were also used to train doctors who were setting up reading clinics in hospitals around the country to help cure "dyslexia." Yet, Orton's warnings were disregarded by Gray, Gates, Thorndike, Judd and others who knew—or should have known—what psychologists like Pavlov, Luria, Lewin, and others were doing in their laboratories. Certainly the Russians were well aware of the work of their American and European counterparts. Vygotsky was well aware of Piaget's work, and Luria drew attention to Lewin's work in Berlin, and they were all well acquainted with Dewey's writings. Dewey and a group of his colleagues had visited the Soviet Union in 1928, and Prof. George Counts of Teachers College had toured the Soviet Union in 1927 and 1929.[11]

In fact, in 1934, a group of about 200 Americans spent the summer in the Soviet Union attending the Anglo-American Institute of Moscow University. They were offered a variety of courses in education, psychology, economics, and sociology, all taught by Soviet professors in English. We do not know if there were any teachers of reading among them, but the *New York Times* of July 23, 1934 reported that politically and socially the students were "of many types, ranging from members of students' radical organizations to Groton graduates planning to enter Harvard or Yale next Fall."

All of this had been arranged by Stephen P. Duggan, director of the Institute of International Education, which sponsored the Moscow summer schools. He explained how these arrangements had been made in a letter to the *New York Times* published May 4, 1935:

> In the Fall of 1933 I was invited by the Soviet Government to go to Moscow to advise with it as to the best methods to develop cultural relations between the United States and the Soviet Union. . . . Before leaving for Russia I invited a number of distinguished educators to form an advisory council. Every one invited accepted the invitation, and during the following years two meetings of the advisory council were held.
>
> In order to discover from those who attended the Moscow Summer session the relative success of the enterprise, I requested a confidential report from each student at the close of the session. These reports were very illuminating. One criticism upon which there was almost unanimous agreement was that each professor who conducted a course thought it necessary to give the background of the Soviet philosophy of political and social organization to show how his particular course fitted it. As there were thirteen courses, the students naturally grew tired of the repetition. Hence this Fall a subcommittee of the advisory committee conferred with the representatives of the Soviet educational authorities as to ways in which the Summer School might be improved. I suggested that one fundamental

course on the principles of the collective society should be given which would be a prerequisite for all students who did not give evidence of a previous familiarity with that system. . . .

Among Duggan's advisors were such academic luminaries as John Dewey and George E. Counts of Columbia University; Frank P. Graham, president of the University of North Carolina; Robert M. Hutchins, president of the University of Chicago; Charles H. Judd, dean of the School of Education at the University of Chicago; and William F. Russell, dean of Teachers College, Columbia University. It was Judd's protégé, William Scott Gray, who had brought out the new look-say Dick and Jane books in 1930 and it was Arthur Gates, Thorndike's protégé at Teachers College, who had brought out his own look-say series at the same time.

The summer school of 1935, which was promoted by a full page ad in the *Journal* of the National Education Association, was abruptly cancelled by the Soviet government shortly after the arrival of about 200 Americans in Moscow. Apparently, some of the Soviet professors had fallen victim to Stalin's massive purge of the Communist Party. It was probably also feared that some of the Americans might be Trotskyite agents. In any case, the purge of the Trotskyites and Old Bolsheviks hardly seemed to put a dent in the ongoing infiltration of American institutions by communists. Nor did the purges deter American progressives from pursuing their socialist goals.

As for Prof. Duggan, who was obviously sympathetic to the Soviet Union, his son Laurence succeeded him as director of the Institute of International Education. Laurence Duggan evidently shared his father's views toward the communist utopia, for on December 20, 1948, at the age of 43, he fell, jumped, or was pushed from the window of his sixteenth floor office in New York after having been implicated by Whittaker Chambers as belonging to a communist spy ring. Duggan had already been interviewed by the

FBI and was scheduled to testify the next day before a Congressional committee investigating the infiltration of the U.S. government by communist agents.

It should be noted that Alexander Luria survived Stalin's purges and reign of terror as well as World War II. During his visit to the United States in March 1960 he lectured at the Postgraduate Center for Psychotherapy in New York under the sponsorship of the Samuel Rubin International Seminars on Mental Health. The subject was "Advanced Studies in Neurophysiology and Behavior."

One of the participants in the seminar was Dr. W. Horsley Gantt, Luria's translator who had spent the years 1922 to 1929 working with Pavlov in his laboratories in the Soviet Union. Back in the U.S., Gantt established the Pavlovian laboratory at the Phipps Psychiatric Clinic at Johns Hopkins University in Baltimore. In 1944, he produced a study entitled *Experimental Basis for Neurotic Behavior; Origin and Development of Artificially Produced Disturbances of Behavior in Dogs.* The study represented experiments conducted over a 12-year period at the laboratory. Gantt had translated Luria's important book, *The Nature of Human Conflicts: An Objective Study of Disorganization and Control of Human Behavior,* published in the U.S. in 1932. Subsequent to Luria's visit to the U.S. in 1960, several of the psychologist's other books were then translated into English and published in the U.S., including *Higher Cortical Functions in Man* (1966), *Cognitive Development, Its Cultural and Social Foundations* (1976), *Human Brain and Psychological Processes* (1966), and *Traumatic Aphasia: its syndromes, psychology and treatment* (1970).

As for the Samuel Rubin International Seminars on Mental Health, it should be noted that in 1963, the Samuel Rubin Foundation made a million-dollar grant to help establish the Institute for Policy Studies (IPS) in Washington, D.C., a notorious Marxist think tank which has waged an unrelenting war against conservative economic and social policies and has collaborated closely with America's Marxist enemies in Central and South America.[12]

Actually, it was Samuel Rubin's daughter, Cora Weiss, who used her family's 25-million-dollar fortune to finance the IPS, whose programs over the years have elicited the sponsorship of many left-leaning members of Congress and whose influence was apparent within the Clinton White House.[13] In fact, Derek Shearer, an IPS operative and author (with Martin Carnoy) of *Economic Democracy: The Challenge of the 1980s,* is a close friend of the Clintons and was Bill Clinton's top economic advisor prior to the election.[14] According to Shearer, "Socialism has a bad name in America, and no amount of wishful thinking on the part of the left is going to change that.... the words Economic Democracy are an adequate and effective replacement." (*Nation,* 10/11/75, p. 340)[15]

In their book, Shearer and Carnoy referred to Antonio Gramsci on strategy:

> The vision of economic democracy must begin to emerge as a *majority* viewpoint. This is what Italian social thinker Antonio Gramsci called "ideological hegemony."

Gramsci, of course, was more than just a "social thinker." He was one of the founders of the Italian Communist Party who preached that communism is best achieved in a developed Christian, capitalist society through cultural transformation. No doubt the IPS itself is a manifestation of the Gramsci strategy to create "organic intellectuals" who produce a steady stream of books, articles, position papers, legislative proposals, conferences and seminars to promote the socialist agenda. In fact, one cannot fully understand the strategy of today's American leftists and their permeation of our cultural institutions without understanding the grand Gramsci strategy.

Antonio Gramsci was born in 1891 and died in 1937, spending

the last eleven years of his life in prison where he wrote his famous *Prison Notebooks,* which became essential reading for America's '60s radicals, many of whom today hold tenured positions in American universities.[16] That Gramsci's ideas are alive and well in the whole language movement was indicated in an introduction to Paulo Freire and Donaldo Macedo's book, *Literacy: Reading the Word and the World,* published in 1987. The introduction, written by leftist radical Henry A. Giroux and entitled "Literacy and the Pegagogy of Political Empowerment," asserts that Gramsci appeared "to both politicize the notion of literacy and at the same time invest it with an ideological meaning that suggests that it may have less to do with the task of teaching people how to read and write than with producing and legitimating oppressive and exploitative social relations." Giroux states (pp. 1-2):

> A master dialectician, Gramsci viewed literacy as both a concept and a social practice that must be linked historically to configurations of knowledge and power, on the one hand, and the political and cultural struggle over language and experience on the other. . . . As a terrain of struggle, Gramsci believed that critical literacy had to be fought for as an ideological construct and as a social movement. . . .
>
> . . . For Gramsci, literacy became . . . a referent and mode of critique for developing forms of counterhegemonic education . . . .[17]

Malachi Martin, in his brilliant book, *The Keys of This Blood,* explains that Gramsci, analyzing the West, recognized that Christian culture and values had too great a hold on the proletarian masses, which therefore made an armed and violent revolution impossible. Christian culture had to be thoroughly undermined before communism could take over. Martin writes:

> True to his general blueprint for action, therefore, Gramsci's idea was that Marxist action must be unitary against what he saw to be the failing remnant of Christianity. And by a unitary attack, Gramsci meant that

Marxists must change the residually Christian mind. He needed to alter that mind—to turn it into its opposite in all its details—so that it would become not merely a non-Christian mind but an anti-Christian mind.

In the most practical terms, he needed to get individuals and groups in every class and station of life to think about life's problems without reference to the Christian transcendent, without reference to God and the laws of God. He needed to get them to react with antipathy and positive opposition to any introduction of Christian ideals or the Christian transcendent into the treatment and solution of the problems of modern life....

It was also obvious that such goals, like most of Gramsci's blueprint, had to be pursued by means of a quiet and anonymous revolution. No armed and bloodly uprisings would do it. . . . Rather, everything must be done in the name of man's dignity and rights, and in the name of his autonomy and freedom from outside constraint. From the claims and constraints of Christianity, above all.

Accomplish that, said Gramsci, and you will have established a true and freely adopted hegemony over the civil and political thinking of every formerly Christian country. Do that, he promised, and in essense you will have Marxized the West. (pp. 250-251)[18]

It is obvious that, with the help of secular humanism, Gramsci's anti-Christian program has achieved enormous success in America, particularly in public education where thoroughly anti-Christian sex education and values clarification dominate the affective curriculum. As for the founder of IPS, Cora Weiss, authors Peter Collier and David Horowitz, in their book, *Destructive Generation,* write:

Weiss was typical of the red-diaper babies who remained loyal to the Communist politics they inherited from their parents, even if they did not join the Party itself. The father whose fortune she dispensed was an old-line Stalinist, and she retained the "progressive" commitments that had determined his political course. (p. 151)[19]

All of which suggests that when an old-line Stalinist like

Samuel Rubin sponsors an international seminar on mental health in which the star speaker is Soviet psychologist Alexander Luria, chief experimenter on ways of artificially producing behavioral disorganization, one must wonder what kind of "mental health" they were talking about.

13. Miscue Analysis: Training Normal Children to Read Like Defective Children

Back in the early 1900s, when the professors of education were working overtime to find "scientific" justification for changing reading instruction in American schools from alphabetic phonics to the look-say, sight, or whole-word method, many studies were done to see what kind of effect the new method would have on children's reading ability.

One study done by Myrtle Sholty, published in the February 1912 issue of the *Elementary School Teacher*, revealed that the two methods of teaching reading produce two different kinds of readers: objective and subjective. The alphabetic-phonics method produces fluent, accurate, objective readers while the sight method produces impaired subjective readers who guess at words, omit words, insert words, substitute words, and mutilate words. The sight readers' lack of phonetic knowledge puts them at a distinct disadvantage. They are unable to accurately decode the words since they look at them as whole configurations, like Chinese ideographs, with no connections to the sounds of the language.[1]

Reading researcher Geraldine Rodgers, in an unpublished manuscript on the history of reading instruction (p. 728), states that Sholty's experiment merely confirmed what had been discovered in 1903 by German psychologist Oskar Messmer, who had identified the two types of readers. Rodgers writes:

> When William Scott Gray [future editor of "Dick and Jane"] published his summary of American reading research in 1925, which has been the foundation for all "histories" of "reading research" ever since, he "naturally" omitted Messmer's German work, and "accidentally" misreported Sholty's research in his brief summary so that it was no longer recognizable concerning either its nature or its conclusions.
>
> Sholty was reporting on her tests with three little girls half-way through second grade, so the tests must have been done before 1912, probably after February, 1911. Of the three second-grade girls, two were reading words in parts, for sound, but one was reading only whole words for meaning. However, all three little girls at the University of Chicago experimental school were "helped" by context guessing, which was obviously necessary because of the small amount of phonic training used at the experimental school. Sholty specifically referred to Messmer's research and noted that her research results were in line with his conclusions.[2]

In 1914, psychologist Walter F. Dearborn, who reviewed the Sholty study, wrote about Messmer's observations:

> The chief differences between these types [of readers] are said to be that the objective readers have a rather narrow span of attention in reading, but see accurately what they do see, and seldom guess or "read into" the material perceived, and that the subjective readers have a wider span, are influenced more by words lying in indirect vision, depend on relatively meager visual cues such as large word wholes, and that they are more likely to misread because of the large apperceptive element which they supply to the reading. (p. 42)[3]

And so it was well known by the top psychologists involved in creating the new look-say or sight reading programs that these whole-word instruction methods produced inaccurate subjective readers. Despite this, the professors proceeded to produce and publish the textbooks based on this very defective methodology.

Another very significant study, published in the November 1914 issue of the *Elementary School Teacher*, was done by Clara Schmitt, an assistant in the department of child study at the Chicago Board of Education. She analyzed the errors made in oral reading by two groups of children: one mentally defective, the other normal. She wrote:

> The child may show an ability to recognize words from the printed page to a greater or less extent, but this recognition with the defective child consists, largely, merely of a mechanical type of visual memory which serves as a stimulus for its associated vocal prototype. The child who learns words in this way only is always dependent upon his teacher since he can acquire for himself no new or unfamilair word from the printed page. He can become somewhat independent of his teacher only if he learns phonetic values. Defective children are sometimes capable of acquiring very large visual vocabularies, but show themselves quite deficient in perceiving phonetic relationships. Children of the first grade may be expected to acquire the simplest phonetic elements of the English language. The child who can obtain a visual vocabulary with facility, who gains a perception of the simple phonetic values, and who learns to combine them correctly for the independent learning of new words is considered a favorable reactor so far as the subject of reading in the first grade of the public schools is concerned.[4]

The normal children chosen for the test were average good readers, aged 7 to 11. The defective children were between the ages of 10 and 16 who had been in special rooms for defective children for at least one year. Since at that time the official policy of the Chicago public schools was to teach children to read phonetically, both the normal and defective children had been taught the same way. While the normal children learned to read phonetically with ease, the defective children had problems. Miss Schmitt writes:

> The phonetics which underlie the reading process is the great stumbling-block of the defective child. Seldom is one found who has this accomplishment. He may be able to learn a very few of the simplest combinations, such as consist of one or two consonants and a vowel. The normal child progresses in his knowledge of phonetic values to such an extent that he becomes independent of the teacher in so far as the illogical complexities of our English spelling permit. At the fourth grade the normal child is able to work out new and unfamiliar words with approximate phonetic correctness.

But what is particularly interesting in this study is the discovery that the defective children made very different kinds of errors, even though they had all been taught to read phonetically. Miss Schmitt writes:

> The errors in pronunciation made by the normal children in this and the second reading test were always in favor of a word which had considerable visual or phonetic resemblance to the correct word. The errors made by the defective children with the first selection which was perfectly familiar to them in content, at least, were absurd as far as visual or phonetic values were concerned, but were calculated to fill in the context. The defective child reads, for instance, that the fox saw a vine with *berries* [instead of *grapes*] on it. Because of the great prevalence of this type of variation the performance of the defective group cannot be compared with that of the normal.[5]

In other words, it was easier for the defective child to substitute a word which fitted the context than decode the word accurately, which means that the defective children were reading like nonphonetic sight readers. *And that is the way normal children are being taught to read today!* For example, in *Evaluation: Whole Language, Whole Child,* a book explaining the wonders of whole language, the authors write:

The way you interpret what the child does will reflect what you understand reading to be. For instance, if she reads the word *feather* for *father*, a phonics-oriented teacher might be pleased because she's come close to sounding the word out. However, if you believe reading is a meaning-seeking process, you may be concerned that she's overly dependent on phonics at the expense of meaning. You'd be happier with a miscue such as *daddy*, even though it doesn't look or sound anything like the word in the text. At least the meaning would be intact. (p. 19)[6]

In other words, a whole-language teacher would prefer that a child read more like a defective child than a normal child! But even the early advocates of the whole-word method realized that they would have to teach some phonics. This was obvious from an analysis made by Josephine Bowden in 1912 of how children learned a "sight vocabulary." (See chap. 8.) She found "no evidence in any of the cases studied that the child works out a system by which he learns to recognize the words. That he does not work out phonics for himself comes out quite clearly in the transposition test. Furthermore, only once did a child divide a word even into its syllables." Her conclusion:

Under the methods of instruction employed with this class as outlined above, it appears that these beginners in reading have after two months or more of instruction secured a sufficient concept of the general appearance of a very limited number of words to recognize them as wholes, that in doing this they made use of only very general cues or points of differentiation between words and have not noticed the finer points of distinction between words and parts of words. It appeared very doubtful to the experimenter whether, under this method of teaching words as visual wholes, the pupils would of themselves, have come to make this latter necessary analysis with much success. Without some foregoing analysis and subsequent synthesis, the differences between words are not great enough to be recognized merely from the total visual appearance. The early introduction of phonics may supply, in some measure, this analysis.[7]

Contrast what Josephine Bowden wrote in 1912 about the necessity of teaching phonics in a look-say reading program with what whole-language guru Frank Smith wrote in *Reading Without Nonsense* in 1985 (p. 129):

> Children do not need a mastery of phonics in order to identify words that they have not met in print before. . . . Once a child discovers what a word is in a meaningful context, learning to recognize it on another occasion is as simple as learning to recognize a face on a second occasion, and does not need phonics. Discovering what a word is in the first place is usually most efficiently accomplished by asking someone, listening to someone else read the word, or using context to provide a subtantial clue.[8]

The difference between Josephine Bowden and Frank Smith is that Bowden came to her conclusions after observing real children in a real classroom, whereas Smith writes from theory alone. What is important about the three early experiments conducted in Chicago is that they taught us three important facts about reading instruction. The Sholty experiment confirmed that the two teaching methods—phonics and whole-word—produce two different kinds of readers. Phonics produces accurate objective readers; whole-word methodology produces error-prone subjective readers. The Schmitt experiment reveals that today's normal children who are taught to read by look-say make the same kinds of errors that defective children, incapable of learning to read by phonics, make. In other words, we are training normal children to behave like defective children! And the Bowden experiment proved that without some phonics, the whole-word method was dismally inadequate as a reading instruction system.

Which brings us to the subject of "miscue analysis." Frank Smith explains the concept of the miscue in *Understanding Reading* (p. 151):

The prior use of meaning ensures that when individual words must be identified, for example, in order to read aloud, a minimum of visual information need be used. And as a consequence, mistakes will often occur. If a reader already has a good idea of what a word might be, there is not much point in delaying to make extra certain what the word actually is. As a result it is not unusual for even highly experienced readers to make misreadings that are radically different visually—like reading "said" when the word is actually *announced* or *reported* but which make no significant difference to the meaning. Beginning readers often show exactly the same tendency . . . . The mistakes that are made are sometimes called *miscues* rather than *errors* to avoid the connotation that they are something bad (Goodman, 1969). Such misreadings show that these beginning readers are attempting to read in the way fluent readers do, with sense taking priority over individual word identification.[9]

One could write a book about the utterly perverse reasoning in that paragraph. In the first place only a sight reader could make the kinds of errors Smith illustrates. A phonetic reader will make entirely different kinds of errors, perhaps something on the order of scanning hastily and reading *deported* for *departed*, but then correcting himself because the sentence doesn't make sense. On the other hand, substituting "said" for "announced" is the kind of error that Schmitt found that defective children made even though they had been taught to read by a phonetic method.

I can confirm, from my own experience as a tutor, this tendency on the part of retarded individuals to read as Schmitt observed. For ten years I tutored a retarded young man and taught him to read by intensive phonics. Yet, he often made the kind of errors Schmitt observed. Whenever he came to a word he could not read, he substituted a word which made no sense phonetically. In other words, sounding out the word was not his first means of word attack, even though the word might have been one he had previously read correctly. Whenever he did this, I had him spell out the word, and suddenly his phonetic knowledge came to the fore, and he read the word correctly.

When Frank Smith tells us that normal beginning readers make the same kinds of mistakes that defective children make, what he should tell us is that normal beginning readers *taught to read by the whole-word method* make the same kinds of errors that adult *sight* readers make! It is one of the dishonest tricks that whole-language advocates play, by not telling the reader when speaking of miscues what kind of beginning reading instruction was used with the individuals being examined. The very fact that the word "miscue" is used instead of "error" is a good indication of the intellectual dishonesty at work, the fancy sleight of hand being used to confuse the public.

Apparently, the idea of "miscue analysis" was dreamed up by Prof. Kenneth Goodman and his wife, Yetta. In my opinion, miscue analysis is probably the worst form of educational malpractice ever invented. What they do is take a poor sight reader—a victim of the whole-word method—and try to improve his guessing "strategies." After all, it was Ken Goodman who defined reading as a "psycholinguistic guessing game." In other words, no attempt is made to train the poor sight reader to become an accurate phonetic reader. As long as the sight reader's word insertions, omissions and substitutions relate more closely to the meaning of the text, they are acceptable. In short, the purpose of miscue analysis is to make sure that the pupil remains permanently crippled as a sight reader and never becomes an accurate phonetic reader. Ken Goodman writes in *The Whole Language Catalog* (p. 100):

> Miscue analysis helps people to realise that many of the miscues kids are making are sensible, even remarkable sometimes, in what they reveal about the language processes that the reader would have to go through to have produced them.[10]

Yetta Goodman states in the same article:

> Insertions and omissions can give you tremendous insight into whether a reader is proficient or not. Proficient readers tend to make insertions more than less proficient readers; certain kinds of omissions tend to be things that are acceptable to the syntax and semantic structure of the text, and good readers make them all the time. Other kinds of omissions indicate kids who want to leave out words that they are afraid to try and identify.[11]

Can you believe it? A reader is more "proficient" if he or she reads something that isn't there—that is, inserts a word in the text—than a reader who doesn't! Of course, the Goodmans have no intention of teaching these sight readers to become phonetic readers. Ken Goodman writes:

> The concept I put in the place of "remedial" is "revaluing"; that is where the intent of the teacher is to help the child to revalue himself or herself as a reader and to revalue the process; to help the child move away from the process of sounding out and attacking words, and toward making sense out of print and legitimising the kinds of productive strategies that the kids have been using and had thought were cheating. These kids are often their own worst enemies in that their beliefs about themselves and their ability to learn get in their way constantly; they're very easily discouraged. So a lot of patient time taken to help them revalue themselves is the most essential thing.

In other words, the main therapeutic purpose of miscue analysis is to convince the defective reader that it's okay to be a defective reader, as long as the miscues make sense. Its purpose is "to help the child move away from the process of sounding out and attacking words, and towards making sense out of print." But, of course, in the workplace such nonsense does not hold water. An error is an error no matter what else you may call it, and to try to convince a child that an error is not an error will not serve him well when he is an adult confronting the demands of a technologically advanced economy that requires accuracy and precision in thinking and performing and reading. Ken Goodman writes:

> If you understand reading as a transactive process, and that the sense that the reader brings to the text is at least half of what is going on, then we understand what strategies develop that are necessary to deal with the print in the context of that. You can't make reading easier by pulling the process apart and teaching reading skills as such.[12]

Thus, according to whole-language theorists, "the sense that the reader brings to the text" is just as important as the text itself. But supposing the student picks up a book on a subject he knows nothing about? What "sense" other than ignorance does he bring to the text? Many whole-language teachers know nothing about intensive, systematic phonics. But they bring a "sense" of hostility to any arguments in favor of intensive, systematic phonics. I know this to be true, because I have addressed whole-language teachers whose hostility prevented them from even beginning to understand what I was talking about. And I have no doubt that any of them who might start reading this book as a "transactive process" will probably want to burn it rather than finish reading it.

The quest for truth requires a respect and appreciation for accuracy and precision of thought. If, to begin with, you denigrate accuracy in reading, you denigrate the pursuit of truth.

If you want to get an idea of how miscue analysis works, Yetta Goodman and Wendy Hood give an illuminating case history in *The Whole Language Catalog* (p.102). The subject being analyzed is a 7-year-old second grader by the name of Aaron. Goodman and Hood write:

> The procedure involves listening to the unaided oral reading of a complete story or article, asking readers to reflect and retell following their reading and analyzing the responses they make to the text. . . . The unexpected responses readers make are known as miscues. . . .
> Aaron's miscue analysis provides a wealth of information about his

reading. . . . Rarely does Aaron self-correct his predictable miscues that result in acceptable sentences. But Aaron responds differently when his predictions are unacceptable. . . . Aaron often reads to the end of the sentence with an unacceptable miscue before he decides to reread and self-correct. It seems that he is not yet confident enough to self-correct more quickly and needs the additional context to confirm or disconfirm his miscues. . . . Whenever he can, Aaron produces a real word substitution that results in an acceptable and meaningful sentence. . . . Aaron is comfortable omitting words to maintain the flow of the story, especially adjectives . . . which are not necessary to retain the structure of the sentence.

Aaron's miscue profile allows us to plan appropriate reading experiences for him. . . . We talked about why omitting is sometimes a good strategy. He said it helps him "keep the story going." Looking at some of his substitutions, we also talked about reading through to the end of a sentence and substituting a "best guess" that makes sense.

In short, the whole purpose of the miscue analysis is to help the child become a better guesser instead of an accurate phonetic reader who does not need to guess.

Are reading teachers taken in by this? You'd better believe it. The authors write:

As teachers work with miscue analysis, there are two common responses. Teachers become excited about what they are learning about reading and their students. Reading specialists say that they have never known as much about their students as they know when they do miscue analysis. The second common response is "I will never be able to listen to a student read in the same way again." (p. 103)[13]

All of which indicates that none of these teachers have the faintest idea what an alphabetic writing system is about and how a child should be taught it. In my opinion, miscue analysis is the cruelest hoax ever perpetrated on unsuspecting children. To convince a normal child that it is perfectly all right to read as if he or she had a defective brain is so heinous a form of miseducation as to be nothing short of a crime.

Do these teachers know what they are doing? Undoubtedly, many of them have read Frank Smith's *Understanding Reading*, one of several whole-language bibles. A book note on p. 103 of the *Whole Language Catalog* states:

> Smith deftly dismantles the logic behind the popular traditional approaches to teaching reading, and in uncompromising detail explains what reading is and what teachers can do to support it. Interwoven throughout is his sociopsycholinguistic theory of learning.

Dismantling the logic behind the traditional approaches to teaching reading sounds a lot like deconstruction. And that is the key to the whole-language movement: sociopsycholinguistic deconstruction.

14. Whole Language: Deconstruction in the Primary School

The ultimate goal of the whole-language movement—described by its promoters as "nothing short of a grass-roots revolution in education"—is the replacement of our biblically based Christian civilization by a world pagan, socialist system. This may sound like an extreme statement, but it is clearly the unadorned truth if one examines the importance of whole language as a socio-political weapon in the cultural war between humanism and Christianity. It certainly fits in nicely with the Gramscian strategy for an anti-Christian cultural revolution

Perhaps the silliest anti-Biblical statement to be found in the *Whole Language Catalog* is a quotation from James Moffett's book, *Storm in the Mountains: A Case Study of Censorship, Conflict, and Consciousness.* Mr. Moffett writes (p. 71):

> "God believes in the beauty of phonics" means that those who see themselves as God's spokespeople prefer phonics, precisely, I think, because it shuts out content by focusing the child on particles of language

> too small to have any meaning. In other words, what phonics really amounts to for those who are sure they have a corner on God's mind but are very unsure of being able to hold their children's minds is *another way to censor books* (unconsciously, of course) *by nipping literacy itself in the bud.*

Have you ever read anything quite as ridiculous as that? In the first place, phonics permits a child to become an independent reader, so that he can read anything he wants. In our world of bookstores and public libraries there is no way that any parent can censor a child's reading forever. Phonics does not "shut out content" by focusing the child on letter sounds. Nor do children who are taught to read by intensive phonics spend the rest of their lives reading nonsense syllables. First of all, the phonics phase in an intensive, systematic program is generally completed in six months to a year, after which the focus is indeed not only on content but also on spelling, vocabulary development, grammar, composition, literature, etc. It is not only God's people who prefer phonics, but any individual with common sense, for our writing system is an alphabetic one, and requires a phonetic method of instruction.

Mr. Moffett is considered "a major foundational thinker of the whole language movement." He had his baptism of fire in 1974 when one of his books, published by Houghton Mifflin, became the object of the famous Kanawha County, West Virginia, textbook protest by parents who objected to the anti-Christian content in public school reading materials. From that, Mr. Moffett has made the giant leap to the belief that phonics is a subtle form of censorship, when actually it is whole language that is a not-so-subtle form of censorship by denying children the ability to read the printed word with accuracy and precision.

But one must ask what do people like James Moffett believe in? If he is not a believer in the Bible, what does he believe in besides whole language? Is he a humanist, environmentalist, or eco-pagan? Is he into earth worship or New Age mysticism?

The eco-summit meeting in Rio de Janeiro in July 1992, where the political leaders of the world showed more admiration for Fidel Castro than for George Bush, is a sample of what is to come if the plans of the "environmentalists"—the new name for socialists—come to fruition. Green-theology prevailed at the summit where Senator Al Gore, who led the U.S. Senate delegation, called for a new spiritual relationship between man and earth. According to *New American* reporter William F. Jasper (7/13/92), who attended the summit:

> A centerpiece of the Global Forum opening ceremony was the Viking ship *Gaia,* named for the Greek goddess of earth. At the culmination of that program, a group calling itself the "Sacred Drums of the Earth" struck up a solemn cadence. The ceremony program said that the drummers would "maintain a continuous heartbeat near the official site of the Earth Summit, as part of a ritual for the healing of our Earth to be felt by those who are deciding Earth's fate." (p. 5)[1]

At Rio, President Bush, whether he knew it or not, represented the conservative, Christian resistance to the paganist forces in the environmentalist movement. The pagans know that the strongest center of resistance to their plans lies among believing Christians in the English-speaking world. If they can break that resistance, they will be able to bring about the new world, socialist, pagan order.

The easiest and simplest way to do this is to "educate" Christian children to become pagans. Since humanists and pagans control the government education systems in all of the English-speaking countries, and since 85 percent of Christian parents send their children to these pagan schools, the job can be done in about two generations. The resisting remnant of Christians will be dealt with when the time comes.

Incidentally, the difference between humanists and pagans is that the latter practice pre-Biblical idolatry, while the former are atheists who have made science and reason their gods. But what both have in common is an abiding hatred of Biblical religion, particularly the orthodox Christian variety.

The centerpiece of the liberationist, paganizing curriculum in the primary school is whole language, which is based on the deconstructionist philosophy of language. What is "deconstruction"? *Webster's New World Dictionary (Third College Edition)*, published by Simon & Schuster, Inc., defines *deconstruction* as, "a method of literary analysis originated in France in the mid-20th century and based on a theory that, by the very nature of language and usage, no text can have a fixed, coherent meaning."

And that's exactly how whole-language educators define the reading process. The authors of *Whole Language: What's the Difference?* (Heinemann, 1991) write:

> From a whole language perspective, reading (and language use in general) is a process of generating hypotheses in a meaning-making transaction in a sociohistorical context. ... This view of reading implies that there is no single "correct" meaning for a given text, only plausible meanings. (p. 19)[2]

Note the concept of reading as a "process of generating hypotheses" or as a "transactional process." The process is totally subjective with the text providing some sort of mental stimulus. Obviously, this is a recipe for the destruction of literacy, not its improvement. For further clarification, the authors write:

> Whole language represents a major shift in thinking about the reading process. Rather than viewing reading as "getting the words," whole language educators view reading as essentially a process of creating meanings. ... It is a transaction, not an extraction of the meaning *from* print,

in the sense that the *reader-created* meanings are a fusion of what the reader brings and what the text offers.

. . . In a transactional model, words do not have static meanings. Rather, they have meaning *potentials* and the capacity to communicate multiple meanings. (p. 32)

Compare the above with what is said about deconstruction in the *Academic American Enclyclopedia*, (Vol. 6, p. 76):

Deconstruction is a theory about language and literature that developed in the 1970s . . . . Its initial premises were first formulated by the French philosopher and critic Jacques Derrida, whose works converted a number of U.S. academics. . . .

What most characterizes deconstruction is its notion of *textuality*, a view of language as it exists not only in books, but in speech, in history, and in culture. For the deconstructionist, language constitutes everything. The world itself is "text." Language shapes humanity and creates human reality. . . . Yet, upon close examination, words seem to have no necessary connection with reality or with concepts or ideas.[3]

Note the strange contradiction: language creates human reality, but words have no necessary connection with reality. Whole language educators promote the same sort of contradiction. Children are expected to "read for meaning," but are encouraged to invent any meaning they want. After all, when they speak of "reader-created meanings," what limits do they place on the reader's creativity? The article continues:

. . . Given the numerous hidden links of a text to its cultural and social intertext, the text's content and meaning are, essentially, indeterminate. Texts, therefore, are unreadable, and the practice of interpretation may be defined as *misreading*.

[Derrida attacks] what he calls "logocentrism," the human habit of assigning truth to *logos* — to spoken language, the voice of reason, the word of God. Derrida finds that logocentrism generates and depends upon a framework of two-term oppositions that are basic to Western thinking, such as being/nonbeing, thing/word, truth/lie, male/female. In the logocentric epistemological system the first term of each pair is privileged (TRUTH/lie, MALE/female). Derrida is critical of these hierarchical polarities, and seeks to take tradition apart by reversing their order and displacing, and thus transforming, each of the terms — by putting them in slightly different positions within a word group, or by pursuing their etymology to extreme lengths, or by substituting words in other languages that look and sound alike. . . .

Deconstruction has been regularly attacked as childish philosophical skepticism and linguistic nihilism. Nevertheless, it became the leading literary critical school in the United States during the period following the Vietnam War.

Thus, deconstruction is basically an attack on the notion of absolute truth and literal comprehension of a written text. Western thinking, linear thinking is "logocentric" in that it relies on the word as the means of conveying truth. Critics of traditional teaching methods are keenly aware of the difference between the logocentric approach and the whole-language approach. In an article entitled, "Political Philosophy and Reading Make a Dangerous Mix," published in *Education Week*, Feb. 27, 1985, the authors write:

After spending six years observing the efforts of the self-styled "New Right" to influence education throughout the country, we have found a pattern of activities that could, if some members of the New Right are successful, cause a very limited model for teaching reading to prevail in both public and private schools. The model is based on the belief that literal comprehension is the only goal of reading instruction. Because it trains children to reason in a very limited manner, it is a model that we believe could have serious political consequences in a country where the ability of the citizenry to read and think critically is an essential determinant of democratic governance. . . .

. . . By attempting to control the kinds of materials and questions teachers and students may use; by limiting reading instruction to systematic phonics instruction, sound-symbol decoding, and literal comprehension; and by aiming its criticism at reading books' story lines in an effort to influence content, the New Right's philosophy runs counter to the research findings and theoretical perspectives of most noted reading authorities.[4]

Obviously, the authors of the above, in their rejection of the logocentric model of reading instruction and thinking, agree with the deconstructionists. The common enemy is clearly "literal comprehension" because it represents a Biblical view of the word. An article on Derrida in *Contemporary Authors* (vol. 124, p. 112) states:

> [D]econstructionism emphasizes the reader's role in extracting meaning from texts and the impossibility of determining absolute meaning.[5]

Which is exactly what whole language teaches. In other words, the written word can be nullified by the reader at will. Frank Smith, our whole-language wonderboy, writes (*Phi Delta Kappan,* Feb. 1992, p. 438):

> Authors don't mind if readers skip difficult or boring passages, and they have no temptation to bring a child to order every time attention wanders or a mistake is made. Authors give children *control;* they give them the power to read as they want rather than as a teacher expects.[6]

I don't know how many authors Smith has interviewed, but I would venture to guess that they want to be understood by their readers. Otherwise, why do they write and why do they choose their words so carefully? Apparently authors have something that readers want: information or an interesting story. But if the reader is to regard the author's work as linguistic putty to be molded by the reader, then there is not much point in creating works of literature with precise things to say.

When children are encouraged to "take control" of an author's text, they will no doubt continue to do so as adults—if they bother to read at all. I doubt that Smith himself would approve of readers putting words into his mouth. In fact, we have been overly careful to quote Smith and other whole-language writers and state their positions as accurately as possible. We doubt that whole-language advocates of reading as a subjective process of creating meaning would want that concept applied to their own writings by, say, critics of whole language.

When all is said and done, the aim of the whole-language movement along with deconstructionism is simply to destroy individualism, capitalism, and religion or absolute truth. Individualism is undermined by the classroom emphasis on group work, cooperative learning, and peer dependency; capitalism is undermined by emphasizing collectivist activities; and religion is undermined by attacking the word, logos, the word of God as absolute truth. Religion is also undermined by what the teachers give the children to read: stories about the occult, witchcraft, death, and other depressing, nightmarish subjects.

In other words, if you want to change civilization you must change the way language is learned and used. For example, feminists have already changed our vocabulary with such words as "chairperson," "Ms.," "sexism," etc. Homosexuals have appropriated the word "gay" and coined the word "homophobia." Words describing every facet of perverted sex are now commonly used in sex education classes to educate children about AIDS, and no value judgment is made about such practices except that they may be considered "risky" and contrary to the doctrine of "safe sex." The result is that today's children acquire a vocabulary and concepts of human behavior that would have been inconceivable forty years ago.

Also, the elimination of Biblical terms and concepts from general usage has given American culture a decidedly secular tone. Words like "sin" and "abstinence" are ridiculed as quaint and outdated, and prayerful references to Jesus Christ by professional football players interviewed by the media are met with embarrassment and a quick change of subject. Blasphemy is now commonplace, particularly among comedians and in motion pictures. The prevailing humanist culture shows no respect and little tolerance for Christianity. The inability of humanists to tolerate even the most insipid, watered-down, one-minute prayer at a high-school graduation is indicative of an intolerant, persecutive mindset. Obviously, the public school must be sealed tight against any intrusion of religion, for fear that it will interfere with the process of paganization that goes on for seven hours a day, five days a week, ten months a year, for twelve years.

One of the social scientists considered important in the development of whole-language philosophy is the British-born linguist Michael Halliday, Professor of Linguistics at Sydney University in Australia. In his book, *Learning How to Mean: Explorations in the Development of Language,* Halliday describes the phases a child goes through in learning to speak his own language. He views the entire process as a sociolinguistic one in which the child learns about his social culture as he learns language. He writes:

> Early language development may be interpreted as the child's progressive mastery of a functional potential. . . . Here the concept of meaning, and of learning to mean, is in the last analysis interpreted in sociological terms, in the context of some chain of dependence such as: social order—transmission of the social order to the child—role of language in the transmission process—functions of language in relation to this role—meanings derived from these functions. . . . (p. 5)

> Outside language, we turn to some kind of social theory . . . . Here the most obviously relevant work is that of Basil Bernstein, whose theory of social structure and social change embodies a concept of cultural transmission within which he has been able to identify a number of what he calls 'critical socializing contexts', types of situation involving the use of language which play a key part in the transmission of culture to the child. . . . The fact that in Bernstein's work language is the central factor in

cultural transmission makes it likely that contexts which Bernstein recognizes as critical for cultural transmission will also be critical in the language learning process. (p. 18)[7]

The above provides an important clue as to why whole-language educators insist that children learn to read in the same way they learn to speak. They go through similar sociolinguistic phases without any need for formal instruction. Frank Smith, whose writings are gospel to whole-language educators, believes, as John Dewey did, that "learning is social, not solitary." And, of course, if your aim is to change the culture, then this sociolinguistic doctrine must be applied to reading instruction. Smith writes in the same *Kappan* article already cited (p. 432):

> The original philosophy of whole language, even before it acquired the label, had nothing to do with methods, materials, or techniques. There was no attempt to tell teachers what they should *do* to teach children to read; rather, the aim was to tell teachers what their attitudes should be. The basis of the philosophy was *respect*—respect for language (which should be natural and "authentic," not contrived and fragmented) and respect for learners (who should be engaged in meaningful and productive activities, not in pointless drills and rote memorization). The philosophy has attracted the enthusiastic support of scores of thousands of teachers. It is without doubt the most vital movement in education today, and its political and social influence has been enormous.[8]

In summing up the phases a child goes through in learning to speak his mother tongue, Halliday writes:

> We started with the hypothesis that learning the mother tongue consists of mastering certain basic functions of language and in developing a meaning potential in respect of each. ... It is presumed that these functions are universals of human culture, and it is not unreasonable to think of them as the starting point not only for linguistic ontogeny but also for the evolution of the linguistic system. (p. 33)[9]

In other words, the child, in learning to speak his own language, goes through the same process that the human race did in its evolutionary development of speech. Of course, if you believe the Bible then you believe that Adam was created with a fully developed power of speech and could converse with God in the Garden of Eden. As we read in the Gospel of St. John, "In the beginning was the Word, and the Word was with God, and the Word was God." The absolute Word, or Logos, is the very foundation of Biblical religion. The deconstructionists and whole language advocates know that the future of Christianity depends on this belief in the absolute Word. By destroying this concept in the minds of children, the atheists and pagans can finally destroy Christianity as a cultural and spiritual force.

Another part of the overall paganist plan is to sexualize the children sufficiently so that they will find themselves in emotional conflict with Christian doctrines opposed to premarital, recreational sex. Day in and day out, the entire humanist-hedonist culture wages a relentless campaign in the media to sexualize Americans, to produce sexual addiction to the point that Americans will reject the self-restraining standards of orthodox Christianity. This is done by creating "cognitive dissonance," a conflict between the children's prematurely aroused sexual desires and their family religion. In trying to resolve the conflict, which is painful and stressful, the children will choose the humanist moral philosophy with its sexually permissive creed and reject the values of their families. In short, the purpose of creating cognitive dissonance is to enable the child get rid of his Christian conscience.

Paganism, as we know from history, is associated with perverted sexual practices, phallic worship, temple orgies, etc. Thus, the sexualization of American children is a needed ingredient for the creation of a pagan culture. When you consider that children will now be given sex education in kindergarten as part of the AIDS prevention program, and at the same time will be taught that there is no absolute Word, and that the ultimate purpose in life is social and sexual intercourse, we can expect the rising generation to be the most licentious and depraved in American history.

Pagan societies are characterized by idolatry, occultism, sexual promiscuity, flagrant homosexuality, violence, murder, human sacrifice, incest, infanticide, child abuse, widespread disease, despotism, political instability, a low level of productivity, and a wide disparity between the very rich and the very poor with few in the middle.

The key to paganizing America is by controlling how children learn language, for as Halliday writes, "language comes to occupy the central role in the processes of social learning." He states further:

> A child who is learning his mother tongue is learning how to mean. As he builds up his own meaning potential in language, he is constructing for himself a social semiotic [a system of abstract signs and symbols]. Since language develops as the expression of the social semiotic it serves at the same time as the means of transmitting it, and also of constantly modifying and reshaping it, as the child takes over the culture, the received system of meanings in which he is learning to share. (p. 60)

> In this way a child, in the act of learning language, is also learning the culture through language. The semantic system which he is constructing becomes the primary mode of transmission of the culture. (p. 66)[10]

What all of this means is that those who control the teaching of language to children can control the future of our culture. Since, in this country, we are in a cultural war of increasing intensity between Christians and humanists (i.e. socialists, atheists, pagans, new agers, etc.), it is the height of folly for Christians to put their children in schools controlled by humanists. Obviously many of these children, subjected to twelve years of humanist indoctrination, will forsake their Christian heritage and become the all-American pragmatic pagan for whom a taste in perversion will simply mean living according to an alternate lifestyle.

Thus, the full implications of the whole-language movement cannot be appreciated or understood until we recognize that the cultural war we are in is being waged with an intensity we have never seen before in this country. That its philosophical roots can be traced to the nihilist depths of deconstruction should not surprise us since the academic world has become the spawning ground of every anti-Biblical idea that the human mind can conceive of. Philosophical nihilism in high places preceded the French and Russian revolutions, both of which were unbelievably bloody and cruel.

But not only do the whole-language deconstructionists reject the concept of the absolute word—the logos—but they reject the very system of logical thinking that made Western civilization possible. They not only reject the Bible, they reject Aristotle's A is A. Their new formula is A can be anything you want it to be, which can only be the basis of a pre-literate or non-literate culture in which subjectivism, emotion and superstition prevail as the means of knowing.

That, of course, is simply a form of insanity—the inability not only to deal with objective reality but to recognize and admit that it exists. A mind so inclined is a mind that will lead its owner to destruction.

But I suspect that the leaders of the whole-language movement know all of this. They have not suspended their own ability to deal with objective reality in ways beneficial to themselves. They know how to collect their paychecks, get government grants, arrange seminars, buy airline tickets, rent cars, hire lawyers, read publishers' contracts as they are actually written. After all, in contract disputes, the word is all important. These men and women are no fools even though their ideas are foolish. They are simply conmen and charlatans who fancy themselves as latter-day utopians. The mischief they spread harms millions of children and perverts our culture.

How does whole-language deconstructionism translate itself into classroom practice? First, the educators deconstruct our alphabetic system. That is, the nature of our alphabetic system is ridiculed and its benefits kept from the students. And so the teaching of phonics is strongly discouraged. Frank Smith writes in *Reading Without Nonsense* (p. 129):

> Children do not need a mastery of phonics in order to identify words that they have not met in print before. The very complexity and unreliability of the 166 rules and scores of exceptions make it remarkable that anyone should think that the inability to use phonics explains "Why Johnny still can't read." Once a child discovers what a word is in a meaningful context, learning to recognize it on another occasion is as simple as learning to recognize a face on a second occasion, and does not need phonics. Discovering what a word is in the first place is usually most efficiently accomplished by asking someone, listening to someone else read the word, or using context to provide a substantial clue.[11]

On page 53 of the same book, Smith writes:

> The spelling-to-sound correspondences of English are so confusing that in my judgment children who believe they can read unfamiliar words just by "blending" or "sounding" them out are likely to develop into disabled readers, the type of secondary students who are condemned for being "functionally illiterate" because they do exactly what they have been taught and try to read by putting together the sounds of letters.
>
> Besides, I think it would be difficult to exaggerate the complexity and unreliability of phonics. To take just one very simple example, how are the letters *ho* pronounced? Not in a trick situation, as in the middle of a word like *shop*, but when *ho* are the first two letters of a word? Here are eleven common words in each of which the initial *ho* has a different pronunciation — *hot, hope, hook, hoot, house, hoist, horse, horizon, honey, hour, honest.*

Can anyone really believe that a child could learn to identify these words by sounding out the letters?

Obviously, Smith doesn't know how intensive phonics is taught. Children are taught the letter sounds in their spelling families. Thus, the child knows how to pronounce *hot* because it rhymes with *cot, dot, pot*. He knows how to pronounce *hope* because it rhymes with *cope, mope, rope*. He knows how to pronounce *hook* because it is in the same spelling family as *book, cook, look*. He knows how to pronounce all of these words not because they begin with *ho* but because he knows their spelling families. As for *shop*, after the child has been taught the sound the consonant digraph *sh* stands for, he can decode any number of words beginning with *sh: ship, sham, shell, shut*, etc. If Smith had ever taught intensive phonics he'd know that there are millions of children who have no problem learning how to read these words on the basis of their letters.

What Smith doesn't say in his book is that an alphabetic writing system is a phonetic system that *requires* the reader to develop a phonetic reflex, that is, an automatic association between letters and sounds. And that phonetic reflex can only be acquired by rote memorization so that the child doesn't have to think about the sounds the letters stand for. Our alphabetic system is 85 percent regular with 95 percent of the irregularities consisting of slight variations in vowel pronunciation.

And the reason why children have little difficulty mastering the irregular words is because their pronunciations are obvious. For example, even though the word *was* is in the *as, has* spelling family, a child knows it is pronounced *wuz* simply because *waz* is not a word and doesn't make sense. The spoken word provides the correct pronunciation. It is the same with the word *have*, which is pronounced *hav*, even though it is in the same spelling family as *cave, gave, save*. But in a word like *behave*, the proununciation of the *h-a-v-e* is perfectly regular.

The important characteristic of an alphabetic writing system is that it is a phonetic representation of the spoken language. Meaning is derived when the written letters are articulated in speech or internally vocalized or subvocalized by the reader. Alphabetically written words are not ideographs or hieroglyphics. They are graphic representations of speech. Whole-language theorists reject this simple fact. Smith writes in *Understanding Reading* (p. 27):

> Written language does not require decoding to sound in order to be comprehended; the manner in which we bring meaning to print is just as direct as the manner in which we understand speech. Language comprehension is the same for all surface structures.[12]

In other words, we should all read as if we were deaf and that printed words are little pictures conveying meaning directly. But this is really impossible to do, for if we do not relate the printed word to its spoken equivalent then we cannot think, for the thought process—as opposed to daydreaming—is carried out with language, not a series of still pictures. In other words, whole-language educators see no difference between the word *Men* and the little picture of a man that appears on restroom doors in airports. To whole-language educators, both are little pictures. The authors of *Whole Language: What's the Difference?* write (p. 9):

> Oral language, written language, sign language — each of these is a system of linguistic conventions for creating meanings. That means none is "the basis" for the other; none is a secondary representation of the other.[13]

Unfortunately, saying it doesn't make it so. Alphabetic writing *is* a representation of the spoken equivalent. That's what made alphabetic writing superior to ideographic writing. For educators not to know this is tantamount to an architect not knowing how to read blueprints, or a concert pianist not knowing how to read music.

In fact, alphabetic writing is the same as musical notation in that both forms of writing stand for sounds. The written notes stand for musical sounds. The alphabetically written words stand for their articulated equivalents in speech.

Even Vygotsky understood this quite well. In his book, *Thought and Language,* published in 1934, he wrote:

> Writing . . . requires deliberate analytical action on the part of the child. In speaking, he is hardly conscious of the sounds he pronounces and quite unconscious of the mental operations he performs. In writing, he must take cognizance of the sound structure of each word, dissect it, reproduce it in alphabetical symbols, which he must have studied and memorized before. In the same deliberate way, he must put words in a certain sequence to form a sentence. Written language demands conscious work because its relationship to inner speech is different from that of oral speech . . . .
>
> Inner speech is condensed, abbreviated speech. Written speech is deployed to its fullest extent, more complete than oral speech. . . . The change from maximally compact inner speech to maximally detailed written speech requires what might be called deliberate semantics — deliberate structuring of the web of meaning. . . .
>
> The opinion has even been voiced that school instruction in grammar could be dispensed with. We can only reply that our analysis clearly showed the study of grammar to be of paramount importance for the mental development of the child. . . .
>
> Just as the child realizes for the first time in learning to write that the word *Moscow* consists of the sounds *m-o-s-k-ow* and learns to pronounce each one separately, he also learns to construct sentences, to do consciously what he has been doing unconsciously in speaking. Grammar and writing help the child to rise to a higher level of speech development. (pp. 98-101)[14]

In short, Vygotsky's conception of primary education is much closer to our traditional view of the three Rs than to anything presently advocated by our progressive educators. In other words, whole-language educators are perpetrating a fraud. They are telling parents that whole language is a new and better way of teaching children to read when, in reality, it is nothing of the sort. For all intents and purposes, whole language is a way of preventing children from becoming fluent, accurate phonetic readers. It is a new way of creating reading disability, a new way of creating academic confusion and learning frustration, a new way of crippling the children's linguistic development. Whole-language teachers may think they are doing a wonderful job in their first-grade classes. After all, they don't have to pick up the pieces in the grades that come after.

15. Debunking Whole-Language Myths About New Zealand and Australia

Whenever whole-language proponents are asked where whole language has been tried and successfully used, they invariably cite New Zealand and Australia. For example, Marie Carbo, in her attempt to discredit Prof. Jeanne Chall's pro-phonics book, *Learning to Read: The Great Debate,* in *Phi Delta Kappan,* November 1988, wrote:

> Currently, the U.S. ranks a dismal 49th in literacy out of 159 members of the United Nations. The country that ranks first, New Zealand, teaches reading through the whole-language approach, which integrates literature, story writing, and the arts—and also incorporates some phonics, when needed.
>
> By contrast, phonics has been emphasized in many American classrooms for the past 20 years. . . . If phonics is so effective and so much of it has been taught for the past 20 years, one might reasonably ask why the U.S. ranks 49th in literacy.[1]

Of course, what Ms. Carbo fails to acknowledge is that phonics taught within the context of a look-say or whole-word reading program is practically useless, for children who develop a holistic reflex acquire a block against looking at words phonetically. Also, phonics, for decades, has been taught as phonetic clues, one of the strategies used in whole-word reading. Just as Carbo asserts that schools in New Zealand only teach phonics "when needed," so it is with most U.S. primary schools where phonics is taught only "when needed"—or as a last resort. Phonics is taught in a piecemeal, fragmentary way right up to the sixth grade so that the student can never grasp it as a system or develop the needed phonetic reflex.

As for New Zealand's alleged high rank on the literacy scale, an article in the June 1993 issue of *North and South,* a prestigious magazine published in New Zealand, demolished that myth once and for all. The article, "Our Illiteracy: Reading the Writing on the Wall" by Jenny Chamberlain,[2] states:

> It's a phrase heard so often it now passes for fact — that New Zealand is a "highly literate" nation. . . . It's a comfortable thought — a nation of 3.4 million people who rate among the world's most proficient readers and writers. . . . So it seems churlish, unpatriotic even to reintroduce an offensive term into the vocabulary. The word is illiterate and contrary to popular belief that's what we are becoming.
>
> It's almost as though we've made a national pact with each other to ignore our illiteracy. We want to believe that we're a nation of bookworms, so we disregard the signs that it's there among our very young, our adults, our unemployed and in the workforce—a ball and chain dragging down the performance of a nation. . . .
>
> A national survey, along the lines of those conducted in Britain (1987), Canada (1987) and Australia (1989), has never been done in New Zealand, though ARLA, the Adult Reading and Learning Assistance Federation, is currently pressing hard for one. Information on illiteracy is gathered piecemeal by interested groups but nobody puts it all together to make a picture—if they did it would be composed of facts like these:
>
> Despite the enormous emphasis placed on reading in primary schools our current teaching method fails 25 per cent of new entrants. One in four

six-year-olds requires remedial help after one year at school.

A recent ARLA survey on workplace literacy reveals between 20 and 22 per cent of the New Zealand workforce are not coping well with the literacy demands of employment.

In 1987 a Justice Department survey of 19 prisons showed that 47.8 per cent of inmates had reading ages of less than 10 years.

In 1992 a staggering 17,000 young people (one third of school leavers) went straight from school onto unemployment benefit with no post-secondary education—a national tragedy.

No one is monitoring the number of adolescents who slide through secondary education and leave school unable to read and write adequately, yet our polytechnics and universities are now having to redirect funding into basic literacy and numeracy tuition in learning-support units. Most units report that numbers of students requiring this help are increasing.

People in the employment industry increasingly despair of the illiteracy of the young people they try to match with the positions employers offer. Says Kathy Kostyrko, president of the 75-agency National Association of Personnel consultancies: "Young people coming out of school can't spell, can't write and can't think for themselves. We put them through our tests and they don't get a look in the door. Everyone in industry feels the same."

New Zealand's illiteracy is a huge national problem bubbling away under the lid of our complacency, a problem we mistakenly believe we can ignore but which is about to boil up and burn us any moment.

So if New Zealand has a "huge" literacy problem virtually as bad as ours, where do the whole-language people get this idea that New Zealand is the utopia of literacy? Chamberlain explains:

> In part our reputation is based on a 1970 international reading survey of 15 countries in which our 14 and 18-year-olds ranked top. But this survey is now very out of date.

In other words, Ms. Carbo is using 1970 data to argue against the teaching of phonics when it was probably phonics which made those 14 and 18-year-old New Zealanders become the good readers they were. It is the introduction of whole language into the schools of New Zealand which has brought about the present literacy crisis in that country. Chamberlain writes:

> There is a reading war going on in this country being waged between, on the one hand, teachers and Reading Recovery teachers who use the contextual or "whole language" approach (the way most of our primary school children learn to read) and, on the other, by the phonics faction. The latter are led by a small group of reading experts who dare to challenge the whole-language devotees and say that young children would catch on to literacy earlier if contextual teaching were balanced by teaching the old ABC way—sounding out the letters and letter clusters so that young readers have the code which helps them unlock words for themselves.
>
> The whole-language method (whereby children are immersed in books and the experience of reading and infer the letter-sound rules by which language is constructed rather than sound them out in a formal way) gradually took hold in the New Zealand education system from the 1970s and was part of the holistic and progressive education policy adopted at the time.
>
> The Reading Recovery scheme, also whole-language based, is nationally coordinated from well-appointed headquarters at the Auckland College of Education. Devised by renowned reading expert Marie Clay in the early 70s, it's the jewel in the ACOE crown and the tutors (currently 35 of them) who go on to teach Reading Recovery teachers are trained here. The Reading Recovery scheme is implemented in 61 per cent of state schools with six-year-olds and costs the country $10.4 million annually.
>
> It has brought New Zealand and in particular the Auckland College of Education a great deal of attention and international kudos over the last few years. The scheme was exported to Ohio in 1984, adopted in Surrey, Britain, in 1990 and in September 1992 was being trialled in 20 London education authority areas. Hundreds of American teachers visit the college each year to learn about it and we train overseas Reading Recovery tutors here. . . .
>
> It's hard to avoid the conclusion that New Zealand's reputation for being a world leader in reading really rests on a now superceded 23-year-old survey and superb marketing.

The leading whole-language guru in New Zealand is John McCaffery, senior lecturer in reading and language at the Auckland College of Education. According to McCaffery, literacy is:

a social, cultural, political process which is contexually bound. We now know there is no such thing as universal literacy. You can no longer prepare people to go out into the world as fully functional literate people. Our definition of what literacy is is keeping up with changes in society and being in a position to prepare children for them. What we now undertstand is that there is no such thing as literacy. There are a whole lot of literacies that are valued by people. The forms are specific to occupations and levels.

That sounds a lot like what is being prepared for American children in Outcome-Based Education: literacy for a specific occupation but not for the lifelong enjoyment of books or as a means of access to the wisdom of mankind. In any case, Jenny Chamberlain's article proves that the much vaunted high literacy of New Zealand is another bit of disinformation that advocates of whole language love to spread in order to tout the glories of their abominable teaching practices. As Chamberlain says:

> New Zealand's illiteracy is a huge national problem bubbling away under the lid of our complacency, a problem we mistakenly believe we can ignore but which is about to boil up and burn us any moment.

In Australia, where whole language flourishes, the literacy problem has already boiled over and is the daily subject of the press. When this writer toured Australia in August 1991 he was given a whole sheaf of newspaper clippings about that country's reading problem. Here's a sample of some of them:

The Courier-Mail (Brisbane, Queensland) 8/2/91

Falling standards 'a scandal'

The dramatic decline in the standard of Australian schools since World War II was scandalous, a senior academic said yesterday.
The University of Wollongong pro vice-chancellor, Professor Lauchlan Chipman, told an Australian Family Association lunch in Brisbane there

was an enormous amount of evidence showing the decline.

The "education crisis" would critically affect the Australian economy and its international performance was a direct result of poor quality teacher-training institutions. . . .

Prof Chipman cited the 1989 Australian Army entrance exam—"a basic grade four test", in which 12 percent of males and 4 percent of females holding 10 and 12 certificates failed.

In a comparison of 1974 and 1984: Monash University British history student essays in 1984 had significantly more spelling and grammatical mistakes than in 1974.

Studies showed the "assumed vocabulary" from secondary school text books had declined by 500 words since 1945 and the assumed vocabulary for primary school students was half of that of the 1920s.

"Yet there have never been more newspapers, magazines and books," Prof Chipman said. "The consensus is that the universal level is declining."

Prof Chipman said modern educators placed too much value on self-esteem and the child's feelings at the expense of healthy competition. . . There was too much emphasis on creativity without first equipping children with fundamental skills.

Where have we heard that sort of criticism before? Apparently, Australia has been undergoing the same dumbing down process in education as America. Even the Australian army is having a difficult time with the literacy problem according to the *Adelaide Advertiser* of 4/21/90:

Schools blamed for illliteracy of army recruits

Canberra: Federal Defence Science and Personnel Minister Gordon Bilney has defended the caliber of army recruits and blamed illiteracy problems among would-be soldiers on the education system. Army enlistment officers revealed this week that the number of potential recruits under 21 being rejected because of poor literacy and comprehension skills has risen 150 per cent in the past five years. Almost 12 per cent of men and 8 per cent of women failed the "trainability" tests.

Director of army recruiting Colonel Bernie Sullivan said the tests were aimed at Year 9 level students but candidates with Year 12 certificates had failed. . . .

The army was also having trouble attracting recruits to take on technical training in the electronics trades in particular.

"I think, quite bluntly, too many kids are taking the easy options at school and they're not getting stuck into the more difficult mathematics, physics, chemistry subjects," Colonel Sullivan said.

Not only the army, but the workforce in Australia is also trying to cope with the decline in literacy skills, as revealed in the following article from Melbourne's daily, *The Age,* of 10/23/90:

One in 10 adults have literacy problems

More than one in 10 adults in Australia have trouble with basic reading and writing, a national conference on literacy development and industrial productivity heard yesterday. The president of the ACTU [Australian Council of Trade Unions], Mr Martin Ferguson, told the Melbourne literacy and industry conference that more than one million adult Australians were unable to read a simple sentence in English, understand simple telephone dialing instructions, fill out basic application forms or follow instructions for medication or product use.

More than half a million of those adults had English as their first language. [Australia's total population is only about 16 million people.] ...

The Federal Minister for Resources, Mr Griffiths, said it was estimated that a lack of functional literacy cost Australia at least $3.2 billion each year in reduced productivity because of the additional time taken to communicate instructions.

Higher education in Australia is also suffering because of the low literacy of the students coming out of Australian public schools. An article in the Sydney *Daily Telegraph* of 11/21/88 indicates the seriousness of the problem:

Fury Over Illiterate Students

Thousands of students leaving school to take up technical college courses are so illiterate they cannot read their own textbooks, according to an alarming new survey. The problem is so widespread that special remedial classes in English and mathematics will have to be set up in every college in [New South Wales] to enable apprentices and other students to continue with their courses.

NSW Education Minister Terry Metherell said yesterday a survey of colleges indicated that 10 to 15 per cent of all trade and general studies students had deficiencies in literacy and numeracy.

"That's the equivalent of up to 10,000 students who are lacking in the basic skills," he said. "These people may not be illiterate but some do not have the basic level of English needed to undertake a trade course. They cannot read some of the basic information in their trade manuals or interpret simple mathematical work. . . . The scale of the problem has alarmed college teachers."

Dr Metherell, angered by the survey's results, said some of the worst illiterates were picked up as soon as they sat for college admission tests or tried to fill in enrollment forms. Others were detected in the first few hours of class when it was clear they could not follow their lectures or textbooks.

Intensive remedial classes, running for 10 to 12 weeks, will now be held at all colleges to bring students up to the standard required to enable them to complete their studies. . . .

In a bid to ease the crisis, children as young as eight will undergo special literacy and numeracy tests in Government schools next year. . . . If the results are poor, the State Government will have to require teachers to put more emphasis on core subjects.

Although the foregoing article was published in 1988, this writer during his 1991 tour of Australia visited a number of primary schools and spoke with educators in charge of the government schools' reading programs only to learn that the primary schools in Australia are heavily committed to whole-language methodology and philosophy. Only in Brisbane, in the state of Queensland, did this writer find a teacher in a primary school emphasizing phonics. She was no doubt an exception to the whole-language rule. Meanwhile, the Australian Teachers' Federation, their equivalent of our National Education Association, blames the decline in literacy and numeracy skills to "years of neglect of primary schools" by the Federal and State governments. Their solution, according to the *Sydney Morning Herald* of 1/26/85, is that "more money be spent on primary education to enable smaller classes, with greater individual teacher attention for particular students." No inkling at all in the article that teaching methods may have had something to do with the problem. Two years later, *The Australian* (Sydney) of 7/15/87 reported:

Spelling tests in schools to end

Spelling tests are to be abolished in [New South Wales] schools by 1990 with the introduction of a new method of teaching. Traditional verbal and written tests are to be phased out and replaced by a more holistic approach, primary school teacher Mr Max Green said yesterday.

Mr Green, head of Balarang Primary School on the NSW south coast, has been researching the new spelling curriculum that will be phased in from 1988, before being made mandatory in 1990. Mr. Green, who was attending the Australian Conference on Language and Learning in Sydney, which ended yesterday, said the new method aimed to take the competition aspect out of learning to spell. This aspect often promoted feelings of inferiority and depression. . . .

The new curriculum was written by Ms Rhonda Jenkins, a language consultant from the NSW Department of Education.

The reaction of the business and professional communities was quite strong, as indicated by an article in the Sydney *Telegraph Mirror* of 8/28/91 which reported:

The NSW Chamber of Commerce may soon be forced to issue its own certificates assuring employers that school leavers applying for jobs know how to spell. It would be used by job seekers with—or instead of—school assessments.

And Chamber executive director David Abba said today it might not be long before job advertisements specify: "Must be able to spell."

Mr Abba said the proposed certificates, which would also cover proficiency in typing and other skills, might be necessary because bosses could not be sure school, or even university graduates, were competent in the three Rs.

The uproar over spelling began when it was revealed the Education Deparment will scrap standardized spelling tests in September and introduce the Writing K-12 system in primary schools.

The same newspaper also reported:

Two prominent Sydney solicitors have branded the NSW education system a farce after most young job candidates for a position at their firm could not correctly spell 10 words. The solicitors, Henry Grech and David Bannerman, have slammed the system for not teaching students the basics of spelling and writing. . . .

"There must be something the matter with our schools when they are turning out people who simply cannot spell every day words."

The Blacktown solicitors said they were embarrassed and angry after studying 40 applications from school leavers for a position as a junior with their firm. Part of the interview included a spelling test with words such as urgent, mortgage, solicitor, contract and believe.

Another report in *The Australian* of 7/2/91 indicated the great concern employers have for the furture of Australia if the schools continue to produce such a low level of basic skills. It reads:

Bad education system 'brings economic doom'

The nation's education system has been strongly attacked as a recipe for lower living standards and long-term economic damage. The corporate general manager, technology and development of BHP, Mr Peter Laver, told an Australian Academy of Science national forum in Canberra the educational shift away from excellence towards comfortable mediocrity was a prescription for continuing economic decline.

There were few more critical issues facing industry today, because its employees needed to perform better if it were to become internationally competitive, he said. There was a strong perception among employers that the present education system was meeting neither present nor future need. . . .

A recent community literacy survey had revealed a "startlingly high" level of incapacity to perform simple tasks requiring basic cognitive literacy and numeracy skills.

"This result is a damning indictment of the school system in Australia, and a burden that must be accepted by industry," Mr Laver said. "The consequence of this literacy problem is that industry training resources are being wasted, teaching employees things they should have learned in school." . . .

It was a cardinal rule of business to supply what the customer wanted: the education industry had not fully accepted the need to understrand its market.

The chairman of the Australian Science and Technology Councils (ASTEC), Professor Ray Martin, said he was deeply concerned at the barrier that seemed to exist between schools and the real world.

"The teaching profession is crucial because they talk to our children and give them their perception of what industry is all about," he said.

"Unfortunately school leavers these days seem to have a pretty poor image of business, and almost no concept of its role in generating a healthy economy for Australia. But the teachers also argued that business sees things too narrowly, and that education is about other things as well."

That's the sorry state of education and literacy in Australia, where whole language has been used longer than in any other country. Also, it should surprise no one that the schools of Australia are turning out graduates, or "school leavers" as they call them, who have a "pretty poor image of business." After all, the education system in Australia is controlled by the same Fabian socialists who control education in Britain. In Fact, Mrs. Joan Kirner, former Minister for Education and Premier of the state of Victoria in 1991, is herself a dedicated Fabian socialist. She is quoted in a 1984 Victorian Fabian Society Pamphlet as saying:

> If we are egalitarians in our intention we have to reshape education so that it is: part of the socialist struggle for equality, participation and social change, rather than an instrument of the capitalist system; a vital weapon in the transition to more equal outcomes for disadvantaged groups and classes rather than a ladder to equal educational opportunity for individuals; a catalyst for system change rather than the legitimization of system maintenance.

Mrs. Kirner might have well been speaking for our progressive American psycho-educators as well, who are as determined as she is to bring about a socialist society. And now it ought to be obvious why students in Australia come out of their schools with little understanding of free enterprise or the requirements of business and lack the necessary academic skills required in a high-tech economy.

And so, is literacy flourishing down under where whole language now reigns supreme in the primary schools of the southern hemisphere? Obviously not. But the lie is being spread about by whole-language proponents who are no strangers to fraud and deceit.

But as Abraham Lincoln is reported to have said, you can fool all of the people some of the time, and you can fool some of the people all of the time, but you can't fool all of the people all of the time.

16. The Great American Literacy Disaster

To gain the full sense of what our educators have done to American literacy, one need do little more than read the report released by the U.S. Education Department on September 8, 1993 which revealed that an estimated 90 million American adults—or half the adult population—have such poor reading and writing skills that they can scarcely cope with the literacy demands of our society.

According to the *Boston Globe* of 9/9/93, "These adults cannot write a brief letter explaining an error on a credit-card bill, figure out a Saturday departure on a bus schedule, or use a calculator to determine the difference between a sale price and a regular price."

The $14-million "Adult Literacy in America" study, conducted by the Educational Testing Service for the National Center for Education Statistics, was ordered by Congress in 1988. The data in the survey was gathered through lengthy interviews with 26,000 adults in a dozen states, including some in prisons. A number value to everyday skills was assigned on a 500-point scale.

Some 40 million American adults scored between 0 and 225, indicating that they had only the most meager reading and writing skills. For instance, they could locate the expiration date on a driver's license, but not an intersection on a simple city map. Minorities and poor people were disproportionately at the bottom, but half were white.

An additional 50 million adults did somewhat better but were still considered to have inadequate reading and writing skills. One third of all adults performed at the middle level (scoring 276 to 325), and only 20 percent—34 to 40 million—scored high enough to be considered highly literate, that is, able to handle tasks involving complex documents and information. The *Globe* article relates:

> For years, business executives have said the low level of literacy among tens of millions of Americans was a direct threat to the US economy.... [Education Secretary Richard] Riley and [Labor Secretary Robert] Reich have been warning in cities all around the country of a further divided society, one where the educated get well-paying jobs and the rest have a hard time eking out a living....
>
> "I am not shocked. This reaffirms what we have known," said Keith Poston, spokesman for the National Alliance of Business, a group dedicated to building a competitive workforce through public-education reform.
>
> American business has been paying dearly for the nation's illiteracy problems, Poston said, and it is not unusual for employers to "reject three out of four applications because they cannot read or write well enough to hold entry-level jobs. Half the applications are thrown in the trash."...
>
> The last comprehensive government study on adult literacy was done in 1975, and since then, the same often-quoted estimate for the number of functionally illiterate Americans has stood at between 23 million and 27 million adults....
>
> At no time in American history have so many people earned high-school and college degrees—leading many to describe the country as better educated than ever. However, according to this study, a diploma does not mean a person is functionally literate. More than half of high-school graduates were found to have restricted abilities in math and reading.

And so we now have irrefutable evidence from our own government that our schools have failed so miserably in their job of teaching children to read, that half of America's 191 million adults write and read so poorly that they are unable to function effectively in our technologically advanced economy. Yet, these functional illiterates were all educated at great expense in our government schools, spent more time in classrooms than any previous generation, and emerged from the process with virtually no employable skills. Secretary Riley's reported advice that they go back to school for a "tune-up" is tantamount to advising a victim of medical malpractice to go back to the same doctor that botched the job to begin with.

Nowhere in any of the media reports on this incredible literacy disaster was there any inkling that the educators and their teaching methods were principally responsible for it, even though virtually every astute observer acknowledges that the nation is being "dumbed down" by our education system.

The simple truth is that the American public school system is slowly crippling the country by destroying the brains of its youngest citizens, and by the time the American people wake up to what is being done to them by their psycho-educators, it may be too late. America will be more like Brazil than the America we have known. As the government's survey revealed, those with the lowest scores earned a median weekly salary of $230 to $245 while those with the highest scores had incomes of $620 to $680. In other words, we are creating a society in which the gap between the haves—the highly literate, the cognitive elite—and the have nots—the functionally illiterate—is growing wider and wider, exactly what public education was supposed to prevent from happening.

Even the ranks of the highly literate are diminishing. For example, in 1972 the number of students who achieved the highest verbal score of 750 to 800 on the SAT (Scholastic Aptitude Test) was 2,817. In 1987, that number was down to 1,363, and in 1990 it was down to 1,226. America is literally losing its brains.

That decline was predicted in 1971 by John Gaston, head of the Fort Worth, Texas, branch of the Human Engineering Laboratory, who told *Dallas Morning News* columnist, David Hawkins (8/26/71):

> Do you know that the present generation knows less than its parents? All of our laboratories around the country are recording a drop in vocabulary of 1 percent a year. In all our 50 years of testing it's never happened before. . . . Young people know fewer words than their fathers. That makes them know less. Can you imagine what a drop in knowledge of 1 per cent a year for 30 years could do to our civilization? . . . We also believe that the recent rise in violence correlates with the drop in vocabulary. If they can't express themselves with their tongues, they'll use their fists. . . . We define intelligence as natural aptitudes plus knowledge, which is another word for vocabulary. We cannot establish vocabulary as an aptitude—which means anybody can learn words, though not everybody does. We test many gifted people who are low in vocabulary and we tell them—we tell the world—to learn words. Swallow the dictionary. Brilliant aptitudes aren't worth much without words to give them wings. The one thing successful people have in common isn't high aptitudes—it's vocabulary, and it's within everybody's reach. Success actually correlates more with vocabulary than with the gifts we're born with.

Wise words, indeed! Anyone familiar with American primary reading programs will recognize how thoroughly dumbed down textbook vocabulary has been since the introduction of Dick and Jane in the early 1930s. Of course, the ruling elite believe that a submissive, dumbed-down population, kept amused and titillated by sexual license, TV sitcoms, and cradle-to-grave government-provided security, is just fine. Just as the communist rulers of the former Soviet Union didn't care how miserable and impoverished were the lives of the masses, so the new American ruling class made up of the universitarian elite look down on everyone else as being hopelessly inferior and only worthy of the lives the elite has planned for them.

It was literacy "expert" Thomas G. Sticht, former assistant to Labor Secretary Robert Reich, whose views were reported in the *Washington Post* of Aug. 17, 1987, as follows:

> Many companies have moved operations to places with cheap, relatively poorly educated labor. What may be crucial, they say, is the dependability of a labor force and how well it can be managed and trained—not its general educational level, although a small cadre of highly educated creative people is essential to innovation and growth. Ending discrimination and changing values are probably more important than reading in moving low-income families into the middle class.

That's what Outcome-Based Education is all about: the end of the American dream, the end of real upward mobility. In fact, Prof. Anthony G. Oettinger, chairman of the Center for Information Policy Research at Harvard University and member of the elitist Council on Foreign Relations, told an audience of communications executives in 1981:

> Our idea of literacy, I am afraid, is obsolete because it rests on a frozen and classical definition. Literacy, as we know it today, is the product of the conditions of the industrial revolution, of urbanization, of the need for a work force that could, in effect, "write in a fine round hand." . . .[1]

Prof. Oettinger, of course, is wrong. Widespread literacy was a result of the Reformation which required ordinary folk to be able to read the Bible so that they could live in accordance with God's law. Those ideas were brought to America by the Puritans who established their Bible-based commonwealth in New England. It was the requirements of the Christian religion which led to the establishment of universities in the New World so that a learned clergy could be raised up. It was high literacy which enabled the colonists to write an eloquent Declaration of Independence and create a constitutional form of government for the new republic. The need for high literacy preceded the industrial revolution and urbanization. In fact, farmers were great readers, and the books and journals written for farmers were written at a level which today's college students would find beyond their ability to emulate. For example, here are some excerpts from a letter by one R. Davis, of Plymouth County, Massachusetts, published in the *New England Farmer* of Sept. 13, 1851 (p. 300):

> In my peregrinations in New England for the last few years, my attention has been called to the prevailing disease among potatoes. Of the numerous articles written on the cause of the "rot," I have read liberally, and examined with intense interest the remedies proposed. But, as yet, I am satisfied that all have failed in assigning the true cause; though partial remedies, at very great annual expense, have been proposed.
>
> Having bestowed much thought and experimental labor on this subject for four years past, I think I have ascertained the *cause;* if so, a radical cure may be effected, and the potato restored to its primal pure state and healthy condition; the cause being removed, the effect will cease. . . .
>
> Now, with your leave, I will give you my views of this vegetable epidemic, or contagion, and the results, thus far, of my experiments.
>
> I hold that the potato crop has degenerated in consequence of amalgamation. Northern, southern, eastern and western, early and late varieties, have run together, and produced a kind of hybrid germ. This I hold to be the *fous et origo* of the rot. It is a well-known fact, that within the last half century potatoes of every variety . . . have been introduced among us, and all mixed together; and hence the rot. For instance, there are in my neighborhood a very few old farmers with stiff notions and strong prejudices against innovation, who have always grown the same kind of potato, and have entirely escaped this disease.

There is more to this well-written letter, but the point has been made. The purpose of high literacy is to enable the mind to develop logically and scientifically, so that even farmers can deal with their problems thoughtfully and intelligently. Prof. Oettinger continues:

But as much as we might think it is, literacy is not an eternal phenomenon. Today's literacy is a phenomenon that has its roots in the nineteenth century, and one does not have to reach much farther back to think of civilizations with different concepts of literacy based, for example, on oral, rather than written, traditions.

How far back does Prof. Oettinger want to go? To pre-alphabetic civilizations in which literacy was restricted to a priestly elite who could read the hieroglyphics or ideographs? Is he trying to tell us that because people had to live that way in the pre-alphabetic period that we might find their "oral" literacy preferable to our alphabetic literacy? Prof. Oettinger goes on:

The present "traditional" concept of literacy has to do with the ability to read and write. But the real question that confronts us today is: How do we help citizens function well in their society? How can they acquire the skills necessary to solve their problems?

Do we, for example, really want to teach people to do a lot of sums or write in "a fine round hand" when they have a five-dollar hand-held calculator or a word processor to work with? Or, do we really have to have everybody literate—writing and reading in the traditional sense—when we have the means through our technology to achieve a new flowering of oral communication?

Who is the "we" in Prof. Oettinger's musings? Do "we" really want to teach people to do a lot of sums, etc. Do "we" really have to have everybody literate? The "we" is obviously the elite, the education establishment, and the answer to the questions is obviously "no." I do not know of a parent who sends his or her child to school who doesn't want that child to learn to read and write in the traditional sense. But obviously Prof. Oettinger doesn't care what parents think. His concern is with what the elite wants, not what the parents want, and he is trying to convince the businessmen he's addressing that they should want the same. He goes on:

> What is speech recognition and speech synthesis all about if it does not lead to ways of reducing the burden on the individual of the imposed notions of literacy that were a product of nineteenth century economics and technology?

So now we are being told that literacy is a burden imposed on our children because of some outdated notions. The stark truth is that imposed *illiteracy* is a far greater burden to bear for any individual who must live and work in our literate society. Prof. Oettinger continues:

> Complexity—everybody is moaning about tasks becoming too complex for people to do. A congressman who visited one of my classes recently said, "We have such low-grade soldiers in the U.S. that we have to train them with comic books." And an army captain in my class shot back: "What's wrong with comic books? My people *function.*"
>
> It is the traditional idea that says certain forms of communication, such as comic books, are "bad." But in the modern context of functionalism they may not be all that bad.
>
> We have the potential for using the cathode ray tube to transmit pictorial information and for developing it to a much greater extent than we have as a dynamic form of communication, whose implications for training and schooling and so on are quite different from linear print or "frozen" literacy.

With views like these expressed by Prof. Oettinger, no wonder the schools no longer view literacy as anything but a very limited workaday "function." Indeed, the Harvard professor represents the worst of pragmatic educational philosophy in which the grand purpose of education is merely to produce a "functioning" citizen— whatever that means. The love of pure learning, the striving for wisdom, the ability to expand one's use of language have no place in Oettinger's stunted idea of education. Functional literacy means being able to read comic books but not Dickens or Shakespeare or the Bible. It means having just enough literacy to be able get by, or "function" in our society. Gone is the notion of reading to develop one's intellect, satisfy one's curiosity about the world, enjoy good poetry, know the word of God. Gone is the notion that literacy opens the entire world of the written word to the individual and thereby becomes an inexhaustible source of pleasure and knowledge throughout one's life. Gone is the notion of books being a treasure trove for the mind, a priceless inheritance from all of those who came before us. Man is now to be reduced to a passive viewer of the cathode ray tube, responding to carefully selected stimuli, like Pavlov's salivating dogs. C.S. Lewis, in his *Screwtape Letters,* describes the dumbing down process that all tyrants impose on their people. Screwtape says:

> What I want to fix your attention on is the vast, over-all movement towards the discrediting, and finally the elimination, of every kind of human excellence—moral, cultural, social, or intellectual. And is it not pretty to notice how *Democracy* (in the incantatory sense) is now doing for us the work that was once done by the most ancient Dictatorships, and by the same methods? You remember how one of the Greek Dictators (they called them 'tyrants' then) sent an envoy to another Dictator to ask his advice about the principles of goverment. The second Dictator led the envoy into a field of grain, and there he snicked off with his cane the top of every stalk that rose an inch or so above the general level. The moral was plain. Allow no pre-eminence among your subjects. Let no man live who is wiser, or better, or more famous, or even handsomer than the mass. Cut them all down to a level; all slaves, all ciphers, all nobodies. All equals. Thus tyrants could practice, in a sense, "democracy." But now "democracy" can do the same work without any other tyranny than her own. No one need now go through the field with a cane. The little stalks will now of themselves bite the tops off the big ones. The big ones are beginning to bite off their own in their desire to Be Like Stalks.[2]

Undoubtedly, the universitarian elite is delighted at how well they've succeeded in dumbing down America. The survey proves that their plan has worked better than any of them could have dreamed. Think of it, destroying the literacy of the most powerful and literate nation on earth, and with the help of its own intelligent, freedom-loving citizens to boot. And the plan continues to work like magic. Every September, millions of Americans, like submissive, trusting sheep, willingly place their children in the government's schools where nonsurgical prefrontal lobotomies are performed on the brains of these children with virtually no resistance. And where there is resistance, there is Ritalin. And there is every indication that the process will be speeded up with whole language and OBE.

Of course, the new young psycho-educators coming out of the universities have no idea of how far we have fallen in literacy in this country. In fact, they are not even aware of how inferior their own literacy skills are compared with those of the teachers of previous generations. But it is important that we not forget the past, for that is the only way we can measure the effect of the dumbing down process. Simply compare these two statistics: the first from *School and Society* of January 30, 1915 in which the U.S. Bureau of Education reported that in 1910 only 22 out of 1,000 children between the ages of 10 and 14 in the U.S. were illiterate, a percentage rate of 2.2; the second from the *Boston Globe* of September 9, 1993 reporting that 90 million Americans can barely read and write.

The report also tells us that minorities—blacks and Hispanics—were disproportionately at the bottom of the literacy scale. Yet, literacy statistics from 1890 to 1930 show a steady improvement in literacy among blacks. For example, in 1890, the illiteracy rate among blacks was 57.1 percent, in 1900 it was 44.5 percent, in 1910 it was 30.4 percent, in 1920 it was 22.9 percent, and in 1930 it was 16.3 percent.[3]

We have no doubt that if children had continued to be taught to read by intensive, systematic phonics, the illiteracy rate among blacks today would be close to zero. But with look-say, the statistics began to go in the other direction. Today, black functional illiteracy now stands close to 50 percent, close to what it was in 1900! (*School and Society,* 11/19/21, p. 466; 4/9/32, p. 489)

The most reliable source of statistics on illiteracy in America prior to the introduction of look-say in the schools is *School and Society* of April 9, 1932. It states:

> Illiteracy of the white population in 1930 in urban territory was 2.5 [percent]; in rural-farm territory 3.4; and in rural non-farm territory, 2.9 per cent.
>
> Illiteracy among Negroes in the urban population was 9.2 per cent; in the rural population 23.2 per cent; in the rural non-farm population 20.5 per cent.
>
> The high degree of literacy to be found in the North Central states is suggested by the fact that Iowa registered an illiteracy of but 0.8 per cent. That figure is striking when one considers the fact that the average for the country in 1930 was 4.3 per cent. . . .
>
> In the North and West the percentage of illiteracy for the total population ten years old and over was 2.7; in the South, 8.2. Of the native white population six tenths of 1 per cent were illiterate both in the North and in the West, and 3.7 in the South; of the foreign-born whites 10.5 per cent in the North, 9.8 per cent in the South and 5.1 per cent in the West. In the North 4.7 per cent of Negroes were illiterate; in the South, 19.7 per cent; in the West, 3.3 per cent.

How far we have fallen! There is only one solution to our illiteracy problem: a massive exodus from the public schools. That's the fastest, most effective way to destroy the monster before it destroys us.

17. Functional Illiteracy and Delinquency: The Violent Consequences of Educational Malpractice

In June of 1992, the predominantly black area of South Central Los Angeles experienced a social explosion that ended in death and destruction on a scale that shocked the American people. Innocent motorists, who had nothing to do with the acquittal of the police officers involved in the beating of Rodney King, were dragged out of their cars and beaten to a pulp. Most of the destruction was carried out by young male adults, gang members who, it was said, were acting out their intense frustration with the "system."

But if the anger and rage were supposedly directed toward the Los Angeles Police Department, why did the young black thugs burn down over a thousand Korean-owned businesses? The answer is simple: jealousy, envy and hatred. The Koreans, through hard work and savings, had managed to achieve the American dream in only one generation, despite anti-Oriental prejudice, while the blacks, whose families went back several generations in

America, were relegated to an underclass of poverty and hopelessness.

The big advantage the Korean immigrants had was in not having attended American public schools, and apparently, their children, the inheritors of their parents' businesses, seemed to fare rather well in the public schools. The disadvantage of the blacks is that they had been grossly miseducated in the public schools and were, indeed, their most obvious victims. It is estimated that about fifty percent of the young black males in South Central Los Angeles belong to gangs, and judging from the speech patterns of gang members interviewed on television, most of them lack any substantial vocabulary and are probably functionally illiterate. The gang seems to function as an organizational home for the young male functional illiterates in South Central Los Angeles and gives them a power that ultimately terrorizes the entire community. The fact that these gangs are constantly involved in violence and drugs indicates that its members have a need to live at a very high level of emotional stimuli. This doesn't mean that these functional illiterates lack native intelligence. What it means is that their schools denied them a mastery of the basic academic skills that could have made it possible for them to lead more normal lives and prepare for productive careers in America's high-tech economy.

What is equally interesting in the black-Korean conflict is that Korean students came out on top in mathematics and science in the international testing sponsored by the Center for the Assessment of Educational Progress, while American students—black and white—were near the bottom. And so, the young blacks in South Central Los Angeles are more the victims of a crippling education than of racism, for we know that blacks who have a good command of the language, written and oral, are able to rise in our society to positions of great eminence as in the cases of Chief of Staff Colin Powell, Supreme Court Justice Clarence Thomas, author Thomas Sowell, and many others. In addition, the great success of Marva Collins's West Side Preparatory School in Chicago is due to its strong emphasis on phonics, vocabulary development, grammar, and writing skills.

Which brings us to the heart of the matter: the correlation between reading failure and delinquent behavior. Michael S. Brunner, a researcher at the National Institute of Justice, believes that the link between reading failure and delinquent, anti-social behavior has been well established by researchers in the field. In his book, *Retarding America: The Imprisonment of Potential* (Halcyon House, 1994), Brunner reviews the research evidence collected from studies of juvenile offenders which indicate that the frustration these individuals experienced in not being able to learn to read was a direct cause of their anti-social behavior. Brunner writes:

> What brings about the delinquency is not the academic failure per se, but sustained frustration which results from continued failure to achieve selected academic goals. When frustration can find no resolution into constructive or productive activity, one response, although not necessarily the only one, is aggressive, anti-social behavior. Other responses, which are equally counterproductive academically, are regression, resignation and other maladaptive behaviors that result in fixated responses. These reactions to frustration are not only possible but predictable. They have been well-documented from clinical research conducted both with animals and humans. . . .
>
> All the ingredients necessary to create this anti-social aggression through sustained frustration are present: There is an unachievable goal, in this case academic achievement. It is unachievable because the means of achieving it, the ability to read and comprehend text materials, is, in many cases, absent due to whole-word reading instruction. Though the means of achieving the goal are absent, the student, nevertheless, is continually pressured to achieve it by teachers, parents and peers. As a result, frustration ensues. (p. 30)[1]

Brunner quotes many studies to back up his statements. One

research paper entitled *Program of Research on the Causes and Correlates of Delinquency; Urban Delinquency and Substance Abuse,* issued in 1991 by the U.S. Justice Department, states:

> Low reading levels tend to predict the likelihood of the onset of serious delinquency. Longitudinally, poor reading achievement and delinquency appear to mutually influence each other. Prior reading level predicted later subsequent delinquency . . . [moreover] poor reading achievement increased the chances of serious delinquency persisting over time.

E. E. Gagne writes in the *Journal of Special Education* (1977):

> [The] compulsory school attendance law . . . facilitates delinquency by forcing youth to remain in what is sometimes a frustrating situation in which they are stigmatized as failures . . . . The longer learning-disabled students stay in school, the more likely they are to become involved with the police.[2]

In a Report to the Congress issued in 1977 by the Comptroller General of the United States we read:

> In our society, school is the only major legitimate activity for children between the ages of 6 and 18. If a child fails in school, generally there is little else in which he can be successful. . . . Delinquency and misbehavior become a way for the failing child to express his frustration at those who disapprove of his academic underachievement. This disapproval comes not only from parents and teachers, but also from other children who are keenly aware of the school status based on performance.[3]

Brunner writes (p. 33):

> Significant research has been conducted that investigates reading failure as the major source of frustration that leads to delinquency, based upon three hypotheses:
>
> 1. Continued failure in the most significant educational task challenging

the child (reading) is a deeply frustrating experience when permitted to continue for several years, [especially] when such failure begins prior to the child's developing ability to think rationally (approximately age seven and one-half).

2. Continued frustration over prolonged periods of time will result in aggressive behavior directed outward toward society (delinquency) or inward toward the self (neurosis).

3. Confined delinquent boys who have failed in reading will have behavioral histories showing more anti-social aggression than confined delinquent boys who were able to read.

In investigating two groups of incarcerated delinquents, 48 in each group, in two different states, a significant correlation between reading underachievement and aggression for both groups was found. Though IQ scores correlated with reading success in both groups, it will be shown shortly that IQ scores are not reliable predictors for determining if one will be able to learn to read, rather the ability to read will to some extent determine IQ scores! But this study is remarkable in what it didn't find:

". . . the present study was unsuccessful in attempting to correlate aggression with age, family size, or number of parents present in the home, rural versus urban environment, socio-economic status, minority group membership, religious preference, etc. *Only reading failure was found to correlate with aggression in both populations of delinquent boys.*

"It is possible that reading failure is the single most significant factor in those forms of delinquency which can be described as anti-socially aggressive. I am speaking of assault, arson, sadistic acts directed against peers and siblings, major vandalism, etc."

The study quoted above was written by Dennis Hogenson and published in the *Bulletin of The Orton Society,* vol. 24, 1974, with the title, "Reading Failure and Juvenile Delinquency."

It is quite conceivable that when functional illiterates, in the form of gangs, turn against society and burn down the community, they are directing their hatred at the very system that destroyed their minds, for the correlative of reading failure is retardation. The government school represents the "system" as a whole, and it failed to educate them. They remember how intelligent they felt before they went to school and they remember the humiliating, painful, and frustrating experience of failure while they were in school.

In reality, the whole-word reading instruction methods were devised to do in the classroom what Pavlov did in his laboratory: artificially create frustration and disability in the learner. Such methods are the equivalent of a non-surgical prefrontal lobotomy, for their purpose is to produce a defective individual. And this dumbing down process turns each one of these students into a walking time-bomb, waiting for the right moment to go off. One such time-bomb went off on May 1, 1992 in Oliverhurst, California, when a 20-year-old by the name of Eric Houston returned to his high school ready to kill. The *Boston Globe* of 5/3/92 reported:

> Eric Houston's revenge for flunking history three years ago is four dead, 11 wounded and about 80 terrorized hostages at his former high school, authorities said.
>
> "He was a student here in 1988 and '89. He failed a class," Sheriff Gary Tindel said. "He came back today to vent his frustration and retaliate and shoot people." . . .
>
> Cory Dawson, 16, who was among 80 students held hostage, said Houston, 20, told his captives at one point: "The reason why I am doing all of this is because I didn't graduate from high school. Mr. Brens flunked me, and I just want revenge."
>
> Robert Brens, a history teacher, was among the first to die . . . . After hours of telephone negotiations, Houston released his captives, and surrendered. . . .
>
> "He just kept saying that 'the school failed me,'" said Jason Beissel, 16, another hostage. "He kept repeating it. 'The school failed me. They left me with a crappy job.' He had nothing to live for.". . .
>
> Houston showed up at his old high school with a shotgun and .22-

caliber rifle, authorities said. He found Brens leading students in a discussion of the riots in Los Angeles. Brens and Davis died in the first round of gunfire.

In South Central Los Angeles, a couple of thousand walking time-bombs exploded all at once. We are only beginning to understand the enormously destructive power of reading failure when organized into an anti-social force. When you deliberately dumb down a people, you create a monster unlike any other in history. There is no instance in history that I know of where an education system perversely functioned as a brain-deforming instrument used to subjugate an entire people. Only the genius of American psychology could dream up something so evil, so diabolical, so efficient, and so effective.

The sad truth is that public education has destroyed the American dream for countless numbers of young people, and the way the system has done it is by preventing its students from acquiring those academic skills needed to achieve success. Literacy is the key to upward mobility in our meritocracy. Without it you can't get very far.

18. "The Whole Language Catalog" or The Fetish of the Whole

The Whole Language Catalog, authored by Kenneth and Yetta Goodman and Lois Bridges Bird, and published by American School Publishers, tells you everything you ever wanted to know about whole language and more. After having perused critically every page and every article in this 445-page monster of a book, I can say that I am impressed with the scope and depth of the whole-language movement. With all of the emphasis placed on beliefs and values, one gets the distinct feeling that this is a religious movement, with its high priests, its sacred literature, its disciples and fanatics, its proselytizers. It even has its own canon law. For example: Thou shalt not teach intensive, systematic phonics in a whole language classroom. Thou shalt not correct the spelling of a learner for fear that his or her spontaneity in writing will be thwarted. Thou shalt not teach anything that requires rote memorization. Thou shalt not fragment language for phonic or spelling exercises.

Actually, I agree with some of the things that whole-language educators have done. They've gotten rid of those dreadful basal readers and replaced them with "real literature." They've gotten rid of the inane workbooks where children circle things and fill in blank spaces. Children *should* be permitted to write their own whole sentences. But unfortunately, like so much of the pedagogical nonsense in whole language, the children are encouraged to write before they have been taught to read. They use invented spelling to express their thoughts.

Moreover, in whole language, you don't teach children to read. They learn to read in the same way they learned to speak: naturally. It is assumed that if you read to the children, surround them with texts, immerse them in literature, that somehow they will learn to read through a process known in biology as osmosis. It's supposed to be quite liberating. Ken Goodman, probably America's most famous whole-language advocate, writes (p. 207):

> Whole language classrooms liberate pupils to try new things, to invent spellings, to experiment with a new genre, to guess at meanings in their reading, or to read and write imperfectly. Our research on reading and writing has strongly supported the importance of error in language development. Miscues represent the tension between invention and convention in reading.... In whole language classrooms risk-taking is not simply tolerated, it is celebrated. Learners have always been free to fail.[1]

And fail they do. According to Prof. Jeanne S. Chall, who runs a reading lab at Harvard University's Graduate School of Education, "I see the failures from it already. Children are coming into the lab who were in [whole language] classes." (*Wash. Post*, 11/29/86)

But whole language educators do not acknowledge failure in terms of traditional pedagogy, because to them reading is, in Ken Goodman's words, "a psycholinguistic guessing game." And the reason why they have to guess is because they have not been drilled in intensive, systematic phonics which provides readers with an automatic ability to associate letters with sounds. Oh yes, they are taught some phonics, but only incidentally. As La Donna Hauser, writes (p. 115):

> I want students to realize what they do as they read. I'd like them to discover these word-level strategies: (1) skipping an unknown word, (2) using context clues, (3) looking for structural clues within words, (4) sounding out the word, (5) using a dictionary, and (6) asking for help. I accept all productive strategies that students use.[2]

Notice that "sounding out the word" is just one strategy among many. The children are taught some letter sounds, but not in a systematic way. Judy Peters writes (p. 114):

> A focus on decoding and pronunciation may lead to the idea that correct oral performance is the goal of reading, rather than understanding the text, and minimise the amount of risk-taking attempted.[3]

Risk-taking is a euphemism for guessing. Naturally, if children are not taught the means of easy decoding through intensive, systematic phonics, they will have to rely on "strategies" that are much less reliable. The whole language people do it all backwards. They want children to understand what they are reading before they know how to read. Those of us who advocate "phonics first" know from years of experience that you must know *how* to read before you can understand *what* you are reading. After all, if you didn't know how to decode the Russian alphabet, for example, you would not be able to articulate the words and therefore not know what you were reading.

It's downright criminal to teach children that reading is a guessing game. Some years ago when I was tutoring a youngster with a severe reading problem, I discovered that he believed that good readers were simply good guessers and that his problem was that he was a bad guesser. He had been so badly damaged by this idea that it took months of hard work to get him to see things differently. He had been taught to read in a public school which used the whole-word method.

What led Ken Goodman to define reading as a "psycholinguistic guessing game"? He writes (p. 98):

> In my research I found readers anticipating what was coming. They predicted grammatical patterns; they reworded the text; they inserted, omitted, substituted, and changed the word sequence. Sometimes they lost themselves in the process, but often they produced sensible text readings that differed in remarkable ways from an expected reading.[4]

What Goodman has described in the above paragraph is a disabled reader, a so-called dyslexic. Every disabled reader I've ever tutored read that way, and the only cure was to turn that whole-word guesser into an accurate phonetic reader. And that required teaching the individual our English alphabetic system and how to apply this new phonetic knowledge to his or her reading. Every disabled reader I have ever tutored lacked this basic phonetic knowledge. They had either never been taught it or had been taught it in a fragmentary, incidental manner.

And so when Goodman talks of reading as being a "psycholinguistic guessing game," he is referring to a disabled sight reader, not an accurate phonetic reader. To the latter, reading is not at all a guessing game. It is a highly accurate, automatic process in which the written word is decoded instantaneously into its spoken equivalent which, in turn, transmits meaning to the brain. It is the sight method of teaching reading that produces the kind of hobbled reader Goodman considers to be a normal reader. After years of such reading instruction in American schools, there are indeed millions of Americans who read that way. Goodman writes:

> In the reading guessing game we use strategies to make sense of print.

> We sample or select from the print — it would be too slow and distracting to use it all. We predict what will be coming ahead from what we already know. We make inferences and merge them with what we explicitly know so that we can't tell when we're done what we took from the text and what we put into it. And we have strategies for correcting when we lose the meaning.[5]

No wonder so many Americans don't like to read! Some years ago I tutored a very successful, intelligent man, a graduate of a midwestern university, who couldn't read. He was a typical victim of the whole-word, sight method. He had no phonetic knowledge whatsoever. And when he told me that he would rather be beaten than have to read, I understood for the first time the kind of psychic pain that the sight method can cause. I taught him our alphabetic system, and in a short time he was reading smoothly and easily. He was furious at having been deprived of this knowledge when he was in primary school.

Of course, one of the reasons why the whole-language movement has appealed to so many teachers is the inanity of the basal reading programs in their schools. Kathy O'Brien, who teaches at California State University, San Bernardino, describes what it was like using a basal reading program (p. 392):

> I had a curriculum that consisted of isolated skills taught for the sake of passing a proficiency test at the end of the book, as well as a district achievement test. It was a curriculum entirely prescribed by textbook publishers who didn't know my kids. And my students marched mindlessly through these programs, touched by nothing, including me. I know now that this curriculum went against everything I knew and felt about the way kids learn. I was extremely unhappy with the basal reader and fragmented curriculum I was teaching . . . .[6]

And so Ms. O'Brien fell for whole language hook, line and sinker. Who could blame her? She writes:

> My classroom began to change from a teacher-directed skill-and-drill classroom to a student-centered whole language classroom. . . . I believe learning and students, not basal readers and skill lists, should be at the heart of every classroom.

And, of course, Ken Goodman agrees with her wholeheartedly. He writes (p. 10):

> I know of no other movement in the history of education that has so caught the imagination of teachers and developed so strong a grass-roots base among classroom teachers as whole language. I believe that's because the teaching profession, particularly in the English-speaking world, has come of age. Teachers are taking seriously their responsibilities as decision-makers and as advocates for the young people they teach. . . . They are taking power, as professionals, in their classrooms. . . . We share the belief system that underlies whole language.[7]

And so, it is not difficult to understand why so many teachers find whole language preferable to the workbook-oriented basal programs. They are not pleased with the results they get from the basals and the children are bored. And suddenly there is whole language which promises fun and joy and liberation and empowerment. The belief system tells you that children learn to read by reading. No need to teach them to read. They can do it themselves. The classroom becomes a joy-filled community where everyone helps everyone else. Competition is replaced by cooperation. You don't even have to teach spelling. Children invent their own spelling and eventually correct themselves. There is no such thing as a reading error, only a "miscue."

But what is this belief system they all have? According to Jeanette Veatch of Arizona State University, whole language "is but the newest manifestation of progressive education." (p. 235)[8]

Thomas Newkirk, a professor at the University of New

Hampshire, writes (p. 217):

> The whole language approach is, of course, not new. It has strong similarities to the New Education of the 1880s — the Progressive Education of the 1920s and 1930s, and the open classroom movement that had a short life in the late 1960s and 1970s.[9]

Yetta Goodman writes (p. 387):

> Influences on whole language include the traditions of humanism and science. . . . The educational theories and beliefs that whole language represents today will be foundational to educational understandings and practices in the future. In the same way that those of us who call ourselves whole language proponents today discover our roots in the humanistic and scientific beliefs of those who came before, future humanistic and scientific beliefs will have their roots in the dynamic movement called whole language.[10]

The *Catalog* pays homage to John Dewey, who is considered one of the pioneers of whole language. Of course, it was John Dewey who advocated deemphasizing the teaching of reading in the primary school in favor of a curriculum that emphasized socialization. His essay, "The Primary-Education Fetich," published in 1898, outlined the new primary curriculum. Dewey wrote:

> The plea for the predominance of learning to read in early school life because of the great importance attaching to literature seems to me a perversion.[11]

His recommendations led to the adoption of the look-say, whole-word, sight reading method of instruction that has resulted in millions of Americans becoming functionally illiterate. All of those dull, inane basal readers were designed to implement the Dewey program. Even though they were sight-oriented, they also taught some incidental phonics as phonetic clues, for it was known quite early that children could not learn to read by merely memorizing words by their configurations alone. Today, whole language educators are immersing the children in literature but not teaching them to read! The basals may be missing, but Dewey's progressive psycho-socio-political agenda is still intact.

In fact, the whole language movement is so skewed to the left, that one wonders why no one in the establishment has complained about it. But then the whole establishment is biased to the left, and bringing this fact to the public only gets one branded right-wing extremist.

The whole language pantheon of educators who have contributed to the belief system that shapes the movement include such noted Marxists as Paulo Freire, Noam Chomsky, and Lev S. Vygotsky, who is frequently mentioned in *The Whole Language Catalog*. Luis Moll writes (p. 413):

> Vygotsky regarded education not only as central to cognitive development, but also as the quintessential sociocultural activity.... [H]is work focused primarily on the social origins and cultural bases of individual development. . . . His central educational concept, that of the zone of proximal development, highlights this connection between social activity and individual thinking. . . . The key point of the concept is the interdependence between children's thinking and the social and cultural resources provided to help develop (mediate) that thinking.[12]

Whole language educators certainly endeavor to provide the social and cultural resources that will enable the children to develop politically and ecologically correct thought patterns.

Another progressive educator in the whole language hall of fame is Joseph Neef (1770-1854), a disciple of Pestalozzi. According to Ron Miller (p. 109), Neef emigrated to America in 1806 and in 1808 published one of the first systematic explanations of holistic education, *Sketch of a Plan and Method of Education*. In 1826 Neef became head teacher at the experimental communist colony at New Harmony, Indiana, founded by Robert Owen, the English industrialist. The experiment lasted only two years because, as Owen concluded, people educated under the old system could not become true communists even though they sympathized with the idea. Owen's son, Robert Dale Owen, then launched a movement to create a national government system of public schools in America which would be used to prepare the children of America for a socialist way of life.

Henry A. Giroux is perhaps the most radical of the writers in the *Catalog*. He is a professor of education and director of the Center for Education and Cultural Studies at Miami University (Ohio). He writes (p. 417):

> In the most general sense, literacy can be defined in pedagogical terms that adapt people to existing configurations of power, as in the advocacy of functional literacy. . . . In the most emancipatory sense, literacy is a political and pedagogical process of naming the world, which is biographical, historical, and collective. . . . In short, literacy is about the issues of politics, power, and possibility. . . .
>
> One of the most important projects for teachers in the next decade will be the development of a critical literacy that incorporates the politics of cultural diversity with a view of pedagogy that recognizes the importance of democratic public life. . . . Eurocentric culturally dominated curricula must be rejected as resistant to seeing schools as places for educating students to be critical citizens in a vital, democratic society. On the other hand, progressive views of literacy must openly acknowledge their own politics and commitment to pedagogical practices that deepen the goals of democratic struggle and cultural justice. . . .
>
> Whole language has done much to provide educators with both a language of critique and possibility, particularly in terms of its emphasis on the necessity for teachers to incorporate into their teaching the voices that students bring with them to the classroom.[13]

So whole language is more than just another reading program. It's a call for socialist revolution!

Michael Apple, professor of Curriculum and Instruction and Educational Policy Studies at the University of Wisconsin, Madison, is another leftist concerned about the future of whole language. He is concerned about attacks on public education coming from the political right. He writes (p. 416):

> Conservative groups have nearly always attempted to control the daily lives of teachers and to blame them for serious problems in the larger society over which teachers usually have little control. . . . And there are reasons for the current emphasis on an educationally and politically problematic return to a curriculum based on the "western tradition" and "cultural literacy."
>
> This means that — for all its meritorious goals — the whole language movement cannot insure that its own goals and methods will have a lasting and widespread impact unless it is willing to act not only within the school, but outside it as well. Its proponents need to join with others in the wider social movements that aim at democratizing our economy, politics, and culture, and that act against a society that is so unequal in gender, race, and class terms.[14]

Despite the demise of communism in the Soviet Union, Marxist rhetoric is alive and well in the American university!

Bess Altwerger and Barbara Flores write in an article entitled "The Politics of Whole Language" (p. 418):

> Whole language teaching is subversive, in the best sense of the word, because it seeks to restore equality and democracy to our schools, to our children, and in essence, to our society. . . .
>
> We are not just asking for a change in the teaching of reading, but a radical change in the social and political structure of schooling and society (Giroux and McLaren 1986).[15]

Pretty radical stuff, don't you think? Whole language is also considered part of the holistic education movement. Don Miller, founder and editor of *Holistic Education Review,* defines holistic education as follows (p. 427):

> Holistic education seeks to nurture the development of the whole person. It is not enough to educate for academic achievement and vocational skills alone; the human personality is an integrated complex of intellectual, physical, social, moral, emotional, and spiritual possibilities. All of these must be taken into account in the education of children. . . .
>
> Holistic education is a spiritual worldview rather than a materialist one. It is belief in, and a reverence for, a self-directing life force that lies beyond our rational, intellectual understanding.[16]

Miller goes on to say that holistic spirituality is not religion, but "self-actualization," the process outlined by humanist psychologist Abraham Maslow. What is quite clear however is that holistic education gets into areas that public schools have no business getting into: the spiritual and emotional lives of its students. Miller continues:

> The holistic perspective is an inclusive, phenomenological, ecological, global perspective that seeks to encompass all aspects of human experience. . . . [H]olistic education is a radical break from traditional ways of understanding human development. . . . [It] represents a new paradigm. In essence, it is the educational approach of a new culture — an emerging postindustrial, post-technocratic civilization, in which the whole human being may yet be nurtured.

And you thought kids go to school just to learn to read and write! Perhaps what makes whole language so appealing to so many teachers is that the atmosphere in the classroom is more homelike than schoollike. It deals with the whole child, it nurtures, it cuddles. There is no ability grouping, older kids help younger kids, and the kids are active learners reading real books not textbooks. There's lots of dialogue, lots of "critical thinking." It's as if the classroom were transformed into a surrogate home, replacing the child's real home by offering so much more "enrichment" than parents can provide. A perfect scheme for weaning children away from their traditional religious upbringing and inculcating them in the liberating, empowering dogma of holistic, ecological paganism.

19. Dr. Seuss, Edward Miller and Artificially Induced Dyslexia

Ever since *The New Illiterates* was published back in 1973 this writer has argued that the chief, and perhaps only, cause of dyslexia among normal school children has been and still is the look-say, whole-word, or sight method of teaching reading. In that book I uncovered the fact that the sight method had been invented back in the 1830s by the Rev. Thomas H. Gallaudet, the director of the American Asylum at Hartford for the Education of the Deaf and Dumb. He had been using a sight, or whole-word method in teaching the deaf to read, by juxtaposing a word, such as *cat,* with the picture of a cat. And because the deaf were able to identify many simple words in this way, Gallaudet thought that the method could be adapted for use by normal children.

Gallaudet believed that education was a science and could be improved by the same sort of experimentation that went on in chemistry. He wrote in the *American Annals of Education* of August 1830:

> *Mind, like matter, can be made subject to experiment.* If, in this way,

chemistry has arrived to a degree of perfection, as a science, which commands the admiration of all lovers of true philosophy, what may not be expected, also, in the science of education, if the same inductive process is pursued, of eliciting, comparing and arranging the phenomena, which is presented by the subject under examination.

In pursuance of these suggestions, permit me to state the mode which has been pursued in my own family for seven years past, to make my children acquainted with the power and use of letters.

The words *horse, dog, cat* are written, in a very plain and legible hand, on three separate cards. One of them is shown to the child, and the name of the object is pronounced; and then the second and the third in the same manner, *without any reference to the individual letters which compose the word.* After repeating this a few times, the child is asked, 'what is that?' holding up one of the cards, and so of the rest. Let the cards then be placed together, and the child required to select those denoting the several objects, one after the other. Vary the order of doing this until the child becomes perfectly familiar with the words; which will be in a very short time.

The next day, another card containing the name of some other familiar object, may be added, and the child practised in the same manner upon the four cards. The number of cards may soon be increased to six, to ten, to twenty, to fifty.

Here I have been accustomed to stop, and begin to teach the child the letters of which the words are composed in the following manner. Take the word *horse,* and covering all the rest, show the letter *h,* giving its name. Do this with the other letters in succession, repeating the process, until the child is perfectly familiar with the four [*sic*] letters. Then lay down the fifty cards in order, and ask the child to find the letter *h* among them, then *o, r, s,* and *e.* This will readily be done. He has thus learned four [*sic*] letters of the alphabet. Vary the order in which the cards are laid, and require the child to point out the letters, *h, o, r, s, e.* Let this be done till he is familiar with them. Pursue the same course with the card containing the word *dog,* and so on, until the child is perfectly acquainted with all the letters on the cards. They may then be written down in the order of the alphabet, and the child taught to repeat them in that order.[1]

And that's how the look-say, whole-word, or sight method was invented. It was based on the notion that an instruction method suitable for the deaf was also suitable for normal children. Gallaudet's look-say primer, *The Mother's Primer,* was published in 1836 and was adopted by the Boston Primary School Committee in 1837. Horace Mann was then Secretary of the Board of Education of Massacusetts, and he favored the new method.

Gallaudet's primer was imitated by other textbook writers, and the children of Massachusetts were taught to read by this new sight method. By 1844 the defects of the new method were so apparent to the Boston schoolmasters, that they issued a blistering attack against it, and urged a return to intensive, systematic phonics. I reprinted the full text of that historic critique in *The New Illiterates,* in order to demonstrate how early the defects of the look-say, whole-word method were recognized by educators who were not seduced by the siren songs of the reformers.

In that book, I also did a line-by-line analysis of the Dick-and-Jane reading program and came to the conclusion that any child taught to read by that method exclusively would exhibit the symptoms of dyslexia. The cause was obvious: when you impose an ideographic teaching technique on an alphabetic writing system, you get reading disability. By eliminating the sense of sound from the reading process, one is breaking the crucial link between the alphabetically written word and its spoken equivalent. Also, by using sound symbols as ideographic symbols, one creates symbolic confusion.

The schoolmasters of Boston had recognized this phenomenon in 1844, and it was also recognized in 1929 by Dr. Samuel T. Orton, a neuropathologist in Iowa who was seeking the cause of children's reading problems. After considerable research, he came to the conclusion that their problems were being caused by the new sight method of teaching reading. The results of his research were published in the February 1929 issue of the *Journal of Educational Psychology* with the title, "The 'Sight Reading' Method of Teaching Reading as a Source of Reading Disability."

And so, there has been no doubt in my mind as to the cause of dyslexia among perfectly healthy, normal school children. However, in recent years I have heard stories of children entering the first grade already exhibiting the symptoms of dyslexia, before they have had any formal reading instruction. It was said that these children, who had never been to school, were having a terribly difficult time learning to read by phonics. The phenomenon was somewhat inexplicable, until sometime in 1988 when I received a phone call from a man in North Wilkesboro, North Carolina, by the name of Edward Miller. It turned out that he had the key to the mystery.[2]

Miller had called to tell me of his theory of "educational dyslexia," that is, how dyslexia could be artificially induced. I was delighted to know that there was someone else in America who agreed with me. He had seen me on a television interview in 1984 and was so astounded by my assertions about dyslexia that he decided to get my book on the NEA. What I had said on TV sounded crazy to him, but he said I looked too sane to be crazy.

Miller was particularly interested in this subject because he himself was dyslexic and had been so since the first grade. He had been taught to read in a rural school in North Carolina by a young teacher fresh out of college who used the sight method. At first Miller thought it was his stupidity that was causing his reading problem. But in the fourth grade he proved that he was not stupid by memorizing the multiplication table and winning a prize in class. From then on he simply saw his reading problem as a handicap that had to be compensated for by all sorts of tricks. For example, he found that he could pass many essay tests by writing short, simple sentences in which all of the words were spelled correctly. He might earn a C for his efforts, but C's were better than F's.

Eventually, Miller made it through North Carolina State College. In fact, despite his reading disability, he was able to become a mathematics teacher and finally an assistant administrator in a high school in Hollywood, Florida.

It was by reading an excerpt from Rudolf Flesch's book, *Why Johnny Can't Read,* in a newspaper in 1956 that Miller had become aware of the two ways of teaching children to read: the phonetic method and the sight or look-say method. He realized that he had been taught by the sight method.

But it wasn't until 1986, when his young grandson, Kevin, then in the first grade, developed a reading problem, that Miller was motivated to investigate the matter in greater depth. In the suffering and pain of his grandson he saw a repeat of himself. He knew that Kevin had learned to read by look-say, and that was easy to prove because Kevin could read his little sight-vocabulary books rapidly, without error. But when faced with reading matter not in the controlled vocabulary, he had extreme difficulty. Miller could see that Kevin was trying to guess the words. The boy found the process of sounding out words irritating and painful.

Miller recalled what he had read in my NEA book about the Russian psychologists, Luria and Pavlov, and of how they had devised a way of artificially inducing behavioral disorganization by introducing two conflicting stimuli to the organism. Miller believed that he was seeing the same process at work in Kevin. He was sure that Kevin had learned something at an early age that was interfering with his attempt to decode the little phonetic books which Miller had bought him.

"I knew about the two methods of teaching reading," relates Miller, "and suspected that he had learned a non-phonetic method of looking at words. I tried to help him sound out the words in the little books, but the books seemed to be hurting him."

It was obvious to Miller that his grandson had learned a method of reading that conflicted with the phonetic method and that it was causing what is commonly known as "dyslexia." Miller thought he could demonstrate how this cognitive conflict could be artificially induced by way of a very simple experiment. Drawing on his extensive knowledge of mathematics, he devised an experimental problem whereby an individual trained in the base-ten arithmetic system would be required to do his calculations in a base-twelve system. The individual would experience great difficulty, confusion and frustration trying to suppress his base-ten reflex as he attempted to do simple arithmetic in a base-twelve system. This was what the sight reader experienced in trying to apply a phonetic method of looking at words when the automatic tendency was "spatial-holistic" in orientation.

The key to the problem, Miller believed, was in the automaticity involved in each method. If a child's first-learned way of reading was configurational and not phonetic, and if the child could read this sight vocabulary in an out-of-context word list at more than 30 words per minute, that child would develop educational, or artificially induced, dyslexia. However, if the child's first-learned way of identifying words was phonetic, and if that ability had become automatic, that child would never become dyslexic.

But Miller wondered how Kevin could have developed such a strong automatic configurational way of identifying words without any formal reading instruction. He had noticed that Kevin had in his room many children's books, including many of the Dr. Seuss books which children often learn to read by memorizing the words. If Kevin had developed an automatic configurational way of identifying words by having memorized the Dr. Seuss books, then he could have entered the first grade with an already learned way of reading that would conflict with the phonetic approach.

Most people are not aware that the Dr. Seuss books were created to supplement the whole-word reading programs in the schools. Most people assume that Dr. Seuss made up his stories using his own words. The truth is that the publisher supplied Dr.

Seuss with a sight vocabulary of 223 words which he was to use in writing the books, a sight vocabulary in harmony with the sight words the child would be learning in school. Thus, the children would enter the first grade having already mastered a sight vocabulary of several hundred words, thereby making first-grade reading a breeze.

Because the Dr. Seuss books are so simple, many people assume that they were easy to write. But Dr. Seuss debunked that idea in an interview he gave *Arizona* magazine in June 1981. He said:

> They think I did it in twenty minutes. That damned *Cat in the Hat* took nine months until I was satisfied. I did it for a textbook house and they sent me a word list. That was due to the Dewey revolt in the Twenties, in which they threw out phonic reading and went to word recognition, as if you're reading a Chinese pictograph instead of blending sounds of different letters. I think killing phonics was one of the greatest causes of illiteracy in the country. Anyway, they had it all worked out that a healthy child at the age of four can learn so many words in a week and that's all. So there were two hundred and twenty-three words to use in this book. I read the list three times and I almost went out of my head. I said, I'll read it once more and if I can find two words that rhyme that'll be the title of my book. (That's genius at work.) I found "cat" and "hat" and I said, "The title will be *The Cat in the Hat*."[3]

And that is how the Dr. Seuss preschool, sight-word books were born. The publishers believed that if the children could memorize the words in the books, they would be better prepared for the sight-reading instruction they would get in the first grade. An ad for The Beginning Readers' Program states:

> The words are just right for young readers, too. They're in large, clear type. They often tell the story in rhyme. And they're so closely related to the pictures that, with a little help from Mom and Dad, even pre-schoolers can start reading all by themselves. And when a pre-schooler is turned on

to reading by Dr. Seuss and his friends he generally stays turned on to reading for life.

What the ad didn't tell parents is that if the child was permitted to develop an automatic holistic, configurational way of identifying words, then that child would be dyslexic when dealing with the much larger reading vocabulary beyond the few hundred words he or she had memorized. And with the advent of audio cassettes, the child could learn to memorize the words even without the help of Mom or Dad. But if the child had been taught to read phonetically from the very beginning, he or she would never become dyslexic.

Miller had, indeed, made a very significant discovery, one that could save millions of children from falling into the dyslexia trap caused by memorizing the sight vocabularies in their preschool readers. But the problem now was how to make this discovery public?

The publishers of the Beginner Books were making millions of dollars, and the books themselves were extremely popular with parents and children alike. Some children are taught to sound out words by their parents, and these children, of course, are not harmed by these little books since they look at all words phonetically. But since most preschoolers are not taught to read phonetically at home before they go to school, they are in great danger of becoming dyslexic. And the better they get at memorizing the words, the greater the danger, for it is when the child develops an automatic ability to identify words configurationally, that he or she develops the cognitive blockage that produces dyslexia.

The publishers of the Beginner Books have also produced a picture dictionary. The purpose of the dictionary is to make the child "recognize, remember, and really enjoy a basic elementary vocabulary of 1,350 words." We wonder how many hundreds of thousands of children have become dyslexic by memorizing the sight words in this picture dictionary.

But how was Miller going to get this information to the public? He decided to contact some of the educational officials in the Florida public school system. Having retired from the system in 1982, he was acquainted with many of these educators. They listened politely and seemed to understand what he was talking about. But he could arouse no real interest or enthusiasm about his discovery.

He then went to IBM, which had developed a costly computer reading instruction program called Writing to Read which teaches children a modified phonetic writing system. After many phone conversations, they referred him to Dr. Larry Silver, director of the National Institute of Dyslexia in Bethesda, Maryland. Miller called Silver who said he would like to see Miller's materials on the artificial induction of dyslexia. Several days after sending the materials, Miller called Silver's office. The secretary said that the materials had arrived, that a complete copy of them had been made, and that they were being returned to Miller with a letter from Dr. Silver.

Silver's letter was quite perfunctory. He offered no evaluation of Miller's theory on the artificial induction of dyslexia, but advised Miller to team up with someone at a university working in special education. Apparently, Miller's lack of academic "credentials" was the new handicap he had to deal with.

But Miller had already contacted someone at Appalachian State University for help. He had spoken with the dean of the school of education who recommended that he contact Dr. Gerald Parker, professor of special education. In August 1988 Miller made a presentation of his theory to Dr. Parker's graduate students. But he soon realized, by the questions they asked, that they were all committed to the whole-language approach. In fact, Parker expressed the opinion that the best way to avoid creating the cognitive conflict was to teach the child only one way of looking at words: the holistic, configurational way! In other words, the child should only read words that he had memorized as sight words. If he did that, he would never exhibit the symptoms of dyslexia.

But, then, how would the child ever learn to read unknown, multisyllabic words not in his sight vocabulary? Parker told Miller that Frank Smith provided the answer to that question in his book, *Understanding Reading,* the bible of whole-language educators.

Miller got a copy of the book, read it slowly but thoroughly and came to the conclusion that Frank Smith was responsible for the misconception of the century.

Miller's theory was that the two ways of looking at words — the configurational and the phonetic — were mutually exclusive, and that once a child achieved an automatic ability to look at words in a spatial-holistic fashion, it created a cognitive conflict with the phonetic method. Frank Smith, however, insisted that none of these methods were mutually exclusive. But if this were so, then why didn't those who were trained to read phonetically ever become dyslexic, and those who were taught to read ideographically did?

Dr. Parker also told Miller about Dr. Frank Wood, director of the Bowman Gray Learning Disability Project at the Bowman Gray School of Medicine in Winston-Salem, North Carolina. Wood was conducting research on learning disabilities under a $3-million grant from the National Institute of Child Health and Human Development (NICHD). The goal of the project, according to a brochure, was "to understand the causes of learning disability and the methods by which we might forestall or prevent some of the worst consequences in under-achievement." Obviously, if there were anyone who would be interested in Miller's theory about the cause of dyslexia, it would have to be Dr. Wood.

Wood did, in fact, show interest in Miller's theory, and after several visits and phone conversations over a period of about four months, he sent Miller a four-page review of the theory in August, 1988. In essence, Wood agreed that dyslexia was generally characterized by a deficit in decoding skills. But he believed that this deficit was probably due to some children being "genetically predisposed against phonetic processes" rather than their having become phonetically impaired by their preschool learning of a sight vocabulary. Wood wrote:

> There is no evidence of which I am aware that would relate the kinds of early pre-reading experiences you describe to dyslexia in the school years. Perhaps it is fair to say that there has been little attempt to gather such evidence, so that the issue remains unexplored. There is, however, a major series of investigations that establishes the role of genetic factors in dyslexia. To the extent that genetic factors control the dyslexic outcome, preschool experience would be eliminated as any substantial cause of the problem.

In other words, the federal government has spent and is still spending millions of dollars looking for the genetic causes of dyslexia. This line of investigation is the official line of the Interagency Committee on Learning Disabilities which defined "Learning Disabilities" as follows in its 1987 report to the Congress:

> Learning disabilities is a generic term that refers to a heterogeneous group of disorders manifested by significant difficulties in the acquisition and use of listening, speaking, reading, writing, reasoning, or mathematical abilities, or of social skills. These disorders are intrinsic to the individual and presumed to be due to central nervous system dysfunction. Even though a learning disability may occur concomitantly with other handicapping conditions (e.g., sensory impairment, mental retardation, social and emotional disturbance), with socioenvironmental influences (e.g., cultural differences, insufficient or inappropriate instruction, psychogenic factors), and especially with attention deficit disorder, all of which may cause learning problems, a learning disability is not the direct result of those conditions or influences.[4]

In other words, instruction methods are largely irrelevant! Also, note that you can also be learning disabled in social skills, which opens a vast new field of investigation for psychologists seeking government research grants. Wood also wrote:

> The only part of your theory that is undeveloped in research is that having to do with the role of preschool experience in strengthening a natural spatial holistic viewing tendency, to the subsequent detriment of phonemically based reading. That is an interesting research question, and it has not yet been subjected to careful scientific methodology. It seems to me that there would be two separable issues: (1) whether any substantial numbers of dyslexic children owe their dyslexia to the pre-emption by a spatial strategy that was learned or strengethened in the preschool years; and (2) whether this pre-emption by a spatial strategy is even possible (nothwithstanding the question of whether it accounts for a substantial number of dyslexic children's problems).

What this meant was that Miller had to prove, in a manner acceptable to the scientific community, that his theory was correct. Miller believed that he could do so by means of a simple test that anyone could duplicate and verify. He had already seen how dyslexic children could read their controlled-vocabulary books with great speed but were stymied when faced with simple newspaper stories. The question was, at what point did the child become a committed sight reader and develop a block against learning phonics? It took about ten months of experimentation before Miller finally came up with a testing instrument that would indicate clearly whether a child was a sight reader or a phonetic reader and at what point the child's reading mode became permanent. The test would scientifically measure the child's word-identification strategies and accurately measure the severity of the child's dyslexic condition.

The test was composed of two sets of words: the first set consisted of 260 sight words drawn from two Dr. Seuss books,

Green Eggs and Ham and *The Cat in the Hat.* The second set consisted of 260 equally simple words drawn from Rudolf Flesch's word lists in *Why Johnny Can't Read.* The sight words were arranged in alphabetical order across the page. The sight words included such multisyllabic words as *about, another, mother, playthings, something, yellow,* while the words from Flesch's book were all at first-grade level, one syllable and phonetically regular. In other words, for a child who knew his or her phonics neither set of words posed any problem.

The purpose of the test was to measure the speed at which the child read both sets of words and to count the errors, or miscues, made in reading the two sets of words.

The first children Miller tested were the five children of the Newman family, a black family Miller had known for many years. He discovered that the two oldest boys, David and Carl, could read both sets of words with no difficulty, indicating normal, phonetic reading ability. However, their brothers Tyler (11) and Jesse (7) were a different story. Tyler read the sight words at 51 words per minute with no errors, but read the phonetic words at 17 words per minute with 91 errors. Jesse read the sight words at a speed of 44 words per minute with no errors, but read the phonetic words at 24 words per minute with 47 errors.

Obviously, both youngsters had become dyslexic. The fact that they could read the sight words at over 30 words per minute meant that their word-identification mode was automatic and, therefore, permanently fixed. Their cognitive block against phonics had been established by the way they had learned to read. Unless the blockage was undone through intensive remedial intervention, it would remain a major lifelong handicap, preventing them from pursuing careers that required accurate reading skills.

The youngest child, Michelle (6), given a shorter version of the test, read the sight words at 21 words per minute with 8 errors and the phonetic words at 10 words per minute with 16 errors. She had not yet developed that degree of automaticity with the sight words that would have prevented her from becoming a phonetic reader. But Michelle was tested nine months later, and the results indicated that she had developed the needed automaticity. She could now read the sight words at 39 words per minute with 11 errors, and read the phonetic words at 21 words per minute with 50 errors. In other words, she had become educationally dyslexic in a matter of nine months. This outcome could have been prevented had she been taught intensive, systematic phonics at a time when her word-identification mode was still indeterminate.

The test had clearly shown its value as an indicator of a child's way of identifying words: phonetically or holistically. It also indicated the degree of dyslexia, or symbolic confusion, the child was suffering from. It could also identify those children who had not yet made a cognitive commitment to either word-identification mode and could still be saved from becoming educationally dyslexic with the proper instructional intervention.

In January 1990 Miller obtained permission to administer his test to 68 students at the Ronda-Clingman Elementary School, a rural school with an enrollment of about 600 near the town of Ronda in Wilkes County, North Carolina. Of the 68 students, 25 were 4th graders, 26 were 2nd graders, and 17 students were from different grades in Title 1. The results were alarming. Of the 26 second graders, 5 were phonetic readers, 11 were permanent holistic readers (with a sight-reading speed of over 30 words per minute) and therefore already educationally dyslexic, and 10 were in a state of reading limbo, that is, they hadn't yet developed automaticity in either word-identification mode and could either become fluent phonetic readers or educationally dyslexic. The outcome would depend on how they were taught to read in the next few months.

Of the 25 fourth graders, 14 were phonetic readers and 11 were holistic, that is, educationally dyslexic. None were in an indeterminate state. In other words, they had all developed the degree of automaticity in their word-identification mode which made their reading mode permanent. If this fourth-grade class was typical of fourth-grade classes throughout North Carolina, this meant that 44% of all students in the public schools of that state would emerge at the end of their school careers educationally dyslexic, that is, functionally illiterate.

Of the 17 students in Title 1, 6 were phonetic readers, 6 were holistic (educationally dyslexic), and 5 were in limbo. Of the latter, 4 were in first grade, indicating that their reading instruction was leading them into educational dyslexia.

What was happening at the Ronda-Clingman school was going on in every elementary school in North Carolina. Were the authorities concerned? Miller had actually gone to the state education authorities in September of 1989 and demonstrated to them his theory on the artificial inducement of dyslexia. Two months later he received a letter from Betty Jean Foust, the state's Consultant for Reading Communication Skills. She wrote:

> This letter is in response to your request that I review your materials and comment upon your theory of dyslexia. . . . Members of the Department of Public Instruction believe in a multiple approach to teaching reading. We believe that phonics may help the beginning reader if it is done early and kept simple. We do not feel phonics are useful with older students. In my teaching experience, I have encountered several students who could not hear sounds, therefore, we used other methods for learning to read. In my opinion, all students do not need a phonics assessment. We have never promoted reading words out of context as your assessment does. Time is precious in our schools, and we need activities which promote achievement.
> Secondly, I believe all students can be taught to read. Some can read better than others, but all students can learn something. We need to guard against the use of dyslexia as a term for "catch all reading problems."

Thus spake the state reading authority.

In January 1991, Miller gained permission to test 62 students at Dade Christian School, a private school in Miami, Florida. The school, with an enrollment of about 1,000 students, is racially mixed, with many children from Spanish-speaking families.

Of the 62 students tested, 26 were in fourth grade, 19 in second grade and 17 in a special group selected from 2nd and 3rd grades because of the difficulties they were having in reading. Of the 19 second graders, 14 were established phonetic readers, 4 were holistic, and 1 was indeterminate, that is, in the limbo state. Of the 17 children in the special group, 16 were educationally dyslexic. Of the 26 fourth graders, 24 were phonetic readers, and only 2 were educationally dyslexic. In other words, while in the public schools of North Carolina 44 out of 100 students were becoming educationally dyslexic because of their reading-instruction methods, about 8 out of 100 were becoming educationally dyslexic at the private school in Florida. But even that rate was too high. In any case, Miller had not ascertained how those two dyslexic students in the fourth grade had become that way, nor was he given the academic histories of the 17 children in the special group.

The implications to be drawn from Edward Miller's theory on the artificial inducement of dyslexia are most significant. In the first place, they infer that dyslexia is being caused by the reading instruction methods presently being used in most American public schools and that educational dyslexia can be prevented by the teaching of intensive, systematic phonics so that the children will become phonetic readers. As Miller has pointed out, a phonetic reader cannot become dyslexic.

If what Miller has discovered is true, then the millions of dollars the federal government is spending on finding the genetic causes of dyslexia is a total waste.

In addition, the billions of Chapter One dollars the U. S.

Department of Education has spent in support of reading programs that are causing educational dyslexia are more than a waste. The billions are being used to commit a horrible crime against the children of this country.

For years, now, we have been telling the public that the dyslexia that afflicts millions of perfectly normal, healthy children is being caused by the reading instruction methods being used in our schools. Whole language is the latest manifestation of this insane addiction to defective teaching methods. It is sad to know that millions of innocent children will be permanently damaged by these methods, used by teachers who believe they are doing the right thing.

Edward Miller has gone to great lengths to bring his findings to the attention of the government education and research establishment. His letters and phone calls to top officials have been to no avail. What he has found out is what we have known for a long time: they are not interested. They have their own agenda, and it has nothing to do with educational excellence.

At this point, our only hope is to reach enough parents so that as many children as possible can be saved from the fate of functional illiteracy the public schools have in store for them. We are advising all American parents to teach their children the three R's at home or have them taught at a trustworthy private school until at least the fourth grade. The most severe, permanent damage is done to the children in the first three grades of public school. We believe that home-schooling is the best educational alternative for all children. However, we realize that home-schooling is not a viable alternative for many parents. In addition, many parents cannot afford private education. But they must find some way to educate their children correctly in those first crucial three years.

Parents must also be made aware that permitting their pre-school children to memorize a battery of sight words will cause reading problems later on. They should teach their children to read by intensive, systematic phonics before giving them little pre-school books to read. This will "immunize" the child against dyslexia.

But the most significant and sensational data was to come two years later. In April 1992, Miller obtained permission to retest the same students at Ronda-Clingman he had tested in 1990 using the same first-grade test. Fifty-one of the original 68 students were available for retesting. The results showed that none of the students who were holistic readers in 1990 had become phonetic readers in the interim. Most of them were able to read the words faster and their accuracy had increased in the phonetic part of the test. But more than half of the dyslexic students miscalled some of the very same sight words they had read correctly in 1990. One student who as a fourth-grader had made a total of 12 errors in 1990 made 29 errors in 1992 as a sixth-grader. In other words, this student read better in the 4th grade than in the 6th grade. In fact, 17 out of the 27 sixth graders did better in 1990 than they did in 1992 on the very same first-grade test!

And nowhere was the dumbing down process more obvious than among the good phonetic readers in the second and third grades of 1990 who were now in the fourth and sixth grades. Of the 13 students (4 second-graders, 7 fourth-graders, and 2 Title One sixth-graders) who had achieved the best scores in 1990, nine made more errors on the very same test in 1992. One fourth-grader who had made only 2 errors in 1990 made 18 in 1992 as a sixth grader. Whereas he had missed no sight words in 1990, he missed 8 in 1992. And whereas he had missed only 2 of the phonetic words in 1990, he missed 10 in 1992. Remember, this was an elementary test composed of preschool sight words and single-syllable, phonetically regular words. Obviously, whatever was being taught at Ronda-Clingman was not advancing the academic skills of the students.

On the contrary, many of the students had regressed

This data confirmed what Kurt Lewin had discovered in his experiments aimed at determining the behavioral effects of frustration on children. Lewin's biographer, Alfred Marrow, writes: "The experiment indicated that in frustration the children tended to regress to a surprising degree. . . . The degree of the intellectual regression varied directly with the strength of the frustration." (p. 122, *The Practical Theorist)*[5]

Miller's data also showed that 28 of the 51 students tested missed more of the sight words in 1992 than in 1990, indicating that there was a limit to how many sight words an individual could retain in memory. Apparently, the dyslexic will retain only those sight words that are frequently seen. In other words, low frequency words learned by sight are often forgotten.

At Dade Christian, Miller retested only the 24 students who did not do well in 1991. The results showed that the students learned to read faster and more accurately but were unable to completely overcome their handicap—their inability to call 99% of the words correctly. This indicated that they had not made the cognitive switch needed to become phonetic readers.

But one of the most significant pieces of data that Miller was to glean from this second testing is the fact that even the worst of the educationally dyslexic readers has a good deal of phonetic knowledge which he or she can only tap when consciously required to do so.

Miller obtained this data by having the children go back and spell the words they missed. Almost always they were able to reread the words correctly after spelling. Obviously, there was enough phonetic information in the spelling alone that enabled the student to experience the word as a phonetic entity. The problem for the sight reader was that the holistic reflex overrode and thereby suppressed whatever phonetic knowledge the reader may have had. In fact, it was the holistic reflex that was causing the block against the phonetic experience and thereby causing dyslexia. Miller concluded that the only way to remove the block against the phonetic experience was to replace the holistic reflex with a phonetic reflex. He calls this process: making a "cognitive switch."

In trying to find a way to help dyslexics make the cognitive switch, Miller came up with an ingenious but very simple idea. He thought, why not take a text, block out all of the high frequency sight words, and leave only those words which required a conscious use of the phonetic knowledge the reader already had. By exercising that phonetic ability until it became automatic, the sight reader could become a phonetic reader with the necessary phonetic reflex.

The result was the Miller Sight Word Eliminator, an invention that can help turn a dyslexic sight reader into a proficient phonetic reader in a matter of weeks or months depending on the frequency and intensity of the retraining. Presently, Miller is working on a remediation system which includes a phonetic teaching component to help the student develop the needed phonetic reflex.

Through his tests Miller also developed a means of measuring an individual's phonetic knowledge and a scale that measures the severity of the dyslexic's handicap. Just as a physician can measure a fever with a thermometer on a scale of 98.7 to 108, Miller has devised a way of measuring the severity of the dyslexic condition on a scale of 1 to 100, based on the number of words miscalled on the phonetic portion of the word identification assessment.

The scale is applied only to students who have developed a holistic reflex. A score of 1 would signify a very mild reading handicap while a score of 100 would indicate an extremely severe case of educational dyslexia. A score of 8 or 10 may indicate a slight reading problem for a second grader, but for a sixth grader it may represent a more serious handicap since the measuring instrument is a first-grade test. Of the 51 students tested at Ronda-Clingman, 13 had no handicap, 17 showed handicaps from 8 to 13, and 20 students had handicaps from 21 to 128.

Although Edward Miller has gotten no official recognition of his work, this has not discouraged him from continuing his remarkable research and the development of a wholly original remediation system which promises to provide dyslexics with a fast and efficient way to cure their disability. There can be no doubt that his more recent findings not only confirm the validity of his reading assessment methods, but are providing irrefutable data indicating that the reading instruction methods being used in the public schools are causing far greater academic damage among even the brightest students than any of us could have imagined.

Perhaps the best way to end this chapter is to tell the story of Vickie Reid and her third-grade son, Travis, who had been attending Ronda-Clingman where Vickie had been a substitute teacher. Vickie had become concerned with her son's reading problem when he began coming home crying because he had to read. She writes:

"This went on for several weeks. Finally it stopped and I thought things were okay. Later in the year he began going to his room and crying for no reason. When I asked what was wrong he did not know. This happened usually on a weekly basis. As a parent I was distraught. I prayed for understanding."

And Vickie got it when she was asked to help Miller in his testing at Ronda-Clingman. After three days of testing the students and marking the papers, Vickie began to realize that there was a severe reading problem at Ronda-Clingman. She took a copy of the assessment home and tested her son who was then in the second grade. It was obvious that he had a reading problem. He was a sight reader and when he came to a word he had not memorized, he simply called it anything.

She wondered how he had gotten that way. Her older son had learned to read very well at Ronda-Clingman, and Travis had learned phonics in kindergarten as a four-year-old and was reading phonetically at age five But his phonetic skill had not reached automatic speed and was being replaced by a holistic view of words. She writes:

"My son had started out on the right track with intensive phonics, but a few miles down the road had been switched to holistic sight reading or a mixture of both and after three years was totally confused and hated school or anything that had to do with reading."

Vickie immediately removed her son from Ronda-Clingman and put him in a Christian school in Statesville where they teach intensive phonics. She writes:

"He has made great improvement, loves school, and hasn't cried once because he had a reading assignment. At the present time, my children are not being affected by these programs, however, I have come to know and love lots of children at Ronda-Clingman who are truly, in my opinion, being ruined, because their parents are not as fortunate as I in finding out there was a problem and then working on the cure."

Vickie's story sums up why Ed Miller's work is so important. He is the only researcher in America who, without the help of any government agency or grant, has proven that dyslexia is being artificially induced in our public schools to the great detriment of American children. The question is: why are those in positions of responsibility so reluctant to even consider, let alone investigate, the possibility that it is the teaching methods that are causing dyslexia and not some central nervous system dysfunction? The honesty and integrity of our educators will be sorely tested in the years ahead as they seriously consider Miller's findings and react to them.

20. Outcome-Based Education *or* How to Turn a Dinosaur into an Octopus

In some of my past writings I have called public education a "sick dinosaur" being kept alive by a life-support system known as the education establishment. The latter, through considerable political power, has managed to keep this ailing, obsolete, nineteenth-century anachronism alive because so many careers not only depend on it but must continue to use it as their means to wield power over society. We have predicted the demise of this dinosaur because, like its extinct ancestor, public education has a huge body, a voracious appetite, and a tiny brain. And the establishment knows this.

And so, they have worked out a new plan, not merely for survival, but for a major enhancement of their power which, if successful, will transform the doomed dinosaur into a huge octopus with tentacles so large, so blood-sucking, that it will embrace the entire American people. The plan is called "Outcome-Based Education" or OBE for short. It can also be described as the last nail in the coffin of traditional education, not that there is much of it left by now.

231

The most radical feature of OBE is that it does away with the traditional requirements for graduation based on the Carnegie units. Under the Carnegie units, you were required, for example, to take 4 years of English, 2 years of American history, 3 years of math, etc. Each unit was worth a number of credits, and when you obtained the necessary credits you were eligible for graduation with a diploma attesting to the fact that you had covered all of these subjects successfully.

The success of the system was based on the effective teaching of these subjects by competent teachers who knew what they were doing, with the students passing a number of tests to verify that they had learned whatever it was they were supposed to learn. All of us who went through the system remember studying, or cramming, for the midterms or finals. You hoped to get an "A" or a "B plus", or a "B." If you got a "C" you passed. If you got a "D" or an "F," you were required to do some sort of makeup or repeat the class.

All in all, the system, with its compulsory attendance laws requiring children to attend school from the age of 6 to 16 or 18, seemed to work fairly well as long as the schools taught the subjects properly. But when the schools started teaching look-say in reading, and students began having serious reading problems, the system began to break down. It became impossible to expect the ever-increasing number of nonreaders to do the kind of reading required to pass the more difficult subjects in the higher grades. The result was social promotion, grade inflation, and a general deterioration of academic standards.

What we have learned from all of this is that the traditional system cannot work if its academic heart has been cut out and replaced by teachers pretending to teach and students pretending to learn. In fact, it is now quite possible to get through twelve years of public schooling and emerge at the end of the process knowing virtually nothing. That's why there's been so much public clamor for back-to-basics reform in the last 30 years. But so far, there hasn't been any real improvement in the system, mainly because the educators don't want to get back to basics.

And so the educators have had to come up with a new idea to appease the public, an idea, however, that permits the educators to keep their progressive revolution in education intact while making sweeping changes. The idea is: "Let's change the system. Let's get rid of the whole traditional system and start afresh."

And what exactly is to replace the old system? Outcome-Based Education. I found a very good description of the new OBE program in a project manual which was given to me during a recent visit to North Carolina, where the Gaston County schools were in the process of implementing an OBE program called Odyssey. The program document reads:

> The Odyssey Project describes a formal system of basic schooling for students ages 3 to 18 with a developmental prenatal to age 3 component. The project will use an outcome-based education model that focuses on the knowledge, skill, and attitudes that students should possess when they graduate from Odyssey learning centers.[1]

So first we learn that OBE begins with the prenatal child and not only focuses on knowledge and skill, but also on attitudes. Will new compulsory attendance laws be required to include prenatal children? Since the educators have so badly botched up teaching children from 5 to 18, what makes them think they can do better with infants from 0 to 5? And what kind of attitudes do the educators think the students ought to have when they leave the "learning center"? Humanistic ones, no doubt. The summary continues:

> Five basic exit outcomes will provide the focus for the instructional program proposed by the project: (1) Communicator; (2) Collaborator; (3) Creative Producer; (4) Critical Thinker; (5) Concerned and Confident Citizen.

Odyssey schools will subscribe to the theory of multiple intelligences and will seek to develop each student's unique talents. . . .

Performance outcomes set for each level of Odyssey schooling will include substantive assessment of each student's mastery of English, social studies (including geography), science, and mathematics objectives. . . . Each Odyssey student will study a second language, music, art, drama, and kinesthetics at each level of schooling. The computer will be used as a basic tool for instruction and management in all the disciplines. The curriculum will emphasize critical thinking and problem solving, and students will examine relevant ethical issues and learn how to make sound choices. In all curriculum areas an emphasis will be placed on understanding global issues.

Notice that "critical thinking" is a very important component in Outcome-Based Education, not logical thinking, or clear thinking, but critical thinking. Critical thinking was the primary method the philosophers of the Enlightenment used to destroy faith in Christianity in eighteenth-century Europe. Peter Gay, in an introduction to his anthology of Enlightenment writings, in which he used the French word "philosophe" to represent the critically minded Enlightenment philosopher, writes:

What united [the philosophers] was the common experience of shedding their inherited Christian beliefs with the aid of classical philosophers and for the sake of a modern philosophy. . . . And what united the philosophes above all was confidence in the critical method.

Here we have reached the core of the eighteenth-century Enlightenment as a movement. The philosophes of all countries and all persuasions were lyrical in their single-minded praise of criticism. . . .

For the philosophes, criticism . . . was an act of aggression. The Christian centuries through which Western civilization had passed, and the Christian faith in whose grip the civilization still found itself, had erected protective walls around the most important areas of human actitivity, notably religion, politics, and sexual morality. Now criticism impartially claimed the right to criticize everything . . . . "Everything must be examined," Diderot wrote in the *Encyclopedia,* "everything must be shaken up, without exception and without circumspection."

The philosophes' passion for criticism has led historians to charge them with a passion for destruction, with equating negative criticism with good thinking. . . . But the philosophes would have found the charge incomprehensible. . . . The philosophes were destructive because they thought one must clear the ground before one can build; one cannot construct the city of man under fire from the enemy, on rubbish, or on a swamp. The world that religion had shaped for so long was—in the philosophes' language—prey to the wild beasts of fanaticism and enfeebled by the poisonous fruits of the tree of superstition.[2]

And so, to the Enlightenment philosophers, Christianity was nothing but superstition which had to be wiped away by unrelenting criticism so that a new atheist-humanist civilization could be built. The political results in Europe were the French Revolution with its reign of terror, the rise of socialism, Nazism, and Communism, two world wars, concentration camps, gulags, slave labor, and millions of corpses.

The Rev. Richard Wurmbrand, who was imprisoned for 14 years in Europe for his outspoken views against communism, wrote a remarkable book, *Marx & Satan* (Crossways Books, 1986), in which he convincingly shows the close relationship between Marxism and satanism. On page 80, he writes:

Just as Satan came to Jesus with Bible verses, so Marx used texts of Scripture, though with much distortion.

Volume 2 of *The Works of Marx and Engels* opens with Jesus' words to His disciples (John 6:63), as quoted by Marx in his book *The Holy Family:* "It is the spirit which gives life." Then we read:

"Criticism [his criticism of all that exists] so loved the masses that it sent its only begotten son [i.e., Marx], that whosoever believes in him should not perish but have a life of criticism. Criticism became masses and lived among us, and we saw its glory of the only-begotten Son of the Father. Criticism did not consider it robbery to be equal with God, but made itself of no reputation, taking the form of a bookbinder, and humbled itself up to nonsense—yes, critical nonsense in foreign languages."

Those knowledgeable in Scripture will recognize this as a parody of Biblical verses (John 3:16; 1:14; Philippians 2:6-8). Here again, Marx declares his own works to be "nonsense," as well as "swinish books."[3]

And so, critical thinking has been at the core of anti-Christian philosophy among socialists and Marxists. For example, one finds the theme of critical thinking central in the writings of Paulo Freire, the Brazilian Marxist educator-philosopher and exponent of Liberation Theology. His works are widely read and admired by American radical educators. Radical professor Henry A. Giroux writes in his introduction to Freire's book, *The Politics of Education* (Bergin & Garvey, 1985):

Central to Freire's politics and pedagogy is a philosophical vision of a liberated humanity. The nature of this vision is rooted in a respect for life and the acknowledgment that the hope and vision of the future that inspire it are not meant to provide consolation for the oppressed as much as to promote ongoing forms of critique and a struggle against objective forces of oppression. By combining the dynamics of critique and collective struggle with a philosophy of hope, Freire has created a language of possiblity that is rooted in what he calls a permanent prophetic vision. (p. xvii)[4]

Freire's book was reviewed by the *Harvard Educational Review* which commented:

The Politics of Education contributes to a radical formulation of pedagogy through its revitalization of language, utopianism, and revolutionary message. . . . Freire not only heightens our awareness but invites us to engage in the emancipatory process brought about by critique. His politics puts history back into our hands. Beyond the power of the alphabet is the power of knowledge and social action. This book enlarges our vision with each reading, until the meanings become our own.

The reviewer in *Contemporary Sociology* wrote:

The Politics of Education is an affirmation of Freire's prodigiously activist approach to popular education and its capacity for securing transformation change.

Paulo Freire himself writes: "There is no way to transformation; transformation is the way." And there is no greater transformation taking place in American education today than Outcome-Based Education where the emphasis is on "critical thinking."

OBE also radically changes the school calendar. According to the project document:

All learning centers [schools] will have common characteristics. All will operate on a year-round schedule. Four terms of ten-weeks each will comprise the learning year. Learners will attend each of the four terms for a total of 200 days each year. At the end of each term, a three-week mini-term will be provided. Learners who accomplish all performance outcomes during the regular ten-week term may attend enrichment or extension sessions or may take leave time from their schooling. Learners who do not accomplish all performance outcomes will attend a five to seven day mini-term that extends their learning time.

Nowhere in the document are we given much of a hint as to what the "performance outcomes" are to be. The crucial question in all of this is: "What will the children be taught?" They say that the learners will be required to master English, social studies, geography, science and mathematics. They tell us that the OBE curriculum will conform with international curriculum standards. But that still doesn't tell us what the contents of these courses will be. How will they teach reading: by whole language or intensive phonics? How will they teach writing: print first or cursive first? How will they teach spelling: invented spelling or correct spelling? How will they teach arithmetic: through concept and problem solving or memorization and practice first?

What will they teach in social studies? That collectivism is superior to individualism? That socialized medicine is better than private medicine? That abortion is a woman's right and that the fetus is just a blob of protoplasm? That the Enlightenment was more important than the Reformation?

And what will they teach in science? That evolution is truth and that creationism is based on myth and superstition? And what happens if your performance outcome is not what the educators want? Will you have to proclaim evolution as truth before you can pass? These are questions that parents must ask before they put their children under OBE control.

We are also told that grade levels are to be replaced by a new system. The document states:

> In the five levels of schooling proposed by The Odyssey Project, traditional designations of grade levels will not be used, rather a Greek letter will designate an age range for learners who attend a particular center. "Alpha" will designate the preformal component of schooling for children ages 0 - 3; "Beta" will be the center for learners ages 3 - 6; "Gamma" for learners ages 7 - 10; "Delta" for learners ages 11 - 14; and "Odyssey" for learners ages 15 - 18. At all levels movement in and out of learning cadres will be determined by accomplishment of performance outcomes not by age, grade levels, or time frames.

Note that OBE takes charge of your child's education from birth onward! This means the psycho-educators must get into your home even before the child is born. Does that mean that you will have to register with the government "learning center" when you become pregnant? The document states:

> Centers will contract with many different agencies to provide health care, social services, wellness and other essential support programs. Many of the agencies will be housed at the centers. This interagency arrangement will provide holistic support services to learners and their families.

In other words, when you enroll your child in school you will actually be enrolling your entire family. A "holistic" approach is a total approach. The psycho-educators will want to know everything about your child and your family. The document spells it out quite clearly:

> Family involvement with their child's schooling will be a primary goal of The Odyssey Project. Family members will provide service hours at each Odyssey center and will attend a minimum number of progress conferences with center professionals each year their child attends the center.

Nor will the OBE program leave you alone after you "graduate." The educators intend to help you develop "life-long liesure activities." The document states:

> If Odyssey is developing individuals who can balance themselves spiritually, intellectually and physically, then life-long liesure activities have to be seen as a basic part of public schooling.

Note the psycho-educators' interest in the learner's spiritual well being. That's part of the holistic concept of education. According to Ron Miller, who publishes the *Holistic Education Review*:

> Holistic education is a spiritual worldview rather than a materialist one.... It seeks to support and nourish the natural unfolding of the human soul within the lives of individuals.... [It] is a radical break from traditional ways of understanding human development.... [T]he holistic approach represents a new paradigm. In essence, it is the educational approach of a new culture—an emerging postindustrial, post-technocratic civilization, in which the whole human being may yet be nurtured. (*Whole Language Catalog*, p. 427)[5]

In short, holistic education is part of the new cultural revolution, the new humane totalitarianism in which the psycho-educators involve themselves in the child's intellectual, physical, social, moral, emotional and spiritual life. A "new paradigm." According to *Webster's New World Dictionary* (Simon & Schuster, 1988), a paradigm is "a pattern, example, or model; an overall concept accepted by most people in an intellectual community, as a science, because of its effectiveness in explaining a complex process, idea, or set of data." The Odyssey document states:

> The Odyssey Project not only breaks the mold of traditional schooling, but it also breaks the mold of traditional thinking about school governance.

Naturally, a program as radical as this will require the considerable retraining of teachers who will become known as "facilitators." The document states:

> The Odyssey Project requires teacher training programs that are solution-centered, with theory and practice integrated through classroom application. The training will be a joint effort of university instructors, school unit specialists, and consultants from public and private sectors.

How will classes be conducted in an OBE setup? We get something of an idea from the Odyssey document:

> All centers will use Paideia concepts as the primary instructional delivery system. The appropriateness of the three levels of instruction — didactic, coaching, and seminars — will be understood, properly balanced, and consistently used during basic schooling.
>
> At the four formal Odyssey levels — Beta, Gamma, Delta, and Odyssey — learners will stay with the same cadre of learners and facilitators for CORE learnings during their years at each center. During CORE-PLUS time learners from different cadres will work together. . . .
>
> For all students at all levels a Learning Support Center will be provided. Located in proximity to the information center, the LSC will play a key role in learners' accomplishment of performance outcomes.
>
> At the three upper levels of Odyssey schooling, learners will be required to attend weekly learning seminars that address national and

world citizenship ideals and values. These seminars will focus on multi-cultural issues that prepare learners for living in the global society of the twenty-first century.

That sounds very much like an educational plan to prepare our children for world government. "World citizenship," "multi-cultural issues," and "global society" are the key phrases and concepts that run throughout OBE documents. Notice also that the school is a "learning center," the student is a "learner," the teacher is a "facilitator," the class is a "cadre," and a grade is a "level." The use of these new terms will help parents and teachers adjust to the new system. A new paradigm requires a new vocabulary.

CORE, by the way, is defined in the document as "the common learnings for all learners." As for the CORE-PLUS curriculum, the document explains it as follows:

> Odyssey's CORE-PLUS curriculum will provide opportunities for learners to extend, explore, enrich or expedite CORE curriculum learnings by creating a responsive environment for learners, helping them make interconnected discoveries about the physical, cultural and social world. The curriculum will be organized around major topics and developmental tasks. Learners will be able to choose from (or based on learners' needs, learning facilitators will assign learners to) a wide range of course offerings that focus on areas such as: technology mastery and understanding, cooperative living, basic survival skills, development of life options, self-directed learning, thinking, creative problem-solving and decision-making, communications, national and world-wide citizenship, current national and international issues and problems, and character building.

Sounds like one long, open-ended bull session with lots of room for values clarification, death ed, sex ed, drug ed, lifeboat survival games, and anything else that can be thrown into the hopper. How will "learners" be graded in the new system? The document states:

> The basic grading system will most likely be based on standards

ranging from 1 to 4, with 1 meaning the learner does not meet the standard, 2 meaning the learner is below the standard, 3 meaning the learner has met the standard and 4 meaning the learner has exceeded the standard. This system can easily be converted into a grade point average if one is necessary or desired. . . . A portfolio system determining that the learner is a good collaborator, communicator and so forth will probably be advantageous for the individual applying to college.

How will special education students be integrated in the OBE program? According to the document, very nicely:

Odyssey will strive to reduce the labeling of learners to basically two labels: those who need extended learning time and those who are learning different, which describes every learner. One of the main tenants [sic] of outcome based education is that all children can learn and succeed and that schools control the conditions of that success. . . . So, in a sense, Odyssey will have "special education programs", but will not label children for the purpose of teaching as they are now labeled.

In Gaston County, the Odyssey project was to be implemented by a 10-member design team, a 9-member support team, and a project director. The description of the teams in the project document reads like something out of Star Trek:

The support team is responsible for the planning, implementation and dissemination of the project during Phases I, II and III, and has been divided into three teams: Archimedes, Diogenes and Epsilon. Team Archimedes derives its name from the Greek scientist, mathematician and inventor, who is credited for saying: "Give me a place to stand and a lever long enough and I will move the earth." Team Archimedes is responsible for project operations and provides technological, research and communications support services. Team Diogenes, named for the Greek cynic who was said to have carried around a lantern looking for truth, is the direct link between the school system and Odyssey. The team is responsible for curriculum and instruction development and training for both Odyssey team members and other personnel from Gaston County schools. Team Epsilon was so named because it represents the missing Greek letter in Odyssey's five levels of basic schooling. The team serves as the critical link in the organization, providing the administrative and clerical support for the effective functioning of the Odyssey Project.

The Odyssey Project team members are visionaries who believe that a "New Generation of American Schools" must be viewed, not as a final destination, but as the beginning of a life-long pursuit for ever-evolving standards of excellence. Their vision is to create a prototype of a world class system of basic public schooling that prepares America's children for life-long learning in the global community of the future.

After reading that, you would expect these "visionaries" to have pointed ears and wear space-cadet uniforms and carry laser-beam guns. This whole OBE Odyssey plan is about as divorced from reality as a picnic on Mars. And this is being sold with a straight face to the American people who are expected to believe that this absurd plan is the best thing that's come down the pike since sliced bread. Even the legislators of North Carolina bought the whole shooting match without so much as asking the public what it thought of the idea. House Bill 1340 of the 1991 session reads:

The General Assembly believes that all children can learn. It is the intent of the General Assembly that the mission of the public school community is to challenge with high expectations each child to learn, to achieve, and to fulfill his or her potential. With that mission as its guide, the State Board of Education shall develop and implement an outcome-based education program. The State Board of Education shall select four sites to participate in the program for five fiscal years beginning with the 1992-93 fiscal year.

That's the same Board of Education that has mandated the teaching of whole language in the primary schools which will produce functional illiteracy on a scale hitherto unimagined. But that's all part of the dumbing down process so that the elite space cadets with their Greek letter names can brainwash the Bible believing children of North Carolina. It reminds me of a book written by a Russian revolutionary in 1870 entitled *The Catechism of the Revolutionist* quoted in Richard Wurmbrand's *Marx & Satan*. The author's plan smacks of what our psycho-educators are doing to the American people. He wrote:

> Mankind must be divided into two unequal parts. One tenth receives personal liberty and unlimited rights over the other nine tenths. The latter must lose their personality and become a kind of herd.[6]

And that's what the public schools are producing, a kind of illiterate herd that will be ruled over by a universitarian elite. Outcome-Based Education is just the latest phase in the long-range plan to destroy Christianity in America by taking full control of the children and the family. It is presently in various stages of adoption throughout the United States. The entire education establishment seems to have been mobilized to push this scheme through by hook or by crook. But opposition by parents is growing, and there is more than enough compelling reason to see to it that the whole idiotic scheme is derailed.

21. OBE and Mastery Learning *or* Educational Revolution by Stealth

Now that the educationist planners have decided that the traditional model of public education is ineffective and obsolete and cannot meet the demands of the future, they are busily paving over the last 150 years of educational experience with their new concept for the government schools: Outcome-Based Education (OBE). According to William G. Spady, chief wizard behind OBE, the idea for this revolutionary new concept of schooling started in 1968 with an essay written by psycho-educator Benjamin Bloom entitled "Learning for Mastery." According to education researcher Charlotte Iserbyt who formerly worked for the U.S. Department of Education, mastery learning is based on B. F. Skinner's behaviorist conditioning techniques. In an article on mastery learning in the November 1979 issue of *Educational Leadership*, Carl D. Glickman writes:

> Mastery learning is built on the assumption that the majority of children can become equal in their ability to learn standard school tasks. As

245

Bloom has written, "To put it more strongly, each student may be helped to learn a particular subject to the same degree, level of competence, and even in approximately the same amount of time." . . .

What mastery learning does is replace "page 55" with "criterion-referenced materials" or "learning modules." As Bloom describes it, the more advanced students who finish the work quickly are busy with enrichment materials; the middle third use the full 40 minutes to do the work; and the other third need extra time for reinforcing work, peer tutoring, and individual teacher consultations. Ideally, mastery learning works so that the previously faster, average, and slower students eventually reach the same levels of proficiency, and from that point on students can be taught together as a group, mastering the same materials at the same time.[1]

Does mastery learning actually work? A mastery-learning experiment involving reading instruction was conducted in the public schools of Chicago beginning in the mid 1970s. Concerning the new program, the *Chicago Tribune* of November 16, 1977 reported: "It has been ten years in the making, but Chicago school officials now believe they have in place a complete, sweeping program to teach children to read — a program that may be a pacesetter for the nation."

An article in *Learning* magazine of November 1982 explained how the program, dubbed Continuous Progress - Mastery Learning (CP-ML), operated:

The program worked like this: Each elementary school student was accompanied by a "skill card" listing various reading skills at different levels from kindergarten through eighth grade. The traditional K-8 elementary school organization had been abolished; instead, students progressed from level A through level N during their nine years in elementary school. Teachers were required to teach each skill to individual children [or reading groups]; then the children were tested on each skill. Those who scored 80 percent or better on a skill test moved on to the next skill; those who mastered 80 percent of the skills at any given level moved on to the next level; and those who mastered 80 percent of all the skills moved on to high school, theoretically able to read.

How well did this method work? The article goes on:

> Pupils, for their part, were becoming very astute at taking and passing subskill tests, but not at reading. A growing number of students, many teachers said, were entering high school having successfully completed the CP-ML program without ever having read a book and without being able to read one.[2]

It didn't take long before parents began to discover that their children weren't learning to read under the program and they filed a lawsuit demanding the removal of the program from the Chicago public schools because, in their view, the program constituted "educational malpractice."

In 1981, Ruth Love, the Superintendent of the Chicago public schools, asked the school board to replace the Continuous Progress - Mastery Learning program with a new one called Chicago Mastery Learning Reading (CMLR). As for the CP-ML program, Benjamin Bloom told a reporter: "The original Continuous Progress - Mastery Learning curriculum had little of continuous progress in it and no mastery learning. I was never consulted."

In other words, no one was willing to take responsibility for the fiasco. But was the new program any better than the old one? The same article in *Learning* states:

> But as the school year progressed, school officials made fewer and fewer claims that CMLR was completely different from Continuous Progress. The behavioral objectives were the same, although in some instances two objectives had been subsumed under one criterion-referenced test. The skills sequence was the same. The criteria for "mastery" were the same. In fact, CMLR culminated the streamlining of Continuous Progress - Mastery Learning. First the school system established objectives; then it wrote tests for each objective; and finally, it produced materials to teach the answers to the tests that tested the objectives.

It didn't take too long before parents began to realize that the new program was, indeed, no better than the old one. The children weren't reading books. The curriculum simply consisted of 5000 pages of materials that taught behavioral objectives. But even the content of the lessons troubled parents. *Learning* states:

> A fourth grade comprehension lesson, for example, featured a story called "Whiskey and Sweets," which depicted a drunken father tricking his son into buying him whiskey and sweets by feigning a heart attack.
>
> A third grade spoof on Cinderella ended with the hero fitting the slipper on the foot of "an ugly forty year old lady who weighed three hundred pounds" and living "unhappily ever after." Junk food was mentioned frequently ("A Big Mac is heaven on a bun"); lessons of urban life were reduced to the basest levels.

What were the final results of this five-year experiment with mastery learning? The article spelled it out in stark, unequivocal terms:

> On April 21, 1982, Chicago's superintendent of schools, Ruth Love, released the results of the city's first high school reading test in seven years. The scores were abysmally poor. . . . On the Tests of Academic Progress (TAP) administered in the fall of 1981, Chicago's eleventh graders in 64 high schools scored at the 25th percentile — a drop of 5 percentile points from the last time the test was given, in 1975.

The details were appalling. Only 4 of the 64 high schools scored above the 50th percentile, 34 scored below the 20th percentile, and 5 schools, with a total enrollment of more than 7,500, scored at the 10th percentile (a score students could have achieved by simply answering the questions at random). In other words, learning by "behavioral objectives" does not produce true learning.

Will Outcome-Based Education do any better? To get that answer we have to know more about Bill Spady who not only coined the term Outcome-Based Education but has worked for the last twenty years to promote its use throughout North America.

In an interview published in *Educational Leadership* (Dec. 1992), Spady tells us that while as a graduate student at the University of Chicago and a member of the admissions staff, he recruited a student by the name of Jim Block, a "bright, intense, athletic young man," and they became fast friends. After Block got his bachelor's degree, Spady introduced him to Benjamin Bloom. Spady says: "Block became Ben Bloom's graduate student just as Bloom was developing the 'Learning for Mastery' idea. Block did a lot of the basic research in 'Learning for Mastery' and I was one of the earliest to know about it because I'd heard it straight from Jim, as it was unfolding."

Spady then moved on to Harvard to teach social relations and education. He also got interested in organizational theory. He says:

> So, when Block told me about the the fundamental changes associated with mastery learning — turning time into a variable instead of time being a constant, and having what I now would call a criterion base for standards instead of comparative standards — I found the ideas theoretically compelling, and I took them immediately to the educational system level — because to me the fundamental barriers to making the mastery learning idea work were at the organizational and institutional level. So I said to Jim Block — I mean we literally made an agreement that day — "You fix the classrooms, I'll work on the total system."[3]

And so, Outcome-Based Education was born. Note that Jim Block's mastery learning methodology would be the classroom mode of instruction, and Spady would reorganize the entire education system to make mastery learning work. In other words, the systemic barriers to learning that were part and parcel of traditional education would have to be removed.

The plan, obviously, was based on the assumption that the traditional school was an obstacle to learning. But was that true?

There was a time, and this writer remembers it well, when the public schools did a pretty decent job of teaching children the basic academic skills along with history, geography, foreign language, touch typing, etc. That was certainly the case in the 1930s and '40s when this writer attended public schools in New York City.

It was only after the introduction of the new Dewey-inspired progressive curriculum, with its whole-word, look-say reading program and its shift in emphasis from the development of the intellectual skills to the development of the social skills that the traditional model begin to fall apart. Traditional education relied on intensive phonics in reading, cursive penmanship in writing, memorized arithmetic facts, and separate subject matter for its academic success. Today, nothing works in public education, not merely because of the way the system is organized, but because of its psychology-driven teaching methods, its obsession with the affective domain, and its perverse and corrupted content.

And so an entirely new kind of system must be created in order to make behaviorist mastery learning work. If it failed in Chicago, OBE theory tells us, it was because of the system, not the program. Outcome-based education *is* the new system.

According to Spady, our present traditional instruction system (which produced the most literate nation in history until 50 years ago) is a relic of the industrial age, therefore we need a new delivery system based on mastery learning techniques (with no known record of success anywhere); the present school calendar is a relic of the agricultural age, therefore we need a year-round school calendar that sweeps the sacrosanct two-month summer vacation into the dustbin of history; and the present traditional philosophy of education is a relic of the feudal age (because it respected religion and parental rights) and is no longer suitable for the information age. What we need, says Spady, is a total revolution, a paradigmatic change.

Spady is an establishment operative who knows how to organize a revolution from the top, a revolution planned and funded by the wealthy humanist foundations (Carnegie, Ford, Rockefeller), the graduate schools of education, the state departments of education, and the federal government: clearly a revolution from the top, which is not exactly the democratic way of doing things. In fact, parents across the nation are up in arms over the new plan.

But that's how it's been in public education from the very beginning. The academic elite foisted government education on the American people in the 1830s, '40s, and '50s. The progressive academic elite imposed its socialist, humanist "reforms" on the public schools during most of the 20th century, and the new psycho-educationist elite will destroy whatever is left of the traditional system and replace it with an expansionist, New Age, holistic system of total control bearing the OBE label.

How does OBE work? That's the crucial question in outcome-based education. How do we decide what the outcomes should be? According to Spady, "We are starting with what the research suggests about the future and we design down, or design back, from there. We're talking about a systematic process called Strategic Design: determining as well as we can from studying the literature and available data about future trends and conditions what our kids will be facing out there in the world."

And so the first thing you must know about outcome-based education is that is based on a new, glorified form of fortune telling. Instead of using a crystal ball to predict what a student will be doing twenty years hence, they will use Strategic Design. And on the basis of that vision of the future the entire curriculum will be designed.

But what happens if the future turns out differently? Tough luck.

The simple truth is that nobody can predict the future with any great degree of accuracy. We couldn't even predict ten years ago that the entire communist system in Eastern Europe would collapse. No one could have predicted the Gulf War, even six months before it started. To base an entire education system on visionary assumptions about the future is not only foolish but dangerous. What students should be taught are basic academic skills that they can use under any circumstances as well as the timeless spiritual and moral values that only the Bible provides. The Bible has endured for over 2,000 years as the unchanging standard and guide to a moral, healthy, and productive life regardless of the forms civilization has taken.

But the visionaries of OBE have a different view. In Spady's seminar guide entitled "Transformational Outcome-Based Restructuring," we read:

> The visionary purpose reflects the rapidly changing social, economic, political, cultural, and environmental context in which our current students will live. As a result, Transformational OBE is inherently future-oriented and focuses on students' life-long adaptive capacities. It requires a fundamental shift in the prevailing paradigm of educational leadership, policy-making, priority setting, outcome defining, curriculum design, instructional delivery, assessment and credentialing, decision making, and implementation strategies.[4]

The key word is "visionary," and success in the OBE school is measured in terms of how well the student achieves the "visionary higher-order exit outcomes."

What is an "outcome"? According to Spady, an outcome is "a culminating demonstration of learning." The emphasis is on performance, not content, on behavior, not knowledge. A "high-level culminating outcome" is a "complex role performance." Curriculum and instruction are geared to "what we want the kids to demonstrate successfully at the end."

Will the traditional subject-based curriculum be abandoned? Yes, says Spady, "But content itself can't disappear; we just develop a fundamentally different rationale for organizing and using it; one that is linked much more to the significant spheres of successful living rather than to separate disciplines and subjects."

In that case, how will history be taught? Spady's view is that there should not be a separate course called history "that starts at some ancient time and moves forward to the present." The students should "thoroughly examine current problems, issues, and phenomena in depth and ask why, why, why, about their origins and relationships."

Which means that somewhere along the line, perhaps at home without the psycho-visionaries breathing down one's neck, the student will have the chance to study history if he wants to understand the origins of today's problems which only a chronological study of history can elucidate. With history being taught in the OBE school only as an adjunct to current events, the student will not be learning history as an ongoing drama of human action.

So what becomes the purpose of education under OBE? The seminar guide states:

> Transformational Outcome-Based Education exists to equip all students with the knowledge, competence, and orientations needed for them to successfully meet the challenges and opportunities they will face in their career and family lives after graduating.[5]

What are "orientations"? They are "the affective and attitudinal dimensions of learning" that deal with the student's emotions, motivation, "attitudes," and relationships. The wrong attitudes — the spiritually and politically incorrect attitudes — will no doubt be taken care of by values clarification. The seminar guide states:

> Teaching, mentoring, and advising lie at the heart of close personal relationships . . . and represent the core aspects of close interpersonal

bonding, respect, and friendship. Teachers and mentors can successfully change the thinking, skills, orientations, and motivation of others through the explanations they provide, the counsel they give, and the example they set.

A key premise of OBE is that all students can learn and succeed and that the school can control the conditions of success. In other words, time will no longer decide how long a student remains in school. He will remain there as long as he has to in order to be able to demonstrate in an "authentic context the outcomes of significance." As the pro-OBE policymakers in Minnesota said when Spady told them that not every student would be in school for the same length of time or take the same courses, "If they can't demonstrate the outcomes of significance, then we shouldn't be letting them out of school."

Apparently, changes in the compulsory attendance laws will have to be made to accomodate this feature of OBE. In fact, OBE is a good reason why compulsory school attendance laws should be repealed because they violate the civil rights of a specific age-group of Americans who will be forcibly subjected to brainwashing of the most blatant kind. There is no room in a free society for an education system that forces children to undergo unspecified attitudinal changes in order to conform to the values and standards of an empowered elite.

And what happens after the student has jumped through all the hoops and can demonstrate a "higher order competency in a complex role performance"? According to Hillary Clinton and Ira Magaziner in an article in *Educational Leadership* (Mar. 92, p. 12):

Students passing a series of performance-based assessments that incorporate this new standard would be awarded a Certificate of Initial Mastery. Possession of the certificate would qualify the student to choose among going to work, entering a college preparatory program, or studying for a Technological and Professional Certificate.... The states should take responsibility for assuring that virtually all students achieve the Certificate of Initial Mastery. Through new local employment and training boards, states, with federal assistance, should create and fund alternative learning environments for those who cannot attain the Certificate of Initial Mastery in regular schools.[6]

There you see the makings of a three-tier pyramidal society: a university elite at the top, born to rule; a body of technicians and professionals to keep the wheels of government, industry and the service economy working smoothly; and the "workers" who will be at the bottom of the new caste system. Perhaps this is the kind of system Spady and his fellow visionaries have seen in their crystal balls. They certainly are preparing American students for that kind of society. Spady says:

> In January of 1980 we convened a meeting of 42 people to form the Network for Outcome-Based Schools. Most of the people who were there — Jim Block, John Champlin — had a strong background in mastery learning, since it was what OBE was called at the time. But I pleaded with the group not to use the name "mastery learning" in the network's new name because the word "mastery" had already been destroyed through poor implementation.[7]

Apparently, Spady and his colleagues think that they can do a much better job of implementation. But they are wrong, because mastery learning is not based on a true knowledge of the mind, and that is why it failed so miserably in Chicago. But now the entire nation will be subjected to this insane experimentation. What worked well in the past is being discarded because it represents a God-given view of the mind. The psychologists prefer their own view based on animal behavior. And that makes it more imperative than ever for parents to keep their children out of the government schools.

The psycho-educators know that a large number of children

will not be able to learn to read under mastery-learning methodology, and they are already preparing American industry to accept that reality. In a previous chapter we quoted Prof. Anthony Oettinger of Harvard's Division of Applied Science who told an audience of executives in 1981:

> [D]o we really have to have everybody literate — writing and reading in the traditional sense — when we have the means through our technology to achieve a new flowering or oral communication? It is the traditional idea that says certain forms of communication, such as comic books, are "bad." But in the modern context of functionalism they may not be all that bad.[8]

Obviously, the parents in Chicago who sued the schools using mastery learning for "educational malpractice" were not interested in having their children learn how to read comic books. They certainly were in favor of the traditional concept of literacy and had expected the schools to be in favor of it too. But they were wrong. Prof. Oettinger reveals the true aims of the educational elite when he asks, "Do we really want to teach, etc." The key word is "want" and his implied answer to his rhetorical question is "No, we really do not want to teach children to read and write in the traditional sense." And that is what American parents must come to grips with: the reluctance of American educators to really impart high literacy.

22. Benjamin Bloom: OBE's Godfather. His Writings Tell All

As everyone knows, American public education has been in crisis for at least the last three decades. In fact, it was the famous *A Nation at Risk* report, issued by the National Commission on Excellence in Education in April 1983, that called for drastic measures to be taken if the public schools were to be saved from further deterioration. And the calls for educational reform came fast and furious.

Basically, there were two types of reforms called for. Conservatives called for getting back to basics, for teaching reading by intensive phonics, for strengthening all of the academic subjects, for greater discipline, more homework, etc. The liberal education establishment had other ideas. Besides calling for more money, higher teacher salaries, all of which they got, their view of reform included whole language, invented spelling, no memorization in arithmetic but lots of calculators, a breakdown of traditional subject matter into relevant topics, and above all, a greater emphasis on the affective domain, that is, more emphasis on feelings, beliefs, values, attitudes, socialization, sexuality, group learning, group therapy, peer counseling, death education, drug education, etc.

Obviously, these two views of education are not only mutually exclusive but produce totally different outcomes. The conservative approach represents a traditional Judeo-Christian world view that sees education as a development of intellect and spirit. It sees the school as serving the parents who entrust their children to the educators who are to teach the youngsters the basic academic skills that will serve them in any future field of work or career they may choose. In other words, the function of a free public school is to provide a basic, no-nonsense education.

Vice Admiral Hyman Rickover summed up the non-sectarian traditional view when he said the following to a Congressional committee in 1962:

> [A] school must accomplish three difficult tasks: *First*, it must transmit to the pupil a substantial body of knowledge; *second*, it must develop in him the necessary intellectual skill to apply this knowledge to the problems he will encounter in adult life; and *third*, it must inculcate in him the habit of judging issues on the basis of verified fact and logical reasoning.... [The school's] principal task ... is to develop the mind... . Far too many of our teachers do not possess the intellectual and educational qualifications that would permit them to offer such a course of studies. There is an easy way out, and many of our schools are using it. They teach simpler things that are easy to teach, easy to learn, and more fun besides—how to be lovable, likable, and datable, how to be a good consumer. These aren't subjects you can grade, the way you can grade mathematics or sciences or languages, but they are good for hiding the ignorance of both teacher and pupil.[1]

All of that was said in 1962, long before it was ever dreamed that one day the schools would be handing out condoms. Apparently, the educators didn't listen to Admiral Rickover then, and they have no intention of listening to his counterparts today.

Why? Because the liberal education establishment approaches

education from an entirely different world view, a humanist world view based on the notion that there is no God, that man is an animal, the product of evolution, and that the purpose of education is not to create competent individuals who can stand on their own two feet and think for themselves, but to change society. Humanist education is basically messianic in its outlook. It not only wants to change society, but also erase from human consciousness any dependence on a higher authority, that is, God. Humanist education is at war with the God of the Bible. It wages spiritual warfare in the full sense of the word. And that is why Admiral Rickover's common sense fell on deaf ears.

Outcome-Based Education, or OBE, is a total reform, or restructuring, of American education designed explicitly to further humanist goals. First and foremost, it does away with every last vestige of traditional education, its methods, its curriculum, its objective means of assessment, its time frame, its goals. In fact, it represents a complete takeover of American public education by the humanist sect, with the sole aim of producing young humanists who will forward the humanist agenda. In other words, OBE intends to do for humanists what Catholic schools did for Catholics.

But Outcome-Based Education did not suddenly arise out of nowhere. It has been worked on and planned for by humanist psychologists, sociologists, and behaviorial scientists for years despite parental clamor for back to basics. These educational theorists and planners feel that they have a mission, that they are in every sense of the word true revolutionaries engaged in a true cultural revolution in which traditional values are to be overthrown and replaced by the pagan-socialist values of the New World Order. That is why humanists have never had any intention of getting back to basics, and that is why parents have experienced nothing but frustration in trying to return public education to its earlier, traditional forms and functions.

Of course, the whole departure from the traditional academic curriculum started at the turn of the century when John Dewey and his humanist colleagues decided to use our public school system as the means of changing America from a capitalist, individualistic, believing nation into a socialist, collectivist, atheist society. The humanists, better known as the progressives, spent the next thirty years revising the curriculum and writing new textbooks so that by 1930 they were ready to impose the new socialist-oriented curriculum on the public schools of America. One might call that period the first phase of the humanist reform movement. It was dominated by behaviorist, stimulus-response, animal-tested psychology.

The second phase began in the early 1960s with the emergence of Third Force psychology developed by humanist psychologists Abraham Maslow, Carl Rogers, Sidney Simon and others who tried to inject an emotional and spiritual component in the behaviorist mix. Since the goal of education was now defined as "self-actualization," the emphasis was now on the development of the affective domain through such programs as values clarification, sensitivity training, situational ethics, multiculturalism, pluralism, etc. As part of the human-potential movement, the goal was to "liberate" human behavior from biblical constrants in order to create a humanist society.

Third Force psychology also gave educators a whole new vocabulary to describe the expanded realm of the educator with such terms as change agents, facilitators, critical thinking, self-esteem, cognitive dissonance, experiential learning, congruence, relationship inventory, operant behavior, taxonomy, morphological creativity, behavioral objectives, group dynamics, etc.

All of this has been engineered mainly by psychologists who now own American public education lock, stock and barrel. From 1900 to about 1940 you had G. Stanley Hall, John Dewey, Charles Judd, James McKeen Cattell, Edward L. Thorndike, and their protégés Arthur Gates, William Scott Gray, William Kilpatrick, Harold Rugg, George Counts and others, all psychologists, or educators trained by psychologists, who transformed American education in the progressive mold. In 1933 there appeared the Humanist Manifesto which set the spiritual foundation for the progressive moment. In the 1940s and '50s you had the strong influence of communist social psychology through the work of Kurt Lewin at M.I.T. and in the founding of the National Training Laboratory in Bethel, Maine, under the sponsorship of the National Education Association. That's where sensitivity training was born.

During the 1920s, Lewin had worked in Berlin on experiments on how to artificially create behavioral disorganization. He was so good at it, that A. R. Luria, the Soviet psychologist, wrote the following about Lewin in his book, *The Nature of Human Conflicts: A study of the experimental disorganization and control of human behavior,* published in 1932:

> K. Lewin, in our opinion, has been one of the most prominent psychologists to elucidate this question of the artificial production of affect and of the experimental disorgansation of behaviour. The method of his procedure—the introduction of an emotional setting into the experience of a human, the interest of the subject in the experiment—helped him to obtain an artificial disruption of the affect of considerable strength. . . .[2]

Obviously, Lewin had mastered the art of artificially inducing behavioral disorganization, and we can only conjecture how these techniques have been used by American psycho-educators to create the kind of behavioral disorganization that afflicts so many American public school students.

In 1973 there appeared Humanist Manifesto II, which basically outlined the school curriculum of the future. It called for "the development of a system of world law and a world order based upon transnational federal government." It further stated:

> The world community must engage in cooperative planning concerning the use of rapidly depleting resources. The planet earth must be considered a single ecosystem. Ecological damage, resource depletion, and excessive population growth must be checked by international concord. The cultivation and conservation of nature is a moral value; we should perceive ourselves as integral to the sources of our being in nature. We must free our world from needless pollution and waste, responsibly guarding and creating wealth, both natural and human. Exploitation of natural resources, uncurbed by social conscience, must end. (pp. 21-22)[3]

Should it surprise anyone, therefore, that American students are being brainwashed to believe that concern for the environment is more important than concern for the unborn? Recently, I was told by a proud father that his little daughter in the second grade had already embarked on a crusade to save the world from environmental destruction. It didn't occur to him that his young daughter was being so well indoctrinated in the religion of environmentalism that she might very well become an eco-fanatic. It's all in the Humanist Manifesto which, incidentally, was signed by Alan F. Guttmacher, president of Planned Parenthood, B. F. Skinner, Betty Friedan, and 200 other humanists.

Outcome-Based Education is really, for all intents and purposes, Humanist Parochial Education. And its proponents make no bones about it. Actually, the beginnings of OBE can be traced back to 1948 when a group of behavioral scientists, meeting in Boston at the American Psychological Association Convention, decided to embark on a project of classifying the goals or outcomes of the educational process since, as they said, "educational objectives provide the basis for building curricula and tests and represents the starting point for much of our educational research."

In other words, you cannot build a curriculum until you decide what the outcomes of that education should be. For example, if you want your student to become a humanist, you must teach the child about evolution, environmentalism, feminism, reproductive rights (abortion), sexual freedom (how to have safe sex), alternative values systems, alternative lifestyles, etc. And you must provide tests and assessments along the way to make sure that the desired outcomes are being achieved.

Likewise, the curriculum of a Christian school is determined by the end goal, or desired outcome, of the educative process: a well-educated Christian steeped in the knowledge of God and His law.

The result of the scientists' deliberations has become known as Bloom's *Taxonomy of Educational Objectives*, a humanist-behaviorist classification of outcomes that does away with traditional outcomes, subject matter and teaching methods. The central figure behind all of this is behavioral scientist Benjamin S. Bloom of the University of Chicago. Bloom is one of those obscure professors who work in their graduate schools with their students trying to find ways to change human behavior and thereby change the world. They are imbued with the same messianic mission that motivated Horace Mann, John Dewey, and a hundred other "educators" to bring about their versions of utopia. (R.J. Rushdoony's 1963 book, *The Messianic Character of American Education* provides a fascinating in-depth study of these American educators.[4])

Bloom's taxonomy, which is little more than a humanist-behaviorist straitjacket for public education, is contained in two handbooks, one for the cognitive domain (published in 1956) and one for the affective domain (published in 1964). Bloom writes:

> Curriculum builders should find the taxonomy helps them to specify objectives so that it becomes easier to plan learning experiences and prepare evaluation devices. . . . In short, teachers and curriculum makers should find this a relatively concise model for the analysis of educational outcomes in the cognitive area of remembering, thinking, and problem solving. . . . (p. 2)
>
> A second part of the taxonomy is the affective domain. It includes objectives which describe changes in interest, attitudes, and values, and the development of appreciations and adequate adjustment. . . . It is difficult

to describe the behaviors appropriate to these objectives since the internal or covert feelings and emotions are as significant for this domain as are the overt behavioral manifestations.... Our testing procedures for the affective domain are still in the most primitive stages. (p. 7)[5]

That was written in 1956. But by now their testing instruments have been quite perfected to do their job of monitoring affective change. In devising these highly intrusive tests, Bloom had the help of Ralph W. Tyler of the Center for Advanced Study in Behavioral Sciences at Stanford University. In fact, Bloom dedicated the taxonomy to Tyler "whose ideas on evaluation have been a constant source of stimulation to his colleagues in examining, and whose energy and patience have never failed us." Bloom continues:

This taxonomy is designed to be a classification of the student behaviors which represent the intended outcomes of the educational process. (p. 10) ... What we are classifying is the *intended behavior* of students—the ways in which individuals are to act, think, or feel as the result of participating in some unit of instruction. (p. 12)

The taxonomy is not completely neutral. This stems from the already-noted fact that it is a classification of intended behaviors. ... (p. 15)

By educational objectives, we mean explicit formulations of the ways in which students are expected to be changed by the educative process. That is, the ways in which they will change in their thinking, their feelings, and their actions.... It is important that the major objectives of the school or unit of instruction be clearly identified if time and effort are not to be wasted on less important things and if the work of the school is to be guided by some plan. (p. 26)

The philosophy of education of the school serves as one guide, since the objectives to be finally included should be related to the school's view of the "good life for the individual in the good society." What are important values? What is the proper relation between man and society? What are the proper relations between man and man? (p. 27)[6]

Note that the relationship between man and God is not included in the taxonomy. Also, note that the Humanist Manifesto of 1933 states that "the good life is still the central task for mankind." Obviously, Bloom drew his inspiration from that philosophy.

Bloom's taxonomy of the cognitive domain contains six major classes: knowledge, comprehension, application, analysis, synthesis, and evaluation. Concerning knowledge, Bloom writes:

> Knowledge as defined here includes those behaviors and test situations which emphasize the remembering, either by recognition or recall, of ideas, material, or phenomena. (p. 62)

A sample of the knowledge expected to be learned is given as follows:

> To develop a basic knowledge of the evolutionary development of man.... A knowledge of the forces, past and present, which have made for the increasing interdependence of people all over the world.... Knowledge of a relatively complete formulation of the theory of evolution. (p. 71)[7]

These are just samples of the kind of politically correct knowledge the student will be expected to demonstrate as learned behavior. William Spady, top OBE guru, describes what is involved in such a demonstration:

> First, an outcome is a demonstration of learning that occurs at the end of a learning experience. It is a result of learning and an actual visible, observable demonstration of three things: knowledge, combined with competence, combined with something my colleagues and I call "orientations"—the attitudinal, affective, motivational, and relational elements that also make up a performance. Further, this demonstration happens in a real live setting, and is, therefore, influenced and defined by the elements and factors that make up that setting, situation, or context.[8]

As for the taxonomy in the affective domain, Bloom writes:

> Affective objectives vary from simple attention to selected phenomena

to complex but internally consistent qualities of character and conscience. We found a large number of such objectives in the literature expressed as interests, attitudes, appreciations, values, and emotional sets and biases. (p.7)... [T]he process of socialization, with its development of behavioral controls, is a topic with which the affective domain is much involved. (p. 38)

Bloom then points out that it is often difficult to separate the cognitive from the affective. He writes:

Many of the objectives which are classified in the cognitive domain have an implicit but unspecified affective component that could be concurrently classified in the affective domain. (p. 48)

Which means that you can easily slip in some affective outcomes with your cognitive objectives, thus making it easier to obtain the desired behavioral changes. And, according to Bloom's research, this is better done at an earlier age. He writes:

The evidence points out convincingly to the fact that age is a factor operating against attempts to effect a complete or thorough-going reorganization of attitudes and values. . . . (p. 85)

The evidence collected thus far suggests that a single hour of classroom activity under certain conditions may bring about a major reorganization in cognitive as well as affective behaviors. We are of the opinion that this will prove to be a most fruitful area of research in connection with the affective domain. (p. 88)[9]

If you learn nothing else from reading this book than the fact that the psycho-educators know how to cause a major reorganization of values in the mind of a child in one single hour of classroom activity, then you've learned why it is now so dangerous to put a child in a public school. I know of an 8-year-old second-grader in Michigan who hanged himself because of a film on suicide he was shown in the classroom. It took only one hour in the classroom to change that child's life for good. The taxonomy continues:

> [Psychologist Gordon] Allport (1954) emphasizes the basic reorganization that must take place in the individual if really new values and character traits are to be formed. . . . (p. 89)
> It is not enough merely to desire a new objective or to wish others to be molded in the image that we find desirable or satisfactory. We must find ways of understanding and determining what objectives are central and significant if we are to summon the appropriate effort to achieve these more complex objectives. (p. 90)[10]

Everything in Outcome-Based Education can be found in Bloom's writings. For example, in his book *Human Characteristics and School Learning,* published in 1976, Bloom expounds on his theory of Mastery Learning, which is at the heart of the methodology in OBE. The basic idea is that most students can learn what the schools have to teach "if the problem is approached sensitively and systematically." What makes mastery learning work, says Bloom, is the feedback-corrective procedure. He writes:

> The feedback procedures typically consist of brief formative tests, at the end of each learning task, which indicate what the student has learned and what he still needs to attain mastery of the task. Mastery is frequently defined as something approximating 80 to 85 percent of the items on a criterion-referenced test. (p. 125)[11]

In mastery learning the pupil is required to take as much time as necessary in order to achieve mastery of whatever it is the teacher wants him or her to learn. In fact, the pupil cannot advance to the next task or learning module until the previous task or learning module has been mastered. This means that the pupil may not graduate far beyond the age of 18 until he or she can demonstrate that politically correct learning has taken place.

A key premise of OBE is that, under mastery learning, all students can learn and succeed and that the school can control the conditions of success. In other words, time constraints will no longer decide how long a student remains in school.

This may mean changing the compulsory attendance laws to accomodate this feature of OBE. They may also be changed to force parents to put their preschoolers in the hands of the public educators. The National Education Association passed a resolution on early childhood education at their convention in July 1993. It reads:

> The [NEA] supports early childhood education programs in the public schools for children from birth through age eight. The Association believes that such programs should be held in facilities that are appropriate to the developmental needs of these children. The Association further believes that early childhood education programs should include a full continuum of services for parents and children, including child care, child development, appropriate developmental and diversity-based curricula, special education, and appropriate bias-free screening devices. The Association believes that federal legislation should be enacted to assist in organizing the implementation of fully funded early childhood education programs offered through the public schools. These programs should be available to all childlren on an equal basis and should include mandatory kindergarden with compulsory attendance.[12]

Why this interest in early childhood education? The answer can be found in Bloom's 1964 book, *Stability and Change in Human Characteristics.* He wrote:

> We can learn very little about human growth, development, or even about specific human characteristics unless we make full use of the time dimension. Efforts to control or change human behavior by therapy, by education, or by other means will be inadequate and poorly understood until we can follow behavior over a longer period. (p. 6)[13]

> The absolute scale of vocabulary development and the longitudinal studies of educational achievement indicate that approximately 50% of general achievement at grade 12 (age 18) has been reached by the end of

grade 3 (age 9). This suggests the great importance of the first few years of school as well as the preschool period in the development of learning patterns and general achievement. . . . The implications for more powerful and effective school environments in the primary school grades are obvious. (p. 127)

We believe that the early environment is of crucial importance for three reasons. The first is based on the very rapid growth of selected characteristics in the early years and conceives of the variations in the early environment as so important because they shape these characteristics in their most rapid periods of formation.

Secondly, each characteristic is built on a base of that same characteristic at an earlier time or on the base of other characteristics which precede it in development. . . .

A third reason . . . stems from learning theory. It is much easier to learn something new than it is to stamp out one set of learned behaviors and replace them by a new set. (p. 215)[14]

And that is why the OBE people want to get at the children as early as possible, to indoctrinate them before anybody else can get to them. And that is why the NEA is pushing for early childhood education from *birth* to age eight. It is also important to note that the men in the forefront of the OBE movement were either graduate students of Bloom or closely associated with him. Today, Bloom is Professor Emeritus and in his 80s. No doubt he is pleased with the work of his disciples who have managed to get virtually every state legislature in America to mandate OBE in their public schools. This by far is the most complete cultural revolution ever to hit America, and most Americans are not even aware that it is taking place.

23. Kentucky's OBE Experiment: Conflict, Confusion, and Lower Scores

Kentucky's adoption of Outcome-Based Education in 1990 was the result of the Kentucky Supreme Court's declaration on June 8, 1989, that the state's entire education system, in "all its parts and parcels," was unconstitutional. Presumably the system was unconstitutional because it did not provide equity in funding for all of the schools, and therefore did not give each child an equal education. Of course, the concept of equal education is as phony as the idea that all children have a right to be born to rich, loving parents. But today's courts believe that they can remake reality by judicial declaration. The Supreme Court went on to issue the following directive:

> Since we have, by this decision, declared the system of common schools in Kentucky to be unconstitutional, Section 183 places an absolute duty on the General Assembly to re-create, re-establish a new system of common schools in the Commonwealth. . . . We view this decision as an opportunity for the General Assembly to launch the Commonwealth into a new era of educational opportunity which will ensure a strong economic, cultural and political future.

The judges, giddy with the godlike power of having overturned the state's education system, then issued their "Seven Capacities" which, they said, should define the new curriculum for the schools. The Seven Capacities and their implications were spelled out in a reform proposal drawn up by Betty E. Steffy, Deputy Superintendent for Instruction, dated Aug. 21, 1989, and presented to the legislature. They read as follows:

> 1. Oral and Written Communication for a Complex, Rapidly Changing Civilization. Implies: Knowledge of the liberal arts, use of technology, life-long learning, human relations skills.[1]

Let's deal with that first. The method of teaching reading and writing in OBE is whole language and invented spelling. Whole language produces crippled readers because it trains the child to view words holistically by their configurations instead of phonetically by their syllabic structure. To put it simply, ours is an alphabetic writing system in which letters stand for speech sounds. The way you become a proficient reader is to develop an automatic association between letters and sounds. That's how you develop a *phonetic reflex.*

Whole language, on the other hand, forces children to look at written English as if it were Chinese, an ideographic writing system rather than an alphabetic one. The child is taught to look at words holistically, as if they were little pictures to be figured out by a variety of strategies, thus creating a holistic reflex. These strategies include picture cues, configuration cues, context cues, syntactic cues, and also graphophonemic cues. Now, if you ask a whole-language teacher whether he or she teaches phonics, they will all say yes, because graphophonemic cues refer to letter sounds, usually beginning consonants. But that is not the same as intensive, systematic phonics in which the child learns to read phonetically without the need for other cues. However, the important thing to know about the holistic reflex is that it creates a block against seeing words phonetically. In other words, it causes dyslexia or reading disability.

As for invented spelling, the child is given no instruction on how to hold a pen, how to form the letters correctly, or how to spell correctly. The child is expected to learn all of this on his or her own at some later date. So how is the child going to become a good communicator if he or she can't read or write properly? That's why we know that OBE is a fraud. Because they are not teaching the children intensive, systematic phonics, or proper penmanship and spelling. Let's go on to Capacity Two.

> 2. Informed Decision-Making Based on Knowledge of Economics, Social and Political Systems. Implies: Global knowledge, critical thinking skills, shifts from focus on factual knowledge to focus on the use of knowledge to make decisions.

Now what is critical thinking all about? It's about using the dialectic technique to destroy the child's belief in absolutes. The dialectic method was used by the ancient Greeks and brought into the modern era by the German philosopher, Hegel. He believed that history progresses through a process of unceasing conflict, the dialectic, in which a prevailing view known as the thesis engages in conflict with its opposite, known as the antithesis, and when the thesis and antithesis get done beating each other up, they come up with a synthesis. This synthesis then becomes the new thesis which meets its antithesis, does battle, and creates a new synthesis.

According to Hegel, this process goes on forever and is the means by which God is perfecting Himself. Now, he's not talking about the God of the Bible. Hegel was a pantheist who believed that everything that exists in the universe is God, that we are part of God, and that God is in the process of perfecting himself through the dialectic.

Now the dialectic method is being used in the public schools to destroy the child's belief in Christian absolutes. That's what critical thinking is all about. Critical thinking is not the same as logical or clear thinking. Logical thinking is objective and supports absolute values. Critical thinking is subjective and undermines absolute values.

As for the idea that it is more important to teach how to *use* knowledge rather than to acquire it opens the door to a lot of pedagogical mischief. Knowledge is power and suggests it own uses. There is no such thing as a generic use of knowledge since there are so many different kinds of knowledge. But knowledge must come first. But in OBE the student is trained to become a processor of knowledge, not an accumulator or owner of it. Turning an empty-headed student into an effective processor of knowledge is equivalent to the alchemist's dream of turning lead into gold. Next is Capacity Three.

> 3. Citizens Role in Government. Implies: Understanding of how government and politics function at the local, state and national level, knowledge of how individuals can effect change through the political process.

Note that the emphasis is on effecting *change* through the political process. You can be sure that the change OBE promoters have in mind is changing our political system to one that will fit into the New World Order. Next is Capacity Four.

> 4. Knowledge of Self. Implies: Belief in self, [an] education system that enables students to realize their potential, elimination of schools based on a factory production model, recognition of student diversity and productivity, focus on strategies to promote physical and mental well-being.

The idea that the traditional public school is based on the factory production model of the Industrial Age is an important part of

OBE's critique of traditional education. The OBE school, organized around outcomes, is supposed to be much more in tune with the Information Age. But with whole-language, low-level literacy an integral part of OBE, we find it hard to see how OBE is going to help students succeed in the "information" age. Also, when educators start talking about a child's "mental well-being," watch out. That means the child will be subject to psychological manipulation and therapy. All of that malarky about "belief in self" has no business in the public school house. The school ought not be a psych lab, and teachers ought not be practicing psychiatry without a license. What does "belief in self" mean other than having confidence in one's abilities? It means being able to do things right. But if you are not taught to read properly, and you have little knowledge in your brain, what kind of self-confidence will that build? Next is Capacity Five.

> 5. Fine and Performing Arts for Understanding Cultural and Historical Heritage. Implies: The arts are an integral part of the core curriculum, the arts to include all forms of creative expression.

I thought I'd have no trouble with that Capacity until I was given a little brochure in Kentucky about a forthcoming performance in Louisville of The Joffrey Ballet dancing to music by Prince, entitled "Billboards." The brochure states:

> When the daring Prince of rock meets the ambitious soul of The Joffrey Ballet, the result is an exciting performance blending tradition with cutting-edge rock 'n' roll. . . . Prince has been called "a modern Mozart and one of the most important figures in the history of music," and The Joffrey Ballet has long been considered one of the pre-eminent performing arts institutions in the United States.

Prince, "a modern Mozart and one of the most important figures in the history of music"? Prince is better known for his near pornographic performances than his resemblance to Mozart. But, believe it or not, the brochure explains to teachers how the performance meets the goals of Kentucky's Outcome-Based Education curriculum:

> The cultural experience of seeing a world-renowned ballet company meets several goals and learner outcomes of the Kentucky Education Reform Act (KERA), and provides a positive educational experience through the arts. The following are suggestions for making *Billboards* a part of your KERA activities:
> Goal 1 Basic Communication
> Learner Outcome 1.14 - Construct meaning and emotions through music. Sample High School Activity:
> By analyzing the music composed by Prince for the production of *Billboards,* students will accomplish this goal. . . .
> Learner Outcome 1.3 - Constructing meaning from messages communicated in a variety of ways. Sample Middle School Activity:
> By attending *Billboards,* students will be exposed to the beauty, grace and communicative powers of ballet. After watching the performance, students can be asked to describe the actions observed and the emotions displayed.

We have not seen The Joffrey Ballet nor heard Prince's music but we suspect that the dancers' gyrations to Prince's rock 'n' roll beat will communicate a somewhat steamy message. This is what *The New Republic* of August 12, 1985 had to say about Prince in an article entitled "Sounds of Sex":

> The pop star who seems to shock everyone is Prince, one of the biggest names in rock history, and a very strange young man. Prince helped change the nature of romantic lyrics in pop music—he's a master of the single entendre. "Head," a dance tune from his third album, *Dirty Minds,* has nothing to do with sports equipment. On "Jack U Off," he indelicately, if rather politely, makes the eponymous offer, "If you're tired of masturbating . . . / If you like I'll jack u off." But the song that has parents most outraged is "Darling Nikki," from the Grammy and Oscar award-winning album *Purple Rain* (ten million copies sold), which has a verse that goes, "I knew a girl named Nikki / I guess you could say she was a sex fiend. / I met her

in a hotel lobby / Masturbating with a magazine. / She said 'how'd u like to waste some time?' / And I could not resist when I saw / Little Nikki grind."

This is pretty strong stuff for ten-year-olds, and Prince doesn't stop there. Oral sex, incest . . . and bisexuality are recurring themes in Prince's music.[2]

Apparently, Kentucky's educators feel that exposure to Prince's music will help the students of Kentucky appreciate the arts. More likely, it will turn their young minds to images of raunchy sex. Somehow this writer feels that if students are to be taught to appreciate the arts that it is better to start with our classical heritage of music— the real Mozart, not an obscene rock 'n' roll imitation — and classical ballet. The brochure further informs us that the performance is:

Presented with the support of the Mary and Barry Bingham, Sr. Fund. Made possible in part by Dance on Tour, a special initiative of the National Endowment for the Arts, in partnership with the Southern Arts Federation and the Kentucky Arts Council. The Joffrey Ballet's national tour is sponsored by Philip Morris Companies Inc.[3]

So you can't even trust the educators or the government when it comes to the arts. Also note the sponsorship of a cigarette company at a time when everyone is trying to keep young people away from smoking. Public education wasn't always that insane. When I was in the third grade in public school in New York City in 1933, we had music appreciation. Our teacher set up a portable hand-cranked Victrola on a table and played classical music selections. Although that took place sixty years ago, I still remember most of the selections played. Which simply indicates how well a child can learn and retain in memory what he or she considers to be of great value. And I believe the third grade is where I acquired my taste for classical music. My teacher had good taste. But can we say the same for OBE educators? Here's the next Capacity:

6. Demonstrated Student Competence at Graduation. Implies: Competence in core curriculum linked to diploma, recognizes student differences, calls for acquisition of life skills.

That, of course, is pure OBE. The student cannot graduate until he or she can demonstrate, not by simple written test, but by a behavioral performance that he or she has achieved the visionary higher-order exit outcome. If you have trouble understanding what that's all about, you're not alone. Most teachers can't figure it out either. And that's why OBE is doomed to failure. It makes no sense. Here's Capacity Seven.

7. Kentucky High School Graduate Competitive in National Job Market. Implies: Kentucky high school graduate with skills equal to skill of graduates in other states.

Well if Kentucky's students are not taught to read and write properly, how are they going to graduate with skills equal to graduates in other states? That's easy. The graduates in the other states will be just as illiterate.

And there you have the Seven Capacities articulated by the illustrious Supreme Court of Kentucky. Needless to say, these breathtaking, overpowering ideas were put into the heads of the judges by education-reform "experts"—otherwise known as OBE carpetbaggers and change agents. Does anyone believe the judges dreamt them all up on their own?

Meanwhile, in February 1989, Governor Wallace Wilkinson, by executive order, created a 12-member Council on School Performance Standards to determine what Kentucky's students "should know and be able to do and how learning should be assessed." After six months of "intensive effort" the Council came up with its Report in September 1989 which states:

This report provides a blueprint for a new Common Core of Learning stressing the application of knowledge rather than just accumulating knowledge, ways to measure learning to make sure the new learning objectives are being attained, and curriculum reform that will guide the student toward these objectives. . . . Additional time; resources; and the joint involvement of school staff, the community, business, and industry will be needed to provide the details and ownership for a workable Kentucky education plan.

Six months later, in March 1990, the Kentucky Education Reform Act, popularly known as KERA, became law. That was quite a hustle for legislation that imposed an entirely new philosophy of education on the state, one that required a tax increase of $1.4 billion for the first two years of implementation. And what were they implementing? A totally new system of education with no real track record of success, no guarantee that it would produce its much touted results. And all of this was accomplished in only nine months after the Supreme Court's decision!

Who were the change-agent carpetbaggers who descended on Kentucky to foist OBE on the state before the people even knew what was being done to them? Most of them were brought into the state as paid "consultants" to the Task Force on Education Reform. Probably the most notable among them was David W. Hornbeck, former chairman of the Board of Trustees of the Carnegie Foundation for the Advancement of Teaching. He chaired the foundation's Task Force on Education of Young Adolescents, which, in June 1989, produced its report, "Turning Points: Preparing American Youth for the 21st Century." He was also former president of Carnegie's Council of Chief State School Officers. As of 1993, he was co-director of the National Alliance for Restructuring Education and a senior adviser to the Business Roundtable. The latter represents the collaboration of big business in the OBE movement.

Hornbeck has been credited, both in newspapers and from

members of the Task Force, for single-handedly restructuring Kentucky's schools. KERA swallowed the entire Carnegie reform package. Once his job in Kentucky was finished, Hornbeck went on to Iowa to do the same work there, and then to Alabama. As of August 1995 he was superintendent of schools in Philadelphia.

Mr. Hornbeck is a salesman for the New World Order, and what he is selling is the education system to go with it. That system is Outcome-Based Education, and that's what the Kentucky legislature bought in 1990.

If there is one thing we know about the New World Order it's that it is anti-Christian to the core, for it is based on a humanist view of man and society. That view is clearly stated in Humanist Manifesto I, issued in 1933:

> Religious humanists regard the universe as self-existing and not created. Humanism believes that man is a part of nature and that he has emerged as the result of a continuous process. . . . Humanism asserts that the nature of the universe depicted by modern science makes unacceptable any supernatural or cosmic guarantees of human values. . . . In place of the old attitudes involved in worship and prayer the humanist finds his religious emotions expressed in a heightened sense of personal life and in a cooperative effort to promote social well-being. . . . Man is at last becoming aware that he alone is responsible for the realization of the world of his dreams, that he has within himself the power for its achievement.[4]

What the humanists are telling us, in other words, is that we don't need God! And that's what OBE tells children: We don't need God. Humanist Manifesto II, issued in 1973, reiterates what the earlier Manifesto said:

> As in 1933, humanists still believe that traditional theism, especially faith in the prayer-hearing God, assumed to love and care for persons, to hear and understand their prayers, and to be able to do something about them, is an unproved and outmoded faith. Salvationism, based on mere affirmation, still appears as harmful, diverting people with false hopes of

heaven hereafter. Reasonable minds look to other means of survival.

We believe . . . that traditional dogmatic or authoritarian religions that place revelation, God, ritual, or creed above human needs and experience do a disservice to the human species. . . . As non-theists, we begin with humans not God, nature not deity. . . . [W]e can discover no divine purpose or providence for the human species. . . . No deity will save us; we must save ourselves.

That's the non-theistic religion that's subtly woven through every page, every lesson of OBE. Humanist Manifesto II also calls for the creation of a New World Order. It says:

We deplore the division of humankind on nationalistic grounds. We have reached a turning point in human history where the best option is to *transcend the limits of national sovereignty* and to move toward the building of a world community in which all sectors of the human family can participate. Thus we look to the development of a system of world law and a world order based upon transnational federal government.[5]

To put it as simply and bluntly as possible, OBE is humanism transformed into public school curriculum. In other words, Transformational OBE is turning Kentucky's public schools into humanist parochial schools in which the overriding aim is to deChristianize the children and turn them into humanists.

Another OBE carpetbagger was Frank Newman, president of the Education Commission of the States, a Carnegie supported agency. Newman was quoted in the *Lexington Herald-Leader* (7/28/89) as saying, "It's no longer a question of whether Kentucky can compete with Tennessee. It's a question of whether Kentucky can compete with Korea." He also was hired as a consultant to the Task Force.

Another change-agent of note was a gentleman by the name of Harold Hodgkinson who managed to keep the kettle of reform boiling by way of critical letters and press interviews that stirred up response. In this way it became possible to identify key members in both conservative and liberal education camps, making it easier to discredit the opposition before they knew what hit them. Hodgkinson has the best change-agent credentials: a stint at the Center for Research and Development at the University of California at Berkeley (1968), Director of the Carnegie Commission on Institutions in Transition Study (1968-70), recipient of a Carnegie grant in 1988 for a project by the National Institute of Education.

A key player in the Kentucky reform movement is the Prichard Committee for Academic Excellence, a prestigious citizens' group with political clout, formed to promote change in Kentucky education. In 1991 the Carnegie Corporation of New York awarded the Committee a grant of about $250,000 to help the committee set up watchdog groups across Kentucky to monitor education reform. Robert Sexton, executive director of the group, was quoted in the *Cincinnati Enquirer* of January 22, 1991 as saying: "It's really a turning point for us. We here in Kentucky are getting national attention and support." The Carnegie gift is the largest grant ever received by the Prichard Committee which has an annual budget of $160,000. The watchdog groups were created to make sure that school boards and state officials carried out the KERA reforms. According to the *Enquirer* story:

> The supervision effort was one of the main reasons the Carnegie Corp. financed the Prichard Committee proposal, said Karin Egan, a spokeswoman for the Carnegie Corp. . . .
>
> Three or four people will be added to the Lexington headquarters, and two to five people will be hired as community organizers to help set up watchdog groups across the state.
>
> The watchdog groups will be encouraged to attend meetings of school boards and the newly created school councils to see that school districts make the required reforms.

And on 2/20/91, the *Cincinnati Enquirer* reported that the

Education Accountability Office of the Kentucky Department of Education had hired a retired FBI agent to take charge of investigations that will monitor the KERA school reforms.

In other words, KERA is not the product of the people of Kentucky. It's the product of a small, Carnegie-financed cadre of change agents, aided by local collaborationists, whose job it is to bring all of public education in America under firm control of a centralized power in Washington. The fact that KERA is part of a national plan tied in with Goals 2000 was confirmed by Secretary of Education Richard Riley who called Kentucky a "lighthouse" for the rest of the nation when it comes to education. Speaking at a Southern Regional Education Board conference in Lexington in 1993, Riley said that President Clinton's initiative Goals 2000: Educate America Act would help states "duplicate what Kentucky has done and is doing. . . . Goals 2000 is, in a way, a national version of KERA." In other words, Goals 2000 is OBE on a national scale.

How the change agents did it in Kentucky is simply a model for them to use in doing it elsewhere. For example, in New Hampshire the same strategy is being used by first getting that state's Supreme Court to rule that the state's public education system is inequitable and therefore requires radical reform. And before you know it, as if by magic, there's an OBE reform bill being considered in the legislature.

The American people should know that they are being had. They will be spending billions of dollars on education reform from coast to coast in the expectation that the next generation will be well educated, and when they find out that they are not, who will pay for this fraud? None other than the taxpayer. You can sure that the educators will find reasons why the plan failed. I can just hear them saying it now: the idea of OBE was great. It was just poorly implemented because of lack of money, lack of parental support, and opposition from Christian fundamentalists. It would have worked had not radical rightists misinformed a gullible public about what OBE truly is. That's what they will say, because generally that's what they always say.

Is KERA working? What kind of results are the people of Kentucky getting from OBE which has now been in place since 1990? An extensive article on KERA in *Education Week* of April 21, 1993 provides some illuminating information. It says:

> Although Kentucky is still in the process of developing a full-blown assessment system, interim measures in reading, writing, math, science, and social studies were given to all students in grades 4, 8, and 12 last year.
>
> For the first time in the state's history, how pupils performed was compared not against each other but against absolute standards for what students should know and be able to do.
>
> The state determined how many students performed at the "novice," "apprentice," "proficient," and "distinguished" levels.
>
> The results were startling. Roughly 90 percent of the state's students scored below the "proficient" level, including many who have traditionally done well on other measures of performance. . . .
>
> Gerald Wischer, the president of the Ohio Valley National Bank in Henderson, says, "Those tests didn't come out nearly as well as the community thought they should."
>
> "Maybe," he speculates, "we're not as good as we thought we were."[6]

So there you are. Perhaps it's unfair to judge OBE on the basis of these first tests. After all, KERA has only been in place three years. Kentucky's commissioner of education, Tom Boysen, described KERA as the "second-greatest revolution in American public education." But it's probably the costliest, so far. In the article on KERA just quoted, we read:

> The law specifies six learning goals that all Kentucky students must meet. (Since the law's passage, those goals have been elaborated into 75 "valued outcomes.") It then orders the state to develop a new system of portfolios, performance assessments, and paper-and-pencil tests to measure children's progress. . . .

[The law] requires that nongraded-primary programs be established in every elementary school by [the fall of 1993]; that high-quality preschool programs be provided for all 4-year-olds at risk of educational failure; that a network of family-resource and youth-service centers be created at or near schools in which at least 20 percent of students are eligible for free or subsidized school meals; and that extended-school services, such as before- and after-school tutoring, be provided for youngsters in need of extra help.

By the way, according to a Kentucky education department spokesperson, those 75 "valued outcomes" were taken directly from Bloom's Taxonomy.[7] As you can imagine, all of this is confusing enough to parents. But what about the teachers? How do they feel about all of this?

"Our teachers are exhausted, to be quite frank," says Jim Young, the superintendent of the Russellville Independent School district in southwestern Kentucky. "And I think this is a statewide phenomenon. They are just worn out."

Principals complain that it's impossible to keep up with all of the paperwork and reading materials generated by the law. Phyllis Becker, an English and Latin teacher at Henderson County High School, says, "I've been taken out of my classroom so much for meetings and committees and workshops that I don't feel I'm doing as good a job as I have done in the past."

[Gayle Ecton, Henderson's superintendent, complains], "We've got teachers who've been teaching 20 or 25 years, and then all of a sudden we say, 'Let's do cooperative learning, peer tutoring, and the whole-language approach and use developmentally appropriate materials.' It's overwhelming, and you get more resistance."

There you have it. The whole-language approach being shoved down the throats of teachers and students, an approach that will create even more illiteracy than we have now.

Perhaps the most eloquent complaint about OBE is to be found in *The Hancock Clarion* of 12/30/93, an article by Eddie Price, a 39-

year-old teacher at Hancock County High School. Mr. Price has taught school for 17 years. He writes:

> I agree that education in Kentucky needs reform, but KERA is NOT the answer. I am not working for any particular group; I'm battling alone — one small voice in a wilderness of state-controlled propaganda. This monster is so huge, so complex, so twisted, that it can't be attacked with a simple argument. I can only share my own un-mandated thought in the hope that others will listen and act.... I MUST speak out against what I perceive as a massive wrong in education....
>
> Like most teachers I am enthusiastic about new discoveries, new directions in teaching.... For that reason I resolved to give KERA my sincerest efforts. Schools were literally being forced to undergo change, so I decided to willingly comply....
>
> The perpetrators of KERA began inundating our schools with mountains of regulations, restrictions, and KERA mandates. Most of the guidelines were vague, subjective, and even contradictory; no one in the state department seemed to know what was going on....
>
> Then the state passed down a list of KERA-mandated outcomes — [75] VALUED Outcomes. Everything that would be taught would be reordered to meet these VALUED outcomes. A few weeks later these outcomes were labeled "Learner Outcomes." I learned that this change was effected to quiet concerned groups across the state. Citizens were questioning the concept of the state mandating what values would be taught.... I began to realize that I wasn't in total agreement with the state. ... Our curriculum would have to be pared down and structured around values and attitudes. We were directed by the state to "weed out unimportant material" that did not meet the VALUED (that's what they really are) Outcomes....
>
> In 1992 I applied with a teaching partner for a state grant to develop an interdisciplinary unit which would link World History, World Literature, and other classes together.... We competed with other school teams across the state and tied for the winning unit! ...
>
> Then came the "accountability factor." ... Specific content was not mandated — only the vague and highly subjective Valued Outcomes.... When teachers voiced concerns about not meeting the Valued Outcomes, they were "soothed" with the explanation that schools would be given the chance to improve. "A Kentucky Distinguished Educator will be sent to

your building to help you grow." Then I learned that this official had the absolute power to declare the school "A School in Crisis"! The principal, and individual teachers could be eliminated with the single stroke of a pen....

I pressed on, learning as much about KERA as possible although in disagreement. I began implementing it into classroom. I attended special workshops on Multiple Intelligences .... I was DISMAYED when the KIRIS Tests were administered! These evaluated only one area of intelligence — the linguistic area! One of the questions required the students to discuss pictures of ballet, African tribal dancing and a Spanish folk dance.... [W]hat horrified me was the fact that I as a Social Studies teacher had "failed" to teach those dances.... [N]o way could I have anticipated this question that would, in reality, measure 33% of what I had taught for the '92-'93 school year! ...When Social Studies scores dropped slightly at our school, I initially felt guilt and shame....

This autumn I attended the Kentucky Council for the Social Studies in Louisville, where I found my fears echoed on a much broader scale. Social Studies scores had "dropped" dramatically statewide and teachers who had tried to embrace KERA had been rudely slapped in the face....

When I sat down and read the entire history of KERA's evolution, I realized that our lawmakers and, even worse, our public had been skilfully and strategically duped. KERA had been slickly packaged in a deceptive language of "glittering generalities" that the public seemed eager to swallow in the name of reform....Pro-KERA articles and comments have no problem making headlines while others with opposing views must pay exorbitant sums for "political advertising". Massive public disenchantment and frustration is downplayed as "concern associated with change"; teachers who speak out against perceived wrongs feel threatened and run the risk of being cast as "anti-reformers" or "traditional diehards opposed to improvement," or even "hidebound"! ... For a "dissident," teaching in the public schools today is similar to living under a Stalinist "Reign of Terror." Many teachers submit their horror stories and misgivings to anonymous publications or ask legislators not to quote them — for fear of repercussions....[8]

That's what OBE is doing to Kentucky as seen through the eyes and experience of a dedicated teacher. And that's what the promoters of OBE would like to do in every state in the Union. Can

OBE be stopped? Yes, if the parents and opposing teachers march on their state capitols and read the riot act to their legislators.

Perhaps the best summing up of the educational lunacy in Kentucky was given by Robert Holland in the *Richmond Times-Dispatch* of 1/22/94. He wrote:

> Kentucky is OBE Heaven. . . . Rarely a week passes without the Clintons' Goals 2000 propaganda machine at the U.S. Department of Education cranking out a tribute to the brilliance of Kentucky's reform, a Clintonite model for the nation.
>
> One of the initial outcomes, it appears, will be the cancellation of the Kentucky spelling bee. Officials of the sponsoring *Louisville Courier-Journal* and the Kentucky Education Association recently said, "The event's emphasis on rote memorization and competition contradicted the spirit of the state's school reform law," according to the January 12 issue of *Education Week*. That's not surprising, given the OBEists' idea that students should face no deadlines to pass tests. But, pray tell, how do pupils learn the alphabet without some memorization? And when they write a letter applying for a job, will not graduates of Kentucky schools be in a competition in which their spelling and grammar will count? How is OBE preparing children for "real life" by sheltering them from competition?
>
> Donna Shedd, a Louisville parent, teacher, and education (anti-OBE) activist, has passed along some fascinating information about the new assessment Kentucky uses to gauge how well students have mastered the state's 75 Learner Outcomes.
>
> Tests of reading comprehension would appear to have an obvious political content. In a fourth grade story, children are told that "green plants were able to get along just fine before people arrived on Earth." Another story, entitled "Your Daddy's a Wimp," requires children to write about whether they would like to be part of a family in which the mother works outside the home and the father "stays home and cooks." They are directed to draw from their "personal experiences." On a 12th-grade assessment, students are given this working definition of nationalism: *an idea which indicates a willingness on the part of a country to place its own interest above those of the world community.* No wonder OBE guru Bill Spady told an Oklahoma TV interviewer that "I don't know what patriotism means."[9]

24. Goals 2000 Federalizes Public Education

On March 31, 1994, President Clinton signed Goals 2000 into law which, according to *Education Week* of April 6, 1994, will "set in motion a process that proponents hope will transform the federal role in education." Secretary of Education Riley said in 1993, "Goals 2000 is, in a way, a national version of KERA (Kentucky Education Reform Act of 1990)." What this omnibus educational restructuring bill really does is federalize public education in the OBE mold. It (1) codifies the six National Education Goals into federal law, (2) authorizes $400 million in grant monies to the states to encourage "voluntary" education reform, (3) changes the present private National Education Goals Panel (NEGP) into a federal bureaucracy. The NEGP is to be composed of two Presidential appointees, eight governors, four Congressmen, and four members of State legislatures. (4) The Bill establishes a 20-member (appointed) National Education Standards and Improvement Council (NESIC) which will function as a sort of national school board, setting "opportunity-to-learn" standards with special help for some groups with females included under "gender equity." It will also set "voluntary" national curriculum content and performance standards and certifying national assessments. (5) The Bill also creates a 28-member National Skill Standards Board to identify broad clusters of occupations covering one or more industries that have common skill requirements and to facilitate the formation of "industry partnerships." These partnerships would develop and then act as an approving body for "recommended" standards, assessments and procedures for certification of achievement of skills for each of those occupations.

Clearly, Goals 2000 is Outcome-Based Education enacted into federal law.

The Senate also voted 62-31 to pass the School-to-Work Opportunities bill (S.1361, Paul Simon, D-IL). This bill establishes a partnership between the Department of Education and the Department of Labor to offer students a "performance-based education and training program enabling them to earn portable credentials."

After final passage of the School-to-Work bill, Labor Secretary Robert Reich described the measure "as a venture capital fund." The bill would provide seed money to communities that form partnerships with employers and schools to create a transition system for the 75 percent of all students who do not go to college. The programs are intended to lead a student to a high school diploma, a certificate from a postsecondary institution and an occupational skill certificate.

According to a report in the January 1994 *Congressional Digest:*

> This bill [Goals 2000] reflects the Clinton Administration's commitment to developing a system for lifelong learning and training. Standards for elementary and secondary school students are not enough. America currently has not organized ways to help students prepare for employment after high school.

Goals 2000 will create a mechanism to define what skills workers must have to get a job in key occupational areas. These standards will, in turn, guide job training programs for youth and adult workers.

In case the reader is not familiar with the much touted National Education Goals, here they are as given in a September 1989 National Governors' Association report:

Goal 1 - Readiness

By the year 2000, all children in America will start school ready to learn.

All disadvantaged and disabled children will have access to high-quality and developmentally appropriate preschool programs that help prepare children for school. Every parent in America will be a child's first teacher and devote time each day helping his or her preschool child learn; parents will have access to the training and support they need. Children will receive the nutrition and health care needed to arrive at school with healthy minds and bodies, and the number of low-birthweight babies will be significantly reduced through enhanced prenatal health systems.

Goal 2 - School Completion

By the year 2000, the high school graduation rate will increase to at least 90 percent.

The Nation must dramatically reduce its dropout rate, and 75 percent of those students who do drop out will successfully complete a high school degree or its equivalent. The gap in high school graduate rates between students from minority backgrounds and their non-minority counterparts will be eliminated.

Goal 3 - Student Achievement and Citizenship

By the year 2000, American students will leave grades four, eight, and twelve having demonstrated competency over challenging subject matter including English, mathematics, science, history, and geography, and every school in America will ensure that all students learn to use their minds well so they may be prepared for responsible citizenship, further learning, and productive employment in our modern economy.

The academic performance of elementary and secondary students will increase significantly in every quartile, and the distribution of minority students in each level will more closely reflect the student population as a whole. The percentage of students who demonstrate the ability to reason, solve problems, apply knowledge, and write and communicate effectively will increase substantially.

All students will be involved in activities that promote and demonstrate good citizenship, community service, and personal responsibility. The percentage of students who are competent in more than one language will substantially increase. All students will be knowledgeable about the diverse cultural heritage of this Nation and the world community.

Goal 4 - Mathematics and Science

By the year 2000, U.S. students will be the first in the world in mathematics and science achievement.

Math and science education will be strengthened throughout the system, especially in the early grades. The number of teachers with a sustantive background in mathematics and science will increase by 50 percent. The number of U.S. undergraduate and graduate students, especially women and minorities, who complete degrees in mathematics, science, and engineering will increase significantly.

Goal 5 - Adult Literacy & Lifelong Learning

By the year 2000, every adult American will be literate and will possess the knowledge and skills necessary to compete in a global economy and exercise the rights and responsibilities of citizenship.

Every major American business will be involved in strengthening the connection between education and work. All workers will have the opportunity to acquire the knowledge and skills, from basic to highly technical, needed to adapt to emerging new technologies, work methods, and markets through public and private educational, vocational, technical, workplace, or other programs. The number of quality programs, including those at libraries, that are designed to serve more effectively the needs of the growing number of part-time and mid-career students will increase substantially.

The proportion of those qualified students, especially minorities, who enter college, who complete at least two years, and who complete their degree programs will increase substantially. The proportion of college graduates who demonstrate an advanced ability to think critically, communicate effectively, and solve problems will increase substantially.

Goal 6 - Safe, Disciplined, and Drug-Free Schools

By the year 2000, every school in America will be free of drugs and violence and will offer a disciplined environment conducive to learning.

Every school will implement a firm and fair policy on use, possession, and distribution of drugs and alcohol. Parents, businesses, and community organizations will work together to ensure that schools are a safe haven for all children. Every school district will develop a comprehensive K-12 drug and alcohol prevention education program. Drug and alcohol curriculum should be taught as an integral part of health education. In addition, community-based teams should be organized to provide students and teachers with needed support.

If only wishing could make it so. In spite of all the lofty rhetoric, what all of the above does is federalize the dumbing-down process taking place in American education. Thomas Sticht, an expert on adult literacy, who has worked for U.S. Labor Dept., had his views reported in the *Washington Post* in 1987 as follows:

Many companies have moved operations to places with cheap, relatively poorly educated labor. What may be crucial, they say, is the dependability of a labor force and how well it can be managed and trained—not its general educational level, although a small cadre of highly educated creative people is essential to innovation and growth. Ending discrimination and changing values are probably more important than reading in moving low-income families into the middle class.[1]

That's a clear indication that high literacy for everyone is no longer a goal of public education. It's only for "a small cadre" composed of the university-bound elite. Secretary of Labor Robert Reich is, like Clinton, a Rhodes Scholar, a member of the ruling elite, and his plan for transforming compulsory education into job training reflects the progressive elite's view that anyone who doesn't go to college or drops out of college is a member of the working class proletariat. But, believe it or not, there are many non-college graduates who go into business for themselves, even educate themselves and become millionaires.

Education in America was never meant to be a form of "job training." From the very beginning it had a higher purpose. Its first purpose was to enable the individual to acquire Biblical literacy, so that the people would be able to govern themselves under God's law. That purpose was widened to include general literacy, the acquisition of knowledge, the pursuit of truth.

Today, the student is to be given a comic-book level of literacy by way of whole-language instruction, no spelling skills under invented spelling, and no memorization of the arithmetic facts. In fact, the text of H.R.6, page 20, dealing with Title One, states:

> The disproven theory that children must first learn basic skills before engaging in more complex tasks continues to dominate strategies for classroom instruction, resulting in emphasis on repetitive drill and practice at the expense of content-rich instruction, accelerated curricula, and effective teaching to high standards.

So the new, improved emphasis is away from the acquisition of basic skills to higher order thinking skills. If that's the case, then why don't we just eliminate primary school and start everyone in the fourth grade? The fraud being perpetrated on the American people by the educators with the help of Congress is easily discernable by those of us who know what kind of results we shall get from whole language, invented spelling, and the new new math. But by the year 2000, the American people, in their greater illiteracy and confusion, will have forgotten what the National Education Goals were all about, just as they have forgotten what Rudolf Flesch wrote in 1955 and 1981.

That so many intelligent men and women in Congress have been willing to go along with this fraud is disheartening but not unexpected. Education has become the instrument whereby the shapers of the New World Order intend to control the American people. By manipulating the minds of the young they will be able to control the future. According to *Education Week* (4/6/94):

> Enactment of Goals 2000 is essentially the culmination of a process that began when the National Governors' Association and President Bush agreed at a 1989 education summit to set national goals. Mr. Clinton, then the governor of Arkansas, was a key player in drafting the goals and in setting up the National Education Goals Panel to monitor progress toward them.[2]

In other words, Rhodes Scholar Bill Clinton played a major role in formulating the National Goals which were first brought before the American public by George New-World-Order Bush in his State of the Union message in January 1990. At that time, I wrote in an open letter to Pres. Bush in the *Blumenfeld Education Letter* of February 1990:

> The first goal you stated is that by the year 2000 every school-age child in America must be ready to learn. This is a very peculiar goal, indeed, for as we all know, children are ready to learn the moment they are born. In fact, by the time they are of school age they have learned to speak their own language quite intelligently and fluently. In the years 2 to 6 children master a speaking vocabulary in the thousands of words, all on their own, without the help of schools or teachers. In other words, every child, unless born with a serious handicap, is a very efficient self-teacher and self learner—

a veritable dynamo of language learning. Yet, after one year in a public school, many of these same intelligent children become "learning disabled." How come?

The problem is not that children aren't ready to learn, it's that the teachers aren't ready to teach! They supervise a myriad of classroom activities that give the impression that education is taking place. But what is really happening is that a myriad of psychological obstacles are being placed in the way of learning.

This can be easily proven by simply looking at the performance of black children. In 1930 the illiteracy rate among urban blacks was 9.2% Today it is around 40 or 50%. Yet there are more black children spending more time in school than ever before! Have blacks, for some unknown reason, lost the ability to learn to read in the last 60 years? Obviously not. Then how is it that 60 years ago, without Head Start, without Title One compensatory education, without integration, black children learned so much better than they do today? . . .

In short, the goal ought not to be to make children ready to learn, as if they weren't, but to make teachers ready to teach as they ought to teach, and not in the faulty manner they are presently being trained. If this were being done, we would not even need Head Start or Title One, (now known as Chapter One), thereby saving the taxpayers billions of dollars.

But apparently the last thing the federal government is interested in is saving the taxpayers billions of dollars, for in 1993 and 1994 the Congress enacted more bills on education than during its total previous existence, with each bill costing the taxpayers millions upon millions. Yet, it can be predicted that public education will only get worse, for the money will be used to implement all of the insanity that now passes for "education" in the nation's public schools.

That the ultimate purpose of Goal 1 is the government control of early childhood education was confirmed in April 1994 by the release of the Carnegie Corporation's report on the subject. It was given ample coverage in *Education Week* of April 13, 1994, providing the reader with a pretty good idea of what's ahead in government policy and federal legislation:

Calling the birth-to-3 span the most critical period in a child's development but the most neglected by policy-makers, an expert panel is proposing a broad blueprint for improvements in education, child and health care, and community services to support young children and their families.

In a report scheduled for release this week, a Carnegie Corporation of New York task force highlights compelling research evidence on the importance of the first three years of life.

A "remarkable" consensus is emerging on what it takes to spur healthy development, the 30-member panel says, while warning that a pattern of social neglect has dimmed the prospects of a "staggering number" of children.

"The crucially formative years of early childhood have become a time of peril and loss for millions of children and their families," writes David A. Hamburg, the president of the Carnegie Corporation, in the foreword to the report.

Among the group's recommendations to spur "responsible parenthood" are expanding family-planning services—including birth control and, in some cases, access to abortion and adoption services—and starting parenthood education in elementary school.

The report also calls on educators to incorporate services for the youngest children in "plans for schools of the 21st century" and urges secondary schools and community colleges to provide training and technical aid to child-care providers. . . .

The report signals an increasing awareness "that what goes on in the first three years of life is very important to school readiness," noted Kathryn Taaffe Young, the director of studies for the Carnegie task force and the report's primary author.

"We need a systematic approach," Ms. Young emphasized. While urging a 10-year investment in young children, the panel did not offer a cost estimate. . . .

The document, which Ms. Young described as the first major national report to address the needs of infants and toddlers, is being released at a meeting here that is expected to feature an address by Hillary Rodham Clinton and talks by Cabinet members, policymakers, child-development experts, and business leaders.

Dr. Julius B. Richmond, a professor of health policy at Harvard

University and the first director of Head Start, said the group hopes to spur community-based responses that integrate health, education, and social policy. Dr. Richmond and Eleanor E. Macoby, a professor of psychology at Stanford University, took over as co-chairman of the task force last year after the original chairman, Richard W. Riley, became the Secretary of Education. . . .

The report points to data showing that early brain development is far more rapid, extensive, and vulnerable to environmental influences than once thought. . . .

"Increasing the proportion of planned, low-risk births requires a national commitment" to expand access to both prenatal care and a "full range of family-planning services," the report states. . . .

Other recommendations include:

• Providing, as part of a "minimum health-care-reform package," primary and preventive health-care services; immunizations; and preconception, prenatal, and postpartum services.

• Offering home-visiting services to all first-time mothers with a newborn and more comprehensive visits to families at risk of poor maternal and child health.

• Expanding the federal family-leave law to cover small firms and to provide leave for four to six months with partial pay.

• Channeling substantial amounts of aid to improve child care for children under 3, providing incentives to states to improve child-care standards, and bolstering care-giver training, wages, and benefits.

• Expanding federal nutrition programs to serve all eligible women and children and adapting Head Start to serve poor families with infants and toddlers.

• Expanding programs to teach nonviolent conflict resolution and enacting stringent gun-control laws. . . .

The report urges federal agencies and states to remove obstacles to serving young children comprehensively and urges action by a wide range of social forces, including the media and parents.[3]

Quite an agenda for the nation set by the Carnegie Corporation, formulated by cadres of social engineers from the universities, and passed through to the White House, Congress and government agencies to be enacted into law. This is cultural revolution from above being imposed on an unsuspecting nation busy with the business of economic survival.

Education Week of April 20, 1994 reported the follow up:

> A Carnegie Corporation of New York report sounding the alarm about a "quiet crisis" facing the nation's youngest children evoked a loud and emotional outpouring of support from top government, business, health, and education officials at a meeting here [in Washington] last week.
>
> Hillary Rodham Clinton, the first speaker, conceded that it will take uncommon "political will and institutional fortitude" to fill the report's mandate. But there is reason for optimism, she said, simply because of the players involved.
>
> "This room is filled with people who are willing to work to make it happen," Mrs. Clinton said. . . .
>
> In a pitch for the health-care-reform plan she helped draft, she also argued that the Carnegie panel's goals cannot be met without universal health coverage.
>
> Attorney General Janet Reno, Secretary of Education Richard W. Riley, Secretary of Health and Human Services Donna E. Shalala, and Secretary of Housing and Urban Development Henry G. Cisneros each talked about the steps their agencies are taking.[4]

Apparently, when the Carnegie Corporation speaks, everybody in Washington listens! As for the "loud and emotional outpouring of support" on the part of "government, business, health, and education officials," who is *Education Week* trying to fool? Further follow up was reported in the *Boston Globe* of April 23, 1994:

> Head Start could soon be reaching out to pregnant women, infants and many more working families—three decades after it first touched the lives of the nation's poorest preschool children. In a late-night vote Thursday, the Senate agreed to expand and improve the comprehensive early childhood development program now serving about 720,000 children, most of them 3 to 5 years old. . . .
>
> In another expansion of Head Start's mission, the bill sets aside a small percentage of the program's budget for services for infants and toddlers. . . .
>
> The Senate's vote comes a week after the Carnegie Corp., a New York

philanthropy, warned that the nation's infants and toddlers are in trouble and that their healthy development—and ultimately the country's economic strength—are at risk.

How many private entities in America can get that kind of attention and action out of the White House and the Congress in the course of one week? Why couldn't we get the same attention and action when the Department of Education announced that half the adult population of this country could barely read and write? How come the Carnegie Corporation isn't interested in that crisis? But when it comes to a revolution that will bring the federal government into the bedrooms and nurseries of every home in America, the statist elite must salivate at the thought of such an expansion of bureaucratic power.

That the federal government, through the Department of Education, has been active in promoting the Carnegie-backed OBE reform movement and the new curriculum that goes with it, can be proven by a letter which accompanied a grant proposal addressed to Terrel Bell, Secretary of Education in the Reagan administration. The letter, written by G. Leland Burningham, former Utah State Superintendent of Public Instruction, dated July 27, 1984, reads:

> Dear Ted:
> I am forwarding this letter to accompany the proposal which you recommended Bill Spady and I prepare in connection with Outcome-Based Education.
> This proposal centers around the detailed process by which we will work together to implement Outcome-Based Education using research verified programs. This will make it possible to put outcome-based education in place, not only in Utah but in all the schools of the nation. For those who desire, we will stand ready for regional and national dissemination of the Outcome-Based Education program.
> We are beginning to see positive, preliminary results from some of the isolated schools in Utah which have implemented Outcome-Based

Education. These positive indicators are really exciting!
We sincerely urge your support for funding the proposal as presented.
Warmest regards,
Lee

The grant application was approved, and the Far West Laboratory, of which Spady was director, got the funding in the amount of $152,530. The grant number is G008410025. The project number is 122BH40246A. Education researcher Charlotte Iserbyt asserts that Bell's solicitation of the grant proposal and the creation and promotion of a federally sponsored curriculum violate the Elementary and Secondary Education Act, General Education Provisions Act, Section 432, which states:

> No provision of any applicable program shall be construed to authorize any department, agency, officer or employee of the United States to exercise any direction, supervision, or control over the curriculum, program of instruction, administration, or personnel of any educational institution, school, or school system, or over the selection of library resources . . . .

Did Terrel Bell break the law while serving as Secretary of Education? Only a Congressional investigation would be able to determine that. Meanwhile, dispite the efforts of the new Republican controlled Congress to rein in the liberals, the juggernaut for social revolution through education, financed by the taxpayer, continues unabated.

25. OBE and Big Brother

One of the more disturbing, if not frightening, aspects of the Outcome-Based Education revolution is its obsession with data collection. However, it all makes sense if you see it from the point of view of the educational totalitarians whose aim it is to use behavioral psychology for the purpose of modifying and controlling human behavior. Thus, the National Center for Education Statistics has been designated by the psycho-educators to be the recipient of computer dossiers of every school child and every teacher in America.

According to Beverly Eakman's *Educating for the New World Order,* the super computer already exists. It is called the Elementary and Secondary Integrated Data System and it will be linked with all of the other federal computer networks collecting data on American citizens.[1] Vice President Al Gore has been in the forefront of the effort to create a "national superhighway for computer information," and as Senator, he introduced the Supercomputer Network Study Act of 1985 which Congress enacted into law.

That this data collection program has been in the works for

some time is indicated by the existence of a Handbook issued in 1974 by the National Center for Education Statistics on State Educational Records and Reports. In their section on Student/Pupil Accounting, they list the major categories of student information. A three-digit system is used to categorize the data. For example, Personal Identification falls under 1 00: Name 1 01, Student Number 1 02, Sex 1 03, Racial/Ethnic Group 1 04, etc. Note the use of an identification number which will probably be the individual's Social Security Number, which is gradually becoming the American citizen's all-purpose ID number.

Family and Residence data fall under 2 00, Family Economic Information 2 40, and Family Social/Cultural Information 2 50.

Physical Health, Sensory, and Related Conditions fall under 3 00, starting with the Student Medical Record Number 3 01, and then covering every aspect of the student's physical health and medical life.

Mental, Psychological and Proficiency Test Results and Related Student Characteristics fall under 4 00. All data collected through psychological testing will be placed under that category, with Specific Mental and Psychological Characteristics under 4 30.

Enrollment information falls under 5 00, with Type of Program entered 5 23, and Type of Class for Instructional Grouping 5 24.

Performance falls under 6 00, Transportation under 7 00, and Special Assistance under 8 00.[2]

The most recent version of the *Student Data Handbook for Early Childhood, Elementary, and Secondary Education* was released in June of 1994 (NCES 94-303), and the latest *Staff Data Handbook: Elementary, Secondary and Early Childhood Education* (NCES 95-327) was released in January 1995. But who will have access to all of this information, and for what reason? Will potential employers, recruiters, and police departments be given this data? Is the U.S. government now to become involved in dispensing private information about its citizens as a new information service?

Supposing some of that information leads to negative consequences for the individual. Will he or she be able to sue the government for releasing that information? Who will own that information?

If the government is not going to make this information available to others, then why are the bureaucrats collecting it?

The government of a free people does not collect dossiers on all of its citizens. A police state does. According to the Declaration of Independence, the purpose of government is to secure the unalienable rights of its citizens, of which privacy is one of the most important.

The federal government's rationale for collecting all of this data is that it is needed to see if the nation is reaching the national goals set by Goals 2000. According to the Student Data Handbook for Elementary and Secondary Education developed for the U.S. Department of Education by the Council of Chief State School Officers, the National Cooperative Education Statistics System was established by the Hawkins-Stafford Education Improvement Amendments of 1988 (P.L. 100-297) "to involve state and federal governments in a mutual effort to produce state comparable and nationally uniform data on public and private school systems."[3]

To understand how all of this works, you have to get down into the bowels of Washington's educational bureaucracies. For example, the National Center for Education Statistics (NCES) is the grand overseer of all of this data collection. In 1991, it awarded a three-year contract to the Council of Chief State School Officers (CCSSO) "to facilitate the implementation of a national education data system." The project was called the Education Data System Implementation Project (EDSIP). Two years prior to EDSIP, the NCES began constructing "an interstate student records transfer system, currently called ExPRESS," an acronym for Exchange of Permanent Records Electronically for Students and Schools. The function of ExPRESS is given as follows:

This activity has included the development of standard data elements for inclusion in an electronic student transcript and a pilot exchange of student records across school districts and from districts to institutions of higher education. The system is now ready for further development, including the appointment of a Governing Board, making formal arrangements with a communications network for exchanging the records, and expansion to more sites.[4]

EDSIP also included implementing a Personnel Exchange System for sharing state expertise in solving education data problems, the development of an Information Referral System for sharing information to improve data systems across states, and the development of student and staff data handbooks.

The CCSSO has carried out two other projects for the NCES. The first, the Education Data Improvement Project (1985-88), "analyzed each state's capacity to provide standard, comparable, and timely data to NCES on public elementary and secondary school and school district, staff, students, revenues and expenditures." The second project was the New Education Data Improvement Project (1988-91) to provide technical assistance plans for each state, which addressed the state's problems in responding to Common Core of Data requirements.

All of these projects are being carried out by highly efficient bureaucrats who love to micromanage the details of data collection, with no thought of what all of this means to American freedom.

As has been stated, the government's rationale for collecting all this data is to find out if the nation is achieving its goals as outlined in Goals 2000. Goal 5, for example, states: "By the year 2000, every adult American will be literate and will possess the knowledge and skills necessary to compete in a global economy and exercise the rights and responsibilities of citizenship."

Since the U.S. Department of Education determined through its $14-million survey that about half the adults in America can barely read and write, it makes one wonder how Goal 5 is to be achieved by the year 2000 without all of these poor readers being given crash remedial reading courses in intensive, systematic phonics. That will never happen. So what is the *real* purpose of Goal 5? It has something to do with the "responsibilities of citizenship."

For a better idea of what the government has in mind, let us look into a publication put out in 1975 by the Pennsylvania Department of Education. Its title is *Getting Inside the EQA Inventory.* EQA stands for Educational Quality Assessment and it was meant to be a prototype for measuring national objectives. This is the document that got Anita Hoge, the indefatigable Pennsylvania mother, into a David and Goliath struggle with the federal and Pennsylvania governments over a parent's right to see the psychological tests which were being given to her child in school without her knowledge or consent. Beverly Eakman's book is about Anita Hoge's saga, without which we would know very little about the data collection plans of the government. The document states (p. 19):

> Viewed in its broadest sense responsible citizenship implies a respect for law and proper authority, a willingness to assume responsibility for our own actions and for those of the groups to which we belong . . . .
>
> Opportunities should be provided for pupils to cooperate and work toward group goals and to demonstrate integrity in dealing with others. Pupils should be given the chance to take the initiative and assume leadership for group action as well as lend support to group efforts as followers.[5]

Apparently, according to government bureaucrats, "responsibilities of citizenship" has more to do with collectivist activity, than with an understanding of the U.S. Constitution. In fact, if you analyze what the educators will be testing in order to determine whether or not the student has achieved the desired goal, you will see that they have a very strange idea of what citizenship is all about. For example, the document states:

The mores, codes, laws and social expectations of society provide the reference points for judging which behaviors reflect *responsible* citizenship and which indicate *poor* citizenship. A review of literature revealed that the National Assessment of Educational Progress developed nine general citizenship objectives. The criterion for inclusion of any one objective was its relative importance to society as agreed upon by a committee of scholars and lay people.

These national objectives were used to provide the frame of reference for what was to be measured. Objectives in the factual domain such as (a) knowing structure of government and (b) understanding problems of international relations were not considered in developing the scale.

There, you have it. The psycho-educators are not interested in whether or not the student knows anything about how the government works. Their interest is in attitudes and behavior. "The display of responsible citizenship behaviors like *honesty* or *integrity* are most often situational," says the Pennsylvania Department of Education.

In other words, there is no absolute sense of honesty or integrity. The document continues:

A person's display of good citizenship behavior under one set of motivating conditions tells us little about the way he or she can be expected to act if those conditions are altered. The context in which the behavior is elicited therefore becomes at least as important in determining the outcome as the predisposition of the individual involved.

A very neat bit of psycho-babble. So what's the solution? Read on:

To assess citizenship, a behavior-referenced model incorporating elements related to the psychological notion of *threshold* is used. In reference to citizenship, threshold refers to that set of conditions necessary to bring about the desirable responses. Thus by varying the situation and introducing conditions of reward and punishment we are able to determine the cutoff levels at which the student will display positive behavior. In this way it is possible to assess not only the students' predisposition to behave in a manner consistent with responsible citizenship but also provide some measure of the intensity of that predisposition across a wide spectrum of situations.

What kind of questions are asked in such an assessment? The document continues:

> Fifty-seven items measure willingness to exhibit good citizenship in many social situations under a variety of motivating conditions. Social contexts are given by 19 situations, each posing a problem and suggesting an action predefined as good or poor citizenship. Each story has three items which list positive or negative consequences resulting from the action. Students are asked to decide whether to take the action for each consequence.

> Sample situation (grade 11):

> There is a secret club at school called the Midnight Artists. They go out late at night and paint funny sayings and pictures on buildings. A student is asked to join the club. In this situation, I would JOIN THE CLUB when I knew . . . .
> 1. My best friend asked me join.
> 2. Most of the popular students were in the club.
> 3. My parents would *ground* me if they found out I joined.

The response for each choice is Yes, Maybe, or No. Guess what the politically correct answer is. In the norm-referenced scoring, "Positive Citizenship" was scored as 2 Yes, 1 Maybe, and 0 no. "Negative Citizenship" was scored as 0 Yes, 1 Maybe, 2 No.

These are the kinds of psycho questions that will be asked and tabulated by all of these expensive computer data collection systems. Students will not be tested on their knowledge of the Constitution, or of our political system. They will be tested on how well they relate to the group.

A Christian student would have had a very difficult time responding to the situation posed in the test. First of all, he or she would not have wanted to join a secret club, or stay out late at night, or paint pictures on private property. The situation as posed in the test represents the psychologists' view that honesty and integrity are situational. But that would not be the case with a Christian. If 0 Yes, 1 Maybe, and 2 No equal negative citizenship, what would a 3 No score mean? Hopeless anti-collectivist? Incorrigible Christian?

The situation posed in the test is very much like the lifeboat survival games, or the fallout shelter survival games used in values clarification programs. They are all artificial situations which do not represent reality and provide no useful information about anything. Yet, our government will be spending billions of dollars to collect this "information" so that our socialist educators can determine what kind of brainwashing is needed to create the new socialist man.

There is also the matter of SCANS, the Secretary's Commission on Achieving Necessary Skills. The Secretary in this case is not the Secretary of Education, but the Secretary of Labor. One of the ways the psycho-educators have been able to recruit support from big business for Outcome-Based Education and school restructuring is by promising to turn out well-trained students for the workforce. In other words, the federal government will become involved in training students for specific jobs based on the needs of the economy, which is what the Communist government of the Soviet Union did in the past.

In order to earn a Certificate of Initial Mastery, the student will be required to learn specific skills for a specific job. Which means, that for most American students, public education will become a form of job training, with little emphasis on the academic skills and knowledge which traditionally were considered to be the most important aspect of education, public or otherwise.

Data from the student's computerized record will be used to create a Résumé summing up the student's workplace competency, personal qualities, academic courses, extracurricular activities, etc. In other words, each student will be under total administrative control by the educational and labor bureaucracies, guided, trained, and brainwashed by the psycho-educators to behave in a manner acceptable to the powers that be.

The OBE people have criticized traditional public education as having been structured along the lines of the factory model. What is the new OBE school model? It's the Pavlovian-Skinnerian psych lab based on operant conditioning. The emerging product will be a semi-literate, intellectually crippled human being, with robotlike responses to the demands of the workplace. The superior students, identified early as the gifted and talented, will be shunted off into higher education to be groomed for membership in the ruling elite. They will have the situational honesty, integrity, and sociability of Bill and Hillary Clinton.

Is that what Americans want from their public schools? Probably not. But whether or not they do anything about it is still to be seen.

26. Who Controls American Education?

On June 27, 1993, there appeared in the London *Sunday Telegraph* a lengthy article about Britain's secret education establishment. It was revealed that since 1941 this shadowy group, known as the All-Souls Group and representing some of the most powerful people in the world of British education, has been meeting three times a year in an oak-panelled room at Oxford University. The article states:

> Many believe it is here, rather than at the Department of Education, that crucial questions about schools are raised. One member, who did not want to be named, said that the group had caused frustration to successive Education Secretaries.
>
> "One of the reasons why Margaret Thatcher got so infuriated with the educational establishment was that it seemed to have a private core which she couldn't get her teeth into, and half her civil servants seems to be involved," he said.
>
> Anyone who discloses details of who was present or what was said risks being black-balled. No minutes are kept, no papers or public statements ever emerge, and the membership list has never before been published. . . . Over Saturday evening sherry in the gardens of Rhodes

House, Oxford, and later over dinner, the great and the good speak frankly together about government policy — and they rarely have anything complimentary to say.

They are protected by Chatham House Rules, which dictate proceedings are off the record. Those who do not share the group's Left-wing views are occasionally invited to speak, but rarely receive a sympathetic hearing.

Each member is free to bring a guest, and the result is a volatile mixture of the most powerful and the most radical in today's educational world....

Membership is by invitation and the criteria are shrouded in mystery. Names are put forward by members, and after they have attended a meeting a decision is made on whether they have anything to contribute.... There are about 50 active members and, once in, few leave.

Does such an exclusive, secretive education establishment exist in the United States?

Undoubtedly. That's the reason why President Reagan could not abolish the Department of Education, and why conservatives in the department were pressured out of their positions the moment they started to do anything threatening to the establishment. Who are they in that top controlling group who formulate national education policy? The top foundation heads like Ernest Boyer, top professors of education like John Goodlad, Bill Spady, and Terrel Bell, and top educational operatives in the state and federal governments. They are the ones who decide on policy and coordinate its implementation throughout the United States and provide the funding for it.

Otherwise, how explain the implementation of Outcome-Based Education in state after state as if orchestrated by a central control? How explain the widespread use of whole language in teaching reading when we know that it produces crippled readers? How explain this orchestrated hostility against intensive phonics among educators? As for the actual formation of an education establishment in the U.S., it seems to have started with a confidential meeting called the Cleveland Conference organized in 1915 by

Prof. Charles Judd, head of the University of Chicago School of Education. Judd, who got his Ph.D. at Leipzig under Prof. Wilhelm Wundt, was spearheading the movement to reform education in the psycho-progressive mold. David Tyack writes in his book *Managers of Virtue* (p. 132):

> [Judd] had a vision that both the structure of the schools and the curriculum needed radical revision, but that change would take place "in the haphazard fashion that has characterized our school history unless some group gets together and undertakes, in a cooperative way, to coordinate reforms."[1]

Judd urged the members of the Cleveland Conference to jump into the breach and undertake "the positive and aggressive task of . . . a detailed reorganization of the materials of instruction in schools of all grades." One of the most important reforms promoted by Judd was in the teaching of reading. It was his protégé William Scott Gray who produced the Dick and Jane look-say, whole-word reading program that began America's downward slide into illiteracy.

Among the 19 members who attended the first Cleveland Conference were James R. Angell, a Leipzig alumnus who became president of the University of Chicago and later president of Yale; Leonard Ayres, director of the Russell Sage Foundation; Abraham Flexner of the Rockefeller Foundation; Paul Hanus, director of the Harvard Graduate School of Education; Paul Monroe, founder of the World Federation of Education Associations; Edward L. Thorndike, father of educational psychology at Teachers College, Columbia University; and Ellwood P. Cubberly of Stanford University's School of Education.

Among others who joined in later years were Lyman Bryson of CBS, John Gardner of the Carnegie Corporation, James Bryant Conant of Harvard, Ralph Tyler of Stanford whose pioneering work in psychological testing helped Benjamin Bloom design

Outcome-Based Education. In fact, Bloom's Taxonomy is dedicated to Tyler. David Tyack writes (p. 132):

> Having no constitution, no minutes, no officers save a "factotum," no bylaws, no "public life," the conference was described in 1949 as a club whose "sole object is to make it possible for forty or fifty men to meet once a year and talk about whatever they are interested in for ten or a dozen hours in session and an unpredictable number of hours in lobbies and bedrooms." Members had a chance to "learn about the news behind the news," to get to know leaders in a variety of fields, to share information about new educational progams or jobs or foundation grants or new government programs or regulations. When the Commonwealth Fund decided to give large sums for educational research, for example, its officer Max Farrand outlined the funding program to conference members first.[2]

And now we know why the education establishment is so unresponsive to parental wishes and why the only realistic alternatives for parents is to get their children out of the government schools and into homeschools or decent private schools. Incidentally, the Chatham House Rules mentioned in the *Sunday Telegraph,* which means that all conference proceedings are off the record, refer to Chatham House, the home of the Royal Institute of International Affairs (RIIA), the British counterpart to our Council on Foreign Relations (CFR). And Oxford, where the All Souls Group meets, is also where Bill Clinton studied on his Rhodes Scholarship. The scholarships were founded by Cecil Rhodes, who made his fortune in gold and diamond mining in South Africa in the 1880s and formed a secret society in 1891 with an elite membership to promote the interests of a world government.

Professor Carroll Quigley, Bill Clinton's mentor at Georgetown University in Washington, wrote a book about the secret society entitled *The Anglo-American Establishment.* Quigley wrote:

> The Rhodes Scholarships, established by the terms of Cecil Rhodes's

seventh will, are known to everyone. What is not so widely known is that Rhodes in five previous wills left his fortune to form a secret society, which was to devote itself to the preservation and expansion of the British Empire. And what does not seem to be known to anyone is that this secret society was created by Rhodes and his principal trustee, Lord Milner, and continues to this day. . . .

This society has been known at various times as Milner's Kindergarten, as the Round Table Group, as the Rhodes crowd, as *The Times* crowd, as the All Souls Group, and as the Cliveden set. (p. ix)

The scholarships were merely a facade to conceal the secret society, or, more accurately, they were to be one of the instruments by which the members of the secret society could carry out his purpose. (p. 33)[3]

The group was largely instrumental in changing the British Empire into the British Commonwealth of Nations, a forerunner of the New World Order. Rhodes died in 1902, and the country of Rhodesia, which was named after him, has become Zimbabwe. Obviously, the Rhodes Scholarships are now being used to recruit the future leaders of the New World Order.

An insight into Rhodes's thinking was given by W. T. Stead, one of Rhodes's closest associates, who wrote:

Mr. Rhodes was more than the founder of a dynasty. He aspired to be the creator of one of those vast semi-religious, quasi-political associations which, like the Society of Jesus, have played so large a part in the history of the world. To be more strictly accurate, he wished to found an Order as the instrument of the will of the Dynasty, and while he lived he dreamed of being both its Caesar and its Loyola. . . . The question that now arises is whether in the English-speaking world there are to be found men of faith adequate to furnish forth materials for the Society of which Mr. Rhodes dreamed. (Quigley, p. 36)[4]

An article about Cecil Rhodes in the *Boston Globe* of Feb. 14, 1993 possibly answers that question. It states:

Cecil John Rhodes would have been delighted at the news that Bill

Clinton is president of the United States, for Rhodes specifically intended his scholarships for young men "who have shown during school days that they have instincts to lead [and] esteem the performance of public duties as their highest aim." Moreover . . . he would have been particularly pleased that a Rhodes Scholar was in charge of an administration that included a sizable contingent of his "boys."

In the first years of the scholarships few Americans applied because you had to know Latin and Greek. But these prerequisites were eventually dropped. Today the selection process is conducted by committees of past Rhodes Scholars in different states and regions. According to the *Globe:*

These review the applications and interview the most promising applicants. Prospective scholars describe the interviews as hard but fair; questions can range from fields of study . . . to more personal challenges. . . . At the regional level, applicants are gathered together for an interview process that includes a cocktail party, ostensibly for socialization and hospitality; dark rumors circulate that the party is an occasion for covert assessment of dress, deportment and mastery of the social graces.

What kind of careers do Rhodes Scholars choose when they return to the U.S.? A survey of the first 25 years of scholars found that 33 percent became educators, 24 percent lawyers, 13 percent businessmen, 8 percent doctors, and only 6 percent went into government service. Nowadays, twice as many Rhodes Scholars are entering government service or foundation work.

Some of the Rhodes Scholars who have achieved a modicum of notoriety are J. William Fulbright (1925) U.S. Senator from Arkansas; Daniel J. Boorstin (1934) Librarian of Congress; Walt W. Rostow (1936) national security adviser; Byron R. White (1938) Supreme Court Justice; Nicholas Katzenbach (1947) U.S. attorney general; Stansfield Turner (1947) director of the CIA; Guido Calabresi (1953) dean of Yale Law School; Neil Rudenstine (1956) president of Harvard; Jonathan Kozol (1958) left-wing

316 / The Whole Language/OBE Fraud

author and admirer of Fidel Castro whose book on illiteracy says nothing about the cause of our illiteracy problem: the discarding of phonics in favor of look-say; Lester Thurow (1960) liberal economist, dean of Sloan School at MIT; David Souter (1961) U.S. Supreme Court Justice; David Boren (1963) U.S. Senator; Richard Lugar (1954) U.S. Senator; Paul Sarbanes (1954) U.S. Senator; Bill Bradley (1965) U.S. Senator; Larry Pressler, U.S. Senator; Robert Reich (1968) U.S. Secretary of Labor; George Stephanopoulos (1984) Clinton's White House spokesman; and Thomas F. Birmingham (1972) Massachusetts state senator who sponsored and promoted the state's new OBE reform bill.

According to the London *Sunday Times* of Feb. 27, 1994, other Rhodes Scholars in the Clinton administration include Jim Woolsey, director of the CIA; Joseph Nye, chairman of the National Intelligence Committee; Bruce Reed, Clinton's domestic policy adviser; Ira Magaziner, main architect of Clinton's health reform plan; Strobe Talbott, deputy Secretary of State; Bowman Cutler, deputy assistant to the president for economic policy; and Nancy-Ann Min, associate director of the Office of Management and Budget for health care. As the *Sunday Times* said: "No award has as much kudos or is such an instant passport to the corridors of power in Washington."

As the reader will notice, there isn't a true conservative among them. All of them to some degree or another are promoting the agenda of the New World Order. According to author Malachi Martin, the pagan, free-market New World Order is merely one of three forces vying for hegemony over the human race. He writes in his book, *The Keys of This Blood* (p. 15):

> Willing or not, ready or not, we are all involved in an all-out, no-holds-barred, three-way global competition. Most of us are not competitors, however. We are the stakes. For the competition is about who will establish the first one-world system of government that has ever existed in the society of nations. . . .

The competition is all-out because, now that it has started, there is no way it can be reversed or called off.

No holds are barred because, once the competition has been decided, the world and all that's in it — our way of life as individuals and as citizens of the nations; our families and our jobs; our trade and commerce and money; our educational systems and our religions and our cultures; even the badges of our national identity, which most of us have always taken for granted — all will have been powerfully and radically altered forever. No one can be exempted from its effects. No sector of our lives will remain untouched.

The competition began and continues as a three-way affair because that is the number of rivals with sufficient resources to establish and maintain a new world order. . . . Indeed, the three rivals themselves . . . speak about this new world order not as something around a distant corner of time, but as something that is imminent. As a system that will be introduced and installed in our midst by the end of this final decade of the second millennium.[5]

Who are the three contenders? Martin sees the first as Christian civilization based on Biblical morality and values. He sees the Catholic church as the last remaining world-wide stronghold of these values. Its opposition to abortion in the face of fierce secular humanist pressure indicates that it has not abandoned moral absolutes.

The second contender is communism which is by no means dead. It rules in China, and events in Russia in 1993 and 1994 have attested to the enduring power of the communist establishment which has slowed the transition to a free-market, capitalist system. In addition, Gorbachev has become head of a new world organization called the Green Cross which has as its aim an "ecologically safe future" for mankind. In an interview in *Parade Magazine* of January 23, 1994, Gorbachev said:

The Green Cross is in its infancy but is already drawing strong support. . . . We need a global focus. . . . We have to change our values. We have to educate people. . . . Educational systems all over the world must take up this task, international codes of law must be developed, and the practical work of environmental cleanup must be undertaken. . . . Leaders in religion, politics and science must speak out and point us in new directions, toward a new paradigm for our civilization. . . . If we're going to protect the planet's ecology, we're going to need to find alternatives to the consumerist dream that is attracting the world. . . . We recognize the gradualness of change, as we recognize the urgency of change. . . . We recognize that we will learn as we go. There is no clear answer, except that the old ideologies in our civlization must give way to the new challenges to our civlization. The growing environmental movement in the world must be the vehicle for that.[6]

Note the use of a green cross as an ecological symbol. A good deal of careful thinking and marketing knowhow must have gone into the choice of a cross to symbolize a movement led by Gorbachev.

Concerning the third contender, Martin writes:

The final contender in the competition for the new world order is not a single individual leader of a single institution or territory. It is a group of men who are united as one in power, mind and will for the purpose of achieving a single common goal: to be victorious in the competition for the new global hegemony.

While the acknowledged public leader and spokesman for this group is the current American president, the contenders who compose this assemblage of individuals are Americans and Europeans who, taken together, represent every nation in the Western democratic alliance.

Unremittingly globalist in their vision and their activities, these individuals operate from two principal power bases. The first is the power base of finance, industry and technology. Entrepreneurial in their occupations, the men in this phalanx qualify themselves, and are often referred to by others, as Transnationalist in their outlook. . . .

Members of the second phalanx of this group of globalist contenders — Internationalists, as they are frequently called — bring with them invaluable experience in government, intergovernmental relationships, and in the rarefied art of international politics. . . . Transnationalists and Internationalists can be said for all practical purposes to act as one: to constitute one main contender. . . . Both are so closely intertwined in their membership that individuals move easily and with great effect from an Internationalist to a Transnationalist role and back again. And not the least important in the all-encompassing confrontation that is under way, both groups share the same philosophy about human life and its ultimate meaning — a philosophy that appears, in the surprised view of some observers, to be closer to Mikhail Gorbachev's than to Pope John Paul's.[7]

It's important to understand that what is taking place in American public education today is a direct result of decisions being made at the top by those planning to lead us into a world government. That is why whole language and Outcome-Based Education are being imposed on our schools in a carefully planned, orchestrated manner.

If you doubt that such an organized group of planners exists, let me quote several passages from Carroll Quigley's monumental history of the world in our time, *Tragedy and Hope,* published in 1966 when Bill Clinton was one of his students at Georgetown University in Washington, D.C. Clinton, incidentally, got his Rhodes Scholarship in 1968. Quigley writes (p. 950):

> There does exist, and has existed for a generation, an international Anglophile network which operates, to some extent, in the way the radical Right believes the Communists act. In fact, this network, which we may identify as the Round Table Groups, has no aversion to cooperating with the Communists, or any other groups, and frequently does so. I know of the operations of this network because I have studied it for twenty years and was permitted for two years, in the early 1960's, to examine its papers and secret records. I have no aversion to it and to many of its instruments. I have objected,both in the past and recently, to a few of its policies . . . but in general my chief difference of opinion is that it wishes to remain unknown, and I believe its role in history is significant enough to be known....
>
> It was this group of people, whose wealth and influence so exceeded their experience and understanding, who provided much of the framework of influence which the Communist sympathizers and fellow travelers took over in the United States in the 1930's. It must be recognized that the power

that these energetic Left-wingers exercised was never their own power or Communist power but was ultimately the power of the international financial coterie, and, once the anger and suspicions of the American people were aroused, as they were by 1950, it was a fairly simple matter to get rid of the Red sympathizers. Before this could be done, however, a congressional committee, following backward to their source the threads which led from admitted Communists like Whittaker Chambers, through Alger Hiss, and the Carnegie Endowment to Thomas Lamont and the Morgan Bank, fell into the whole complicated network of the interlocking tax-exempt foundations. The Eighty-third Congress in July 1953 set up a Special Committee to Investigate Tax-Exempt Foundations with Representative B. Carroll Reece, of Tennessee, as chairman. It soon became clear that people of immense wealth would be unhappy if the investigation went too far and that the "most respected" newspapers in the country, closely allied with these men of wealth, would not get excited enough about any revelations to make the publicity worth while, in terms of votes or campaign contributions. An interesting report showing the Left-wing associations of the interlocking nexus of tax-exempt foundations was issued in 1954 rather quietly. Four years later, the Reece committee's general counsel, Rene A. Wormser, wrote a shocked, but not shocking, book on the subject called *Foundations: Their Power and Influence*. (p. 955)[8]

All of which brings us to the real source of control of American education: the big tax-exempt foundations. While a good deal of the money lubricating educational restructuring today comes from federal and state governments, the private foundations were a crucial source of funding for progressive education in the early days. For example in the 1954 Reese Committee Staff Report on Relations Between Foundations and Education, we read:

> According to our compilations, the Carnegie Corp. has contributed to all educational purposes from 1911 to 1950, approximately $25,300,000. . . . The Carnegie Corporation of New York had contributed a total of $1,237,711 to the National Education Association, the Progressive Education Association, the American Council of Education, perhaps the major part of their sustenance in the early years.

In the area of curriculum reform and textbook revision, the Carnegie Corporation provided the American Historical Society with the funds to produce a new set of social studies textbooks with a clear pro-socialist bias.

Norman Dodd, a former banker who had been appointed research director of the Reece Committee, was asked to investigate the tax-exempt foundations. He found that only 12 of the 7,000 foundations in the country represented 80 percent of the capital endowments of all of them. He and his staff decided to concentrate on those 12. He wrote in 1978:

> This brings me to two experiences which I will describe to you. The first was my response to an invitation during November 1953, from President Roman Gaither of the Ford Foundation, to meet in his office in New York. Upon arriving there, I was greeted with the following:
>
> "Mr. Dodd, we invited you to come because we thought that perhaps, off the record, you would be kind enough to tell us why the Congress is interested in the operations of foundations such as ourselves."
>
> Before I could think of how best to reply, he volunteered this: "Mr. Dodd, we operate here under directives . . . which emanate from the White House. Would you like to know what the substance of their directives is?"
>
> My answer was, "Yes, Mr. Gaither, I would like very much to know."
>
> Whereupon he said: "The substance of the directives under which we operate is that we shall use our grant-making power to alter life in the United States so that we can be comfortably merged with the Soviet Union."
>
> Needless to say, I nearly fell off the chair. . . .
>
> I said, "Mr. Gaither, legally you are entitled to use your grant-making power for this purpose but I do not think you are entitled to withhold this information from the American people to whom you are beholden for your tax exemption. So why do you not tell the American people what you have just told me?"
>
> His answer was: "Mr. Dodd, we would not think of doing that."

The next experience Dodd had was with the Carnegie

Endowment for International Peace which had worked hard to get the U.S. Senate to ratify the United Nations treaty. The president of the foundation, Dr. Joseph Johnson, who had succeeded Alger Hiss in that position, was extremely cooperative and offered Dodd's staff access to the corporation's minute books from its inception. Dodd writes:

> My first reaction is that he had lost his mind. I had some suspicion what these minute books might well contain, but there was no objection from their counsel and there seemed to be no disagreement on the part of the vice presidents.
>
> All of them were relatively young. My guess was that none of them had ever read the minutes themselves. As a result, I accepted the invitation and sent a member of my staff to New York. She later brought back to me on Dictaphone belts what she had dictated from the minutes of the board. This information came as a shock to all of us.
>
> In 1908 the trustees had raised this question, "Is there any way known to man more effective than war, assuming that you wish to alter the life of an entire people?" They discussed this question academically and in a scholarly fashion for almost a year and came up with the conclusion that war is the most effective means known to man, assuming that you want to begin concentrating power in government and abandon the dispersion of authority contemplated by the Constitution.
>
> They then raised Question No. 2: "How do we involve the United States in such a war?" This was in 1909. . . . The trustees answered the question this way: "We must control the diplomatic machinery of the United States."
>
> That brings up Question No. 3, which is: "How do we secure control of the diplomatic machinery of the United States?" And the answer comes up, "We must get control of the State Department."
>
> That tied in with prior information our committee had uncovered indicating that the hand of the Carnegie Endowment for International Peace had already become a powerful policy-making force inside the State Department.
>
> Finally, in 1917, we did get in a war — World War I. These trustees then had the brashness to congratulate themselves on the wisdom and validity of their original decision. The impact of our participation in World

War I immediately indicated its capacity to alter our national life. The trustees even went so far as to dispatch a telegram to President Woodrow Wilson, pressuring him to see to it that the war did not end too quickly.

Finally the war was over. The trustees then took up the problem of preventing — as they put it — a reversion of life in the United States to what it was prior to 1914. They came to the conclusion that to gain that end they must somehow get control of education in the United States. They realized this was a prodigious piece of work, so they tried to obtain the assistance of the Rockefeller Foundation.[9]

It should be noted that prominent educators were among the earliest trustees of the various foundations. For example, Nicholas Murray Butler (1862-1947), who was president of Columbia University from 1901 to 1945, was an original trustee of the Carnegie Foundation for the Advancement of Teaching, a trustee of the Carnegie Corporation of New York, and president of the Carnegie Endowment for International Peace. He was also president of the National Education Association in 1895.

Frank E. Spaulding (1866-1960), a Wundtian PhD who organized Yale's department of education and wrote numerous textbooks, was a member of the Rockefeller funded General Education Board from 1917 to 1920. It was a half-million dollar grant from the General Education Board in 1920 which financed the establishment of the Harvard Graduate School of Education. Walter A. Jessup (1877-1944), who got his PhD at Teachers College, Columbia University, and became president of the University of Iowa in 1916, became president of the Carnegie Foundation for the Advancement of Teaching in 1934 and president of the Carnegie Corporation in 1941.

In short, top educators have been part and parcel of the secret elitist network promoting a humanist world government from the very beginning, and they have used the great foundations to finance their plans. In 1985 an American-Soviet education agreement was negotiated by the Carnegie Corporation for the purpose of developing curricula and teaching materials for American schools.

Also in 1985, the Carnegie Corporation of New York established the Carnegie Forum on Education and the Economy. In May 1985 the Forum's advisory Council created the Task Force on Teaching as a Profession. The result of the Task Force's work was a report entitled "A Nation Prepared: Teachers for the 21st Century." In it is the rationale for all of the insanity that now passes for educational restructuring. As the report said, "We do not believe the educational system needs repairing; we believe it must be rebuilt to match the drastic change needed in our economy if we are to prepare our children for productive lives in the 21st century."

What were the solutions offered by the Carnegie Forum? A National Board for Professional Teaching Standards (to control who may or may not teach), an "integrated" curriculum, team teaching, school-based management, life-long learning, critical thinking, higher order thinking skills, etc. And the way for implementation has been well lubricated by grants to the Education Commission of the States, the National Governors Association, the Council of Chief State School Officers, and the National Association of State Boards of Education. And in the previous chapter we revealed the key role the Carnegie group is playing in getting state governments to adopt and implement Outcome-Based Education.

At the same time, the U.S. Department of Education is pumping billions of dollars into educational "research" through its own grant-giving powers. But the Department of Education apparently takes its orders from the Carnegie Foundation, for most, if not all, of its grants support the educational aims and goals of the Carnegie group. And that is why it is so important for the New World Order controllers to keep conservatives out of power.

For example, one of the biggest mistakes made by the first Reagan administration was the appointment of Terrel H. Bell as Secretary of Education. Reagan wanted to abolish the Department of Education, but Bell wanted to preserve it, for he was an establishment educator and, apparently, no one in the Reagan administration had any idea that that would create a problem. The next four years proved to be an endless struggle between Bell and the conservatives, and in the end, the conservatives lost a crucial cultural battle, even though Bill Bennett replaced Bell in the second term.

Incidentally, it was Jim Baker on the White House staff who proved to be Bell's most valuable ally in the war against the conservatives.

There is one other federal education program of very great importance. It's the monster computerized National Data System of Elementary and Secondary Education which will collect personal information about every child in the public system to be used by the government for its own purposes.

This will mean the complete loss of privacy for the American citizen and the ability of government to control everyone through the education system. If you add to that the information the government already has about us in the files of the IRS, state automobile registries, gun licensing bureaus, etc., our rulers will have a complete, detailed dossier on every American citizen which will include psychological, religious, and political data. And we haven't even included the personal data that presently resides in the computers of our banks, credit bureaus, telephone companies, video rental stores, etc., and is available to the government on demand. Potentially, our lives will be subject to more government control than in any other society in history. It will be the end of individual freedom in America.

How can we fight this billion-dollar educational juggernaut determined to destroy our freedom? It's not easy, but it can be done with patience, persistence, and a strategy that finds the weak links in the totalitarian system.

In a way, we are much better prepared today than we were ten years ago. We have much more information than we had then, and we are much more aware of the wily ways of the enemies of freedom. The Republican victories in November 1994, was a start. But there will have to be many more such Conservative victories in the future if we are to regain the freedoms we have lost.

Postscript

It is quite obvious from the preceding twenty-six chapters that public education is now beyond any hope of reform that would return it to basic academic sanity. And that is mainly because of the total takeover of government education by behavioral and Third Force psycho-educators. They have usurped the prerogatives of academic education in favor of psychotherapy, attitudinal change, and politically correct behavior, none of which has anything to do with the development of intellect. As a result, serious damage is being done to the intellectual development of American children, making them mentally unfit to acquire the knowledge and skills needed to live productive and culturally rich lives, unfit to deal with the complexities and abstractions of a technologically advanced civilization.

The only possible and logical course of action for parents is to remove their children from the public schools and to not even think of putting their preschool children in those schools at all. The alternatives are private schools, church and parochial schools and home schools.

The psychologists cannot be removed from the education system because their roots are too deeply imbedded in the process and substance of everything that goes on in the system and they are in complete control of the graduate schools of education where future teachers are taught. They have tenure and own a host of professional associations and publications that solidify their hold on the system. In addition, they have so changed America's philosophy of education, that it would take a true cultural revolution among the educators to change it to what parents would find acceptable. None of this could have been achieved without the government education monopoly, compulsory school attendance laws, and the billions of taxpayer dollars which support the lifestyles of the professionals who live off the system.

All of which brings us to the basic issue of government owned and controlled education. Does the state really have a compelling interest in education? Obviously not, because the state is an abstraction, a fiction, and only human beings can have compelling interests in anything. Parents have a compelling interest in the education of their children, and concerned citizens no doubt believe that all children should be educated. But can the government do the job? Evidentally not, otherwise we would not have 90 million Americans who can barely read and write, even though these millions of individuals spent more years in school than any previous generation, and more money was spent on them than on any previous generation.

If education were completely private, we would have no reading problem, for a primary school that could not teach children to read would not be in business very long. But government schools that can't teach are rewarded for failure with federally funded special education programs that enrich the school instead of closing it down. The sooner we get the government out of the education business, the sooner we will have successful schools and successful students.

But, since there is no going back to the good old days of academic rigor and discipline, we must go forward. Fortunately, parents still have the freedom to decide which road they will take for their children's education. Should they take the public road leading to OBE, whole language, psychological brainwashing, and government monitoring and data collection? Or the road to educational freedom, intensive, systematic phonics, logical thinking, and healthy intellectual development? If you want the latter, you'll have to do it privately, because the government psycho-educators will not do it for you. Freedom requires responsibility. It also has a cost. Our founding fathers paid the original price in blood and privation, but there is still a cost to maintaining and preserving that freedom for ourselves and our children. The government doesn't pay anyone to be free, for it first gets its money from its obedient citizens, and then uses it to try to get more. In the end, government's aim is to turn us into its servants.

The government education system is a perfect example of government at work: it is deliberately dumbing down the children of this nation to turn them into the obedient servants of a new ruling elite of universitarians and bureaucrats.

Educate your children for freedom, not slavery. You can do it. You must do it!

Notes

Chapter 1   A Bit of Important History   (pp. 5-12)

1. "The 'Sight Reading' Method of Teaching Reading as a Source of Reading Disability," *The Journal of Educational Psychology,* February 1929, pp. 135-143.
2. "Dyslexia," *Life,* Vol. 16, No. 15, April 10, 1944, pp. 79-82.
3. Howard Whitman, "Why Don't They Teach My Child to Read?" *Collier's,* Nov. 26, 1954, pp. 102-05.
4. Rudolf Flesch, *Why Johnny Can't Read* (New York: Harper & Row, 1955), p. 12.
5. Jeanne Chall, *Learning to Read: The Great Debate* (New York: McGraw-Hill, 1967).
6. *The New York Times,* July 9, 1975. In this interview, Prof. Goodman outlined his views on reading instruction which eventually became known as whole-language philosophy.
7. Rudolf Flesch, *Why Johnny Still Can't Read: A New Look at the Scandal of Our Schools* (New York: Harper & Row, 1983).

Chapter 2   Whole Language, Lingusitics and the Wittgenstein Connection   (pp. 13-27)

1. Noah Webster, *American Dictionary of the English Language,* 1828.
2. Noam Chomsky, *Language and Mind,* (Harcourt Brace Jovanovich, 1968) pp. 67,70,97.
3. Noam Chomsky, *Language and Problems of Knowledge,* (M.I.T. Press, 1988) p. 131.

4. Carole Edelsky, Bess Altwerger and Barbara Flores, *Whole Language: What's the Difference?* (Portsmouth, NH: Heinemann, 1991), pp. 19-20.
5. Jane Baskwill and Paulette Whitman, *Evaluation: Whole Language, Whole Child* (Scholastic, 1988), p. 19.
6. Ludwig Wittgenstein, *Philosophical Investigations* (The Macmillan Co., 1953, Fifth Printing, 1971). All of the quotations in this chapter are from this book, with pages indicated in the text, and all italicized words are such in the original.
7. Augustine, Saint, Bishop of Hippo, *Confessions* (New York: Liveright 1943)

Chapter 3 What Is Whole Language? (pp. 28-39)

1. Carole Edelsky, Bess Altwerger and Barbara Flores, *Whole Language: What's the Difference?* (Portsmouth, NH: Heinemann, 1991), p. 9.
2. *Ibid*, pp. 3, 7, 8.
3. Frank Smith, *Understanding Reading: A Psycholinguistic Analysis of Reading and Learning to Read* (Hillside, NJ: Lawrence Erlbaum Associates, 1988), pp. 198-99.
4. Carole Edelsky, *et al, op. cit.*, p. 32.
5. Frank Smith, *op. cit.*, p. 153.
6. Barbara Aria, *The Nature of the Chinese Character* (New York: Simon and Schuster, 1991), p. 12.
7. John Edgar Johnson, "The Chinese Language," *The Biblioteca Sacra and Theological Eclectic*, Vol. 30, pp. 62-76.
8. Robert K. Logan, *The Alphabet Effect: The Impact of the Phonetic Alphabet on the Development of Western Civilization* (New York: William Morrow, 1986), p. 55.
9. *Ibid*, p. 57.

Chapter 4 The Alphabetic Method (pp. 39-44)

1. John Taylor Gatto, *The Exhausted School* (New York: The Odysseus Group, 1993), pp. 109-10.
2. George Clarke, *The Education of Children at Rome* (London: Macmillan, 1896), pp. 71-79.

Chapter 5 The Origin of Look-Say (pp. 45-52)

1. "Modes of Teaching Children to Read" by Samuel Stillman Greene was one of

the sections in *Remarks on the Seventh Annual Report of the Honorable Horace Mann, Secretary of the Massachusetts Board of Education,* written by the Association of Boston Masters in 1844. The *Remarks* initiated a year-long dispute between Horace Mann, supported by the Harvard-Unitarian liberal establishment, and the conservative Boston schoolmasters. See Samuel L. Blumenfeld, *The New Illiterates* (Boise, ID: The Paradigm Co., 1973, 1988), pp. 139-155, for a detailed account of the dispute and the full text of Greene's critique, pp. 315-351.

2. James McKeen Cattell is credited with providing the "scientific" basis for the whole-word method. A summary of that scientific experimentation in 1885 in Leipzig, when Cattell was 25 and a student of Prof. Wilhelm Wundt, is given in *The Psychology of Teaching Reading* by Irving H. Anderson and Walter F. Dearborn (Ronald Press, 1952), p. 212.

3. Edward L. Thorndike, "Curriculum Research," *School and Society,* Nov. 10, 1928, Vol. XXVIII, No. 724, p. 575. *School and Society* was a weekly publication edited and published by James McKeen Cattell.

4. Edward L. Thorndike, *Animal Intelligence* (New York: Macmillan, 1911), pp. 104-05.

5. John B. Watson, *Behaviorism* (New York: W.W. Norton, 1930), pp. ix, 2.

6. Walter F. Dearborn and Irving H. Anderson, "A Sound Motion-Picture Technique for Teaching Beginning Reading," *School and Society,* Vol. 52, No. 1347, Oct. 19, 1940, pp. 367-69.

Chapter 6   The Role of John Dewey   (pp. 53-57)

1. John Dewey's views on education are elucidated in Max Eastman's *Companions* (New York: Farrar, Straus and Cudahy, 1942, 1959), pp. 269-78.

2. Katherine Camp Mayhew and Anna Camp Edwards, *The Dewey School* (New York: Atherton Press, 1966), p. 5.

3. John Dewey, "The Primary-Education Fetich," *Forum,* Vol. XXV, May 1898, pp. 315-28.

4. John Dewey, *The School and Society* (Chicago: University of Chicago Press, 1899).

5. Edward Bellamy, *Looking Backward* (Ticknor and Company,1887; Cambridge, MA: Belknap Press of Harvard University Press, 1969).

Chapter 7   Who Was Huey?   (pp. 58-64)

1. Edmund Burke Huey, *The Psychology and Pedagogy of Reading* (New York: Macmillan, 1908; Cambridge, MA: The MIT Press, 1968).

Chapter 8 Did They Know It Didn't Work? (pp. 65-72)

1. G. Stanley Hall, *Life and Confessions of a Psychologist* (New York: 1923), p. 219.
2. G. Stanley Hall, *Educational Problems*, 2 vols. (New York: D. Appleton, 1911). Hall is quoted in Mitford M. Mathews, *Teaching to Read* (Chicago: University of Chicago Press, 1966), pp. 134-138.
3. Walter F. Dearborn, *The Psychological Researches of James McKeen Cattell: A Review by Some of His Pupils*, "Professor Cattell's Studies of Perception and Reading" (Archives of Psychology, No. 30, 1914), pp. 40-42.
4. G. Stanley Hall quoted in Mitford M. Mathews, *op. cit.*, pp. 136-37.
5. Michael M. Sokal, *An Education in Psychology, James McKeen Cattell's Journal and Letters from Germany and England, 1880-1888* (Cambridge, MA: The MIT Press, 1981), p. 161.

Chapter 9 The Making of Whole Language Ideology (pp. 73-90)

1. Kenneth S. Goodman, Lois Bridges Bird and Yetta M. Goodman, *The Whole Language Catalog* (Santa Rosa, CA: American School Publishers, 1991).
2. Kenneth S. Goodman, "Reading: The Psycholinguistic Guessing Game," *The Whole Language Catalog, op. cit.*, p. 98.
3. Frank Smith, *Insult to Intelligence* (New York: Arbor House, 1986), p. 188. The quotes from Frank Smith in this chapter are all from this book.
4. Samuel L. Blumenfeld, "The Philadelphia Story," *Vital Speeches*, Vol. XLVI, No. 24, Oct. 1, 1980, pp. 749-753. This speech was delivered by the author at the 19th Annual Reading Reform Foundation Conference, Champaign, IL, Aug. 11, 1980.
5. Marilyn Jager Adams, *Beginning to Read: Thinking and Learning about Print* (Cambridge, MA: The MIT Press, 1990).
6. Michael S. Brunner, *Retarding America: The Imprisonment of Potential* (Portland, OR: Halcyon House, 1993).
7. *Beginning to Read:* A critique by literacy professionals and a response by Marilyn Jager Adams. "In this feature, literacy educators holding various points of view comment on Marilyn Jager Adams's book *Beginning to Read: Thinking and Learning about Print* and the *Summary* of it produced by the Center for the Study of Reading. *The Reading Teacher*, A Journal of the International Reading Association, Vol. 44, No. 6, February 1991, pp. 370-395.
8. *Ibid*, p. 377.
9. *Ibid*, p. 375.
10. Robert K. Logan, *op. cit.*, pp. 17, 18, 21.

11. Yetta M. Goodman, *The Reading Teacher,* Feb. 1991, p. 377.
12. *Ibid.*
13. *The Reading Teacher,* Feb. 1991, pp. 392-93.

.

Chapter 10 Psychology's Best Kept Secrets   (pp. 91-102)

1. Jerome Bruner, *In Search of Mind* (New York: Harper & Row, 1983), p. 121
2. George Miller, quoted in Bruner, *op. cit.,* p. 122.
3. John B. Watson, *Behaviorism, op. cit.,* pp. 2, 6.
4. Jerome Bruner, *op. cit.,* p. 137.
5. A. R. Luria, *The Nature of Human Conflicts,* An Objective Study of Disorganisation and Control of Human Behaviour, trans. from the Russian and edited by W. Horsley Gantt (New York: Liveright, 1932; Washington Square Press, paperback edition, 1967), p. xi.
6. I. P. Pavlov, *Twenty Years of Objective Study of the Higher Nervous Activity (Behaviour) of Animals,* 6th edition (Moscow, USSR: State Biological and Medical Publishing House, 1938), p. 690. The quoted passage can be found in *Essays on the Patho-Physiology of the Higher Nervous Activity According to I. P. Pavlov and His School* by A. G. Ivanov-Smolensky (Moscow, USSR: Foreign Languages Publishing House, 1954), p. 201.
7. A. R. Luria, *op. cit.,* pp. 206-07.
8. Carl Rogers' statement is quoted in Alfred J. Marrow's biography of Kurt Lewin, *The Practical Theorist,* p. 213. Marrow's source is: C. R. Rogers. "Interpersonal Relationships USA," *Journal of Applied Behavioral Science,* 1968, 4, No. 3.
9. Alfred J. Marrow, *The Practical Theorist: The Life and Work of Kurt Lewin* (New York: Basic Books, 1969), pp. 167, 122.
10. *Ibid,* p. 258.
11. Kurt Lewin, *Resolving Social Conflicts, Selected Papers on Group Dynamics,* edited by Gertrud Weiss Lewin, Foreword by Gordon W. Allport (New York: Harper & Row, 1948), p. 39.
12. Jerome Bruner, *op. cit.,* pp. 145, 144, 29, 30.
13. *Ibid,* p. 194.

Chapter 11 The Political Agenda in Whole Language   (pp. 103-117)

1. James V. Wertsch, *Vygotsky and the Social Formation of Mind* (Cambridge, MA: Harvard University Press, 1985), p. ix.
2. *Ibid,* pp. 10-11.
3. Kenneth S. Goodman, "Whole Language Teachers," *The Whole Language Catalog, op. cit.,* p. 207.

4. *Ibid.*
5. Carole Edelsky, *et al, op. cit.*, p. 67.
6. Dianne Sirna Mancus and Curtis K. Carlson, "Political Philosophy and Reading Make a Dangerous Mix," *Education Week,* Feb. 27, 1985, p. 29.
7. Bess Altwerger, Carole Edelsky, Barbara M. Flores, "Whole Language: What's New?" *The Reading Teacher,* Nov. 1987, p. 152.
8. Frank Smith, "Overselling Literacy," *Phi Delta Kappan,* Jan. 1989, p. 357.
9. Philip Berryman, *Liberation Theology,* (New York: Pantheon Books, 1987), p. 37.
10. Paulo Freire and Donaldo Macedo, *Literacy: Reading the Word and the World* (South Hadley, MA: Bergin & Garvey, 1987), p. vii.
11. Frank Smith, *Phi Delta Kappan,* Jan. 1989, p. 358.
12. Jan Allen, Patricia Freeman, Sandy Osborne, "Children's Political Knowledge and Attitudes," *Young Children,* Jan. 1989, p. 57.
13. William T. Fagan, "Empowered students; empowered teachers," *The Reading Teacher,* April 1989, pp. 572-78.
14. Kenneth S. Goodman, *What's Whole in Whole Language* (Portsmouth, NH: Heinemann, 1986), p. 37.
15. See *Education Week,* Jan. 8, 1992 for a report on three studies by critics of whole language in *Journal of Educational Psychology,* Dec. 1991. The critics are Frank R. Velluntino, of the State Univ. of N.Y. (Albany), Tom Nicholson, of the Univ. of Auckland, New Zealand, and Brian Byne and Ruth Fielding-Barnsley, of the Univ. of New England, NSW, Australia.
16. Marie Carbo, "Debunking the Great Phonics Myth," *Phi Delta Kappan,* Nov. 1988, pp. 226-40.
17. Jeanne S. Chall, *"Learning to Read: The Great Debate* 20 Years Later — A Response to 'Debunking the Great Phonics Myth,'" *Phi Delta Kappan,* March 1989, pp. 521-38.
18. John Dewey, *Democracy and Education* (New York: Macmillan, 1916; Free Press Paperback, 1966), p. 192.
19. *Ibid,* p. 297.
20. John Dewey, *The School and Society, op. cit.,* pp. 90-91.
21. Paulo Freire and Donaldo Macedo, *op. cit.,* p. 59.
22. *Ibid,* pp. 34, 38.
23. *Ibid,* p. 39.
24. Bess Altwerger and Barbara Flores, "The Politics of Whole Language," *The Whole Language Catalog, op. cit.,* p. 418.

Chapter 12   The Hypocrisy of Whole Language   (pp.118-136)

1. "Primer," *Great Soviet Encyclopedia,* A. M. Prokhorov, Editor in Chief, Translation of the Third Edition, Vol. 4, p. 423 (New York: Macmillan, 1974).

2. *Ibid.*
3. Anna Louise Strong, "Education in Soviet Russia," *School and Society,* Mar. 1, 1924, pp. 260-61. Quotes are from Dr. Strong's article, "The new educational front in Russia," *Survey Graphic,* Feb. 1924.
4. Lucy L. W. Wilson, "Newest Schools in Newest Russia," *School and Society,* Vol. 37, No. 944, Jan. 28, 1933, p. 111.
5. William C. Bagley, "The Soviets Proceed to the Liquidation of American Educational Theory," *School and Society,* Vol. 37, No. 942, Jan. 14, 1933, pp. 62-63.
6. Robert P. Carroll, "Thoroughness in Teaching Elementary Reading," *School and Society,* Jan. 1, 1938, pp. 23-25.
7. A. R. Luria, *The Nature of Human Conflicts, op. cit.,* p. 12.
8. James V. Wertsch, *op. cit.,* p. 9.
9. Cecelia Pollack and Victor Mortuza, "Teaching reading in the Cuban primary schools," *Journal of Reading,* Dec. 1981, pp. 241-43.
10. *Ibid.*
11. George S. Counts, *The Soviet Challenge to America* (New York: The John Day Company, 1931).
12. S. Steven Powell, *Covert Cadre, Inside the Institute for Policy Studies* (Ottawa, IL: Green Hill Publishers, Inc., 1987), pp. 15-16.
13. Peter Collier and David Horowitz, *Destructive Generation* (New York: Summit Books, 1989), p. 151.
14. Martin Carnoy and Derek Shearer, *Economic Democracy: The Challenge of the 1980s* (Sharpe, dist. by Pantheon Books, 1980). According to *Book Review Digest* (1980, p. 193), "Among the ideas entertained are establishment of a government holding company, worker control of investment capital, worker cooperatives, forms of codetermination in management, and systematized activist politics."
15. Derek Shearer and Lee Webb, "How to Plan a Mixed Economy," *The Nation,* Oct. 11, 1975, p. 340.
16. Antonio Gramsci, *Letters from Prison* (New York: Harper & Row, 1973).
17. Paulo Freire and Donaldo Macedo, *op. cit.,* pp. 1-2.
18. Malachi Martin, *The Keys of This Blood* (New York: Simon and Schuster, 1990), pp. 250-251.
19. Peter Collier and David Horowitz, *op. cit.,* p. 151.

Chapter 13 Miscue Analysis (pp. 137-148)

1. Myrtle Sholty, "A Study of Reading Vocabulary of Children," *Elementary School Teacher,* Vol. 12, 1911-12, pp. 272-77.
2. Geraldine Rodgers, *A History of Reading Instruction* (Unpublished Manuscript, 1992), p. 728. This is an exhaustive study of a subject that sorely needs it.

Rodgers has done more in-depth research on the differences between whole-word and phonetic reading instruction than any other researcher in the field.

3. Walter F. Dearborn, "Professor Cattell's Studies of Perception and Reading," *The Psychological Researches of James McKeen Cattell: A Review by Some of His Pupils, op. cit.*, p. 42.
4. Clara Schmitt, "School Subjects as Material for Tests of Mental Ability," *Elementary School Journal*, Nov. 1914, pp. 150-61.
5. Clara Schmitt, *ibid.*
6. Jane Baskwill and Paulette Whitman, *Evaluation: Whole Language, Whole Child* (New York: Scholastic, 1988), p. 19.
7. Josephine Horton Bowden, "Learning to Read," *Elementary School Teacher*, Vol. 12, pp. 21-33. Quoted in Walter F. Dearborn, *op. cit.*
8. Frank Smith, *Reading Without Nonsense,* (New York: Teachers College Press, 1985), p. 129.
9. Frank Smith, *Understanding Reading: A Psycholinguistic Analysis of Reading and Learning to Read, op. cit.*, p. 151.
10. Bronwyn Mellor and Michael Simons, "As We See It: An Interview with Kenneth and Yetta Goodman," *The Whole Language Catalog, op. cit.*, p. 100.
11. *Ibid.*
12. *Ibid,* p. 101.
13. Yetta M. Goodman and Wendy Hood, "Kidwatching, Miscues and Aaron's Reading," *The Whole Language Catalog, op. cit.*, pp. 102-03.

Chapter 14   Deconstruction in the Primary School   (pp. 149-166)

1. William F. Jasper, "Eco '92: Launching Pad for International Global Governance," *The New American*, Vol. 8, No. 14, July 13, 1992, p. 5.
2. Carole Edelsky, *et al, op. cit.*, pp. 19, 32.
3. *Academic American Encyclopedia* (Danbury, CT: Grolier, 1990), Vol. 6, p. 122.
4. Dianne Sirna Mancus and Curtis K. Carlson, "Political Philosophy and Reading Make a Dangerous Mix," *Education Week,* Feb. 27, 1985, p. 29.
5. *Contemporary Authors* (Detroit, MI: Gale Research, Inc., 1988), Vol. 124, p. 112.
6. Frank Smith, "Learning to Read: The Never-Ending Debate," *Phi Delta Kappan,* Feb. 1992, p. 438.
7. Michael Halliday, *Learning How to Mean: Explorations in the Development of Language* (London: Edward Arnold, Publishers, Ltd., 1975), pp. 5, 18.
8. Frank Smith, *Phi Delta Kappan,* Feb. 1992, p. 432.
9. Michael Halliday, *op. cit.*, p. 33.
10. *Ibid,* pp. 60, 66.
11. Frank Smith, *Reading Without Nonsense, op. cit.*, pp. 53, 129.
12. Frank Smith, *Understanding Reading, op. cit.*, p. 27.

13. Carole Edelsky, *et al*, *op. cit.*, p. 9.
14. L. S. Vygotsky, *Thought and Language* (Cambridge, MA: The MIT Press, 1962), pp. 98-101.

Chapter 15 Debunking Whole Language Myths (pp. 167-178)

1. Marie Carbo, *op. cit.* (see note 16 in chap. 11).
2. Jenny Chamberlain, "Our Illiteracy: Reading the Writing on the Wall," *North and South* (Auckland, New Zealand), June 1993, pp. 66-76.

Chapter 16 Great American Literacy Disaster (pp. 179-189)

1. Anthony G. Oettinger, "Regulated Competition in the United States," *The Innisbrook Papers*, the edited proceedings of a Northern Telecom senior management conference on issues and perspectives for the 1980's, Feb. 1982, pp. 19-22.
2. C. S. Lewis, *The Screwtape Letters* (New York: Macmillan, Revised Macmillan Paperbacks Edition, 1982), pp. 164-65.
3. *School and Society*, the weekly magazine founded and edited by James McKeen Cattell, is the best source of statistics on literacy in America. See issues dated Jan. 30, 1915 (pp. 179-80), Nov. 19, 1921 (p. 466), Apr. 9, 1932 (p. 489).

Chapter 17 Functional Illiteracy and Delinquency (pp. 190-196)

1. Michael S. Brunner, *Retarding America: The Imprisonment of Potential* (Portland, OR: Halcyon House, 1993), p. 30.
2. *Ibid.*
3. *Ibid.*

Chapter 18 "The Whole Language Catalog" (pp. 197-208)

1. Kenneth S. Goodman, "Whole Language Teachers," *The Whole Language Catalog (TWLC) op. cit.*, p. 207.
2. LaDonna Hauser, "Supporting Emerging Readers," *TWLC, op. cit.*, p. 115.
3. Judy Peters, "Reading Difficulty: A Blueprint for Action," *TWLC, op. cit.*, p. 114.
4. Kenneth S. Goodman, "Reading: The Psycholinguistic Guessing Game," *TWLC, op. cit.*, p. 98.
5. *Ibid.*

6. Kathy O'Brien, "How I Became a Whole Language Teacher," *TWLC*, *op. cit.*, p. 392.
7. Kenneth S. Goodman, "A Letter to Teachers New to Whole Language," *TWLC*, *op. cit.*, p. 10.
8. Jeanette Veatch, "Whole Language as I See It," *TWLC*, *op. cit.*, p. 235.
9. Thomas Newkirk, "Notes from a Worrier: The Vulnerability of the Whole Language Movement," *TWLC*, *op. cit.*, p. 217.
10. Yetta M. Goodman, "History of Whole Language," *TWLC*, *op. cit.*, p. 387.
11. John Dewey, *op. cit.*, (see note 3 in chap. 6).
12. Luis Moll, "Pioneers: Lev S. Vygotsky (1896-1934)," *TWLC*, *op. cit.*, p. 413.
13. Henry A. Giroux, "Literacy, Cultural Diversity, and Public Life," *TWLC*, *op. cit.*, p. 417.
14. Michael Apple, "Teachers, Politics, and Whole Language Instruction," *TWLC*, *op. cit.*, p. 416.
15. Bess Altwerger and Barbara Flores, "The Politics of Whole Language," *TWLC*, *op. cit.*, p. 418.
16. Ron Miller, "Defining Holistic Education," *TWLC*, *op. cit.*, p. 427.

Chapter 19 Dr. Seuss, Edward Miller (pp. 209-230)

1. Thomas H. Gallaudet, *American Annals of Education*, Aug. 1830.
2. Edward Miller, Rt. 3, Box 329C, N. Wilkesboro, NC 28659. Mr. Miller will provide documentation on request.
3. Dan Carlinsky, "a story (it's true) of a Geisel with a view," *Arizona*, June 14, 1981, pp. 48-53. In this interview of "Dr. Seuss," the cogent remarks are on p. 51.
4. *Learning Disabilities*, A Report to the U.S. Congress prepared by the Interagency Committee on Learning Disabilities (Washington, DC: Dept. of Health and Human Services, 1987), p. 222.
5. Alfred J. Marrow, *op. cit.*, p. 122.

Chapter 20 Outcome-Based Education (pp. 231-244)

1. Odyssey Project, Gaston County Schools, 238 Wilmot Dr., Gastonia, NC 28053. Memorandum, Feb. 8, 1993, Edwin L. West, Jr., Superintendent.
2. Peter Gay, *The Enlightenment: A Comprehensive Anthology*, edited with introductory notes by Peter Gay (New York: Simon and Schuster, 1973), pp. 17, 18.
3. Richard Wurmbrand, *Marx and Satan* (Westchester, IL: Crossway Books, 1986), p. 80.

4. Paulo Freire, *The Politics of Education* (New York: Bergin & Garvey, 1985), p. xvii.
5. Ron Miller, *op. cit.*
6. Richard Wurmbrand, *op. cit.*, p. 99.

Chapter 21 OBE and Mastery Learning (pp. 245-256)

1. Carl D. Glickman, "Mastery Learning Stifles Individuality," *Educational Leadership*, Nov. 1979, pp. 100-03.
2. George N. Schmidt, "Chicago Mastery Learning: A Case Against a Skills-Based Reading Curriculum," *Learning*, Nov. 1982, p. 37.
3. Ron Brandt, "On Outcome-Based Education: A Conversation with Bill Spady," *Educational Leadership*, Dec. 1992/Jan. 1993, p. 67.
4. "Standards for Implementing Transformational Outcome-Based Education," *Outcome-Based Restructuring Presentation* (The High Success Network, P. O. Box 1630, Eagle, CO 81631, 1990), p. 42.
5. *Ibid.*
6. Ira Magaziner and Hillary Rodham Clinton, "Will America Choose High Skills or Low Wages?" *Educational Leadership*, Mar. 1992, p. 12.
7. Ron Brandt, *op. cit.*, p. 68.
8. Anthony G. Oettinger, *op. cit.*

Chapter 22 Benjamin Bloom: OBE's Godfather (pp. 257-269)

1. Vice Admiral Hyman G. Rickover, *American Education—A National Failure*, Hearings Before the Committee on Appropriations, House of Representatives, 87th Congress, Second Session, May 16, 1962, pp. 122-23.
2. A. R. Luria, *op. cit.*, pp. 206-07.
3. *Humanist Manifestos I and II* (Buffalo, NY: Prometheus Books, 1973), pp. 21-22.
4. Rousas J. Rushdoony, *The Messianic Character of American Education* (Phillipsburg, PA: The Craig Press, 1963).
5. Benjamin S. Bloom, M. D. Engelhart, E. J. Furst, W. H. Hill, and D. R. Krathwohl, *Taxonomy of Educational Objectives: The Classification of educational goals: Handbook 1, Cognitive Domain* (New York: Longman, 1956, 1984), pp. 2, 7, 10, 12, 15, 26, 27.
6. *Ibid.*
7. *Ibid*, pp. 62, 71.
8. William G. Spady, "It's Time to Take a Close Look at Outcome-Based Education," *Outcomes*, Summer 1992, p. 6.
9. Benjamin S. Bloom, Donald R. Krathwohl and Bertram B. Masia, *Taxonomy of*

Educational Obejctives, Book 2, Affective Domain (New York: Longman, 1964), pp. 7, 38, 48, 85, 88.

10. *Ibid*, pp. 89, 90.
11. Benjamin S. Bloom, *Human Characteristics and School Learning* (New York: McGraw-Hill, 1976), p. 125.
12. National Education Association, "The 1993-94 Resolutions," *NEA Today,* Sept. 1993, p. 26.
13. Benjamin S. Bloom, *Stability and Change in Human Characteristics* (New York: John Wiley & Sons, 1964), p. 6.
14. *Ibid*, pp. 127, 215.

Chapter 23 Kentucky's OBE Experiment (pp. 270-287)

1 Betty E. Steffy, *Curriculum Reform in Kentucky, A Rationale and Proposal,* presented to the Sub-Committee on School Curriculum, Legislative Task Force on Education Reform, Frankfort, Kentucky, Aug. 21, 1989.
2. Terence Moran, "Sounds of Sex," *The New Republic,* Aug. 12, 1985, pp. 14-16.
3. Brochure, Kentucky Center for the Arts, advertising a special School Matinee Performance of The Joffrey Ballet, Friday, April 22, 1994, in line with the curriculum goals of the Kentucky Education Reform Act (KERA).
4. *Humanist Manifestos I & II, op. cit.,* pp. 8-10, 13, 15, 16.
5. *Ibid*, p. 21.
6. Lynn Olson, "Off and Running, While some are stumbling at the gate, other Kentucky schools move to enact ambitious reform law," *Education Week / Special Report,* April 21, 1993, pp. 4-11.
7. A seminar on Outcome-Based Education was held in Louisville, Kentucky, on Saturday, Oct. 9, 1993, at Ballard High School. The spokesman for the Kentucky Dept. of Education was Robert Rodosky who identified the 75 "valued outcomes" as coming directly from Bloom's Taxonomy.
8. Eddie Price, "Hancock teacher attacks Kentucky school reform, A Reign of Terror (impressions of KERA)," *The Hancock Clarion,* Hawkesville, KY, Dec. 30, 1993.
9. Robert Holland, *Richmond Times-Dispatch* (Richmond, VA), Jan. 22, 1994.

Chapter 24 Goals 2000 Federalizes Public Education (pp. 288-300)

1. Lawrence Feinberg, "Illiteracy Crisis Misread, Researchers Say," *Washington Post,* Aug. 17, 1987, pp. A7-A8. Feinberg interviewed David Harmon, an expert on illiteracy from Teachers College, Columbia University, and Thomas G. Sticht, who has conducted research on reading for the U.S. Army and the Ford Foundation. Feinberg writes: "Harmon and Sticht noted that many

companies have moved operations to places with cheap, relatively poorly educated labor. What may be crucial, they said, is the dependability of a labor force and how well it can be managed and trained, not its general educational level—although a small cadre of highly educated, creative people is essential to innovation and growth. Sticht said his studies of the U.S. military indicate that many fairly complicated jobs can be done well by people with low reading levels. That improved reading is crucial to raising the status of the 'underclass.' Both researchers said ending discrimination and changing values are probably more important than reading in moving low-income families into the middle class." As of Oct. 1995, Sticht was president of Applied Behavioral and Cognitive Sciences, Inc.

2. Mark Pitsch, "With Students' Aid, Clinton Signs Goals 2000,"*Education Week,* April 6, 1994, p. 21.
3. Deborah L. Cohen, "Carnegie Corp. Presses Early-Years Policies," *Education Week,* April 13, 1994, pp. 1, 13.
4. Deborah L. Cohen, "Report on 'Quiet Crisis' for Young Children Stirs Loud Response," *Education Week,* April 20, 1994, p. 7.

Chapter 25   OBE and Big Brother   (pp. 301-309)

1. Beverly Eakman, *Educating for the New World Order* (Portland, OR: Halcyon House, 1991).
2. National Center for Education Statistics, Student/Pupil Accounting, Standard Terminology and Guide for Managing Student Data in Elementary and Secondary Schools, Community/Junior Colleges, and Adult Education. State Educational Records and Reports Series: Handbook V, Revised 1974 (Washington, DC: U.S. Dept. of Education).
3. Council of Chief State School Officers (CCSSO), State Education Assessment Center, Education Data System Implementation Project (EDSIP), *Student Data Handbook for Elementary and Secondary Education,* Draft (9/11/92), developed for the National Center for Education Statistics (NCES), Office of Educational Research and Improvement, U.S. Dept. of Education, One Massachusetts Ave., N.W., Suite 700, Washington, DC 20001-1431, (202) 408-5505, fax (202) 408-8072.
4. Exchange of Permanent Records Electronically for Students and Schools (ExPRESS), Barbara S. Clements, Project Director. A Guide to the Implementation of the SPEEDE/ExPRESS Electronic Transcript, Version 1, developed by the Committee on the Standardization of Postsecondary Education Electronic Data Exchange (SPEEDE), American Association of Collegiate Registrars and Admissions Officers, Mar. 31, 1992. National Center for Education Statistics, U.S. Dept. of Education, Washington, DC., hypothetical résumé, p. 65.

5. *Getting Inside the EQA Inventory* (Pennsylvania Dept. of Education, 1975), pp. 19-21.

Chapter 26   Who Controls American Education?   (pp. 310-326)

1. David Tyack, *Managers of Virtue* (New York: Basic Books, 1982), p. 132.
2. *Ibid.*
3. Carroll Quigley, *The Anglo-American Establishment* (New York: Books in Focus, 1981), pp. ix, 33.
4. *Ibid*, p. 36.
5. Malachi Martin, *The Keys of This Blood,* The Struggle for World Dominion Between Pope John Paul II, Mikhail Gorbachev and the Capitalist West (New York: Simon and Schuster, 1990), p. 15.
6. Colin Greer, "My Challenge to the World," an inteview with Mikhail Gorbachev, "The Well-Being Of The World Is At Stake," *Parade Magazine,* Jan. 23, 1994, pp. 4-6.
7. Malachi Martin, *op. cit.*, p. 17.
8. Carroll Quigley, *Tragedy and Hope* (New York: Macmillan, 1966), pp. 950, 955.
9. Norman Dodd, "Norman Dodd Makes an Amazing Discovery," *Freeman Digest,* June 1984, pp. 37-39. This was a reprint of an article originally published in June 1978 in the same magazine.

Index

☐ **Alpha-Phonics: A Primer for Beginning Readers**..........................$29.95
   Complete systematic, intensive phonics reading program. All
   you need to teach any one to read. Priased by thousands. Anyone can teach with it.

☐ **Alpha-Phonics Audio Tapes** (2) 60 min audio tape set.....................$20.00
   All 128 lessons verbally sounded out, all 44 speech sounds
   reproduced. Tapes make Alpha-Phonics easier than ever for anyone
   to effectively teach reading. Tapesmeant to <u>aid</u>, <u>not</u> replace teacher.

☐ **Alpha-Phonics on CD ROM: Phonics Tutor.***   Alpha-.................$139.00
   Phonics now on computer. Interactive, all 128 lessons,
   most with 7 extra practice screens for drill without boredom.
   Price includes a copy of the Alpha-Phonics book.

☐ **Phonics Tutor Demo Disk.*** Look at the first 4 lessons of.............. $5.00
   Alpha-Phonics on computer. See for yourself how great it
   is on computer. Light year advance in teaching phonics.

☐ **Blumenfeld Oral Reading Assessment Test**....................................$19.95
   How well does your child read? Find out easily in privacy.
   Determines grade level. 5 sets of Pre-tests plus 5 After (re-
   mediation) tests.

☐ **Reading Test Pronunciation Audio Tape**.......................................$5.00
   25 min. audio clearly reproduces all 380 words of both tests.

☐ **Alpha-Phonics Readers:** Set 10 **Little Companion Readers**..........$19.95
   to accompany first 77 lessons of Alpha-Phonics. Kids love 'em.

☐ How To Tutor: Teach "3-R's" with one book....................$19.95
   Reading, cursive handwriting, arithmetic (Gr. 1-6) complete.

  How To Tutor Arithmetic Workbooks:
   ☐   Addition, Subtraction...$24.95
   ☐   Multiplication, Division, Fractions....................................$19.95

☐ **Is Public Education Necessary?**...$14.95
   The true history of how we got Pub Ed starting in the 1830's.

☐ **NEA Trojan Horse in American Education**................................$14.95
   The first full length exposé of National Education Assn.

☐ <u>NEW</u>: **The Whole Language / OBE Fraud**....................................$19.95
   "America had better heed his warnings" on these topics, says
   Dr. Walter E. Williams.

For Shipping Add $3.00. <u>Add</u> $1.00 for each extra book or set tapes. For UPS <u>Add</u> $2.00 to your total. Canada: <u>Add</u> $2.00 to your total (No UPS to Canada). Idaho residents <u>add</u> 5% tax.

* Specify: Macintosh _____
               Windows 95 _____

Name _____

Street _____
          Charge My: VISA ——MC——

City_____ State;— ZIP;——
          DISCOVER—— Exp. Date:_____

Phone:_____

    ☐ Send free information packet.

Make Checks payable to:

The Paradigm Co.

P.O. Box 45161 - Boise, ID 83711 - (208) 322-4440 - 24 hr/7day Ans. Mach.

Please Turn Over

☐ **The Whole Language/OBE Fraud...Brand New...1996........$19.95**
The shocking story of how America is being dumbed down by its own
educational system. Lauded by Marva Collins, Dr. R.J. Rushdoony,
Prof. Patrick Groff, Dr. Walter E. Williams, Dr. D. J. Kennedy, and
others..Add $3.00 shipping.

VIDEO TAPES

☐ **Affective Education.** The dangers of "non directed" education: sex-ed, drug-ed, self-esteeem, values clarification, etc. Dr. Wm. R. Coulson, Samuel L. Blumenfeld. Detroit, September 1990. 2 hours. $30.00

☐ **Whatever Happened to Old Fashioned Education?** Samuel L. Blumenfeld. Missoula, MT, September 1989. Video of Fri. night & all day Saturday Conference on both home-schooling and general discussion of the current American Educational Scene. Edited to 2 hours. Very informative. $30.00

☐ **May 1988 Speech on American Education.** 2 Hour Color Video. An in-depth talk on problems of Public Education. Information gained from hundreds of speaking stops across the U.S. up through May. 88. $30.00

☐ **Blumenfeld Explains Difference Between "Look/Say" and Intensive, Systematic Phonics.** 25 minute color video. Makes difference between the two methods easy to understand. Short enough to facilitate showing to service club, church and home school groups. $10.00

☐ **Two Workshops on** *Alpha-Phonics: A Primer for Beginning Readers.* 90 minute color video. Filmed at Teaching Home National Convention, Portland, OR, Oct. 1988. Each workshop approximately 45 minutes and includes extensive questions and answers. Tells about this highly successful, self-explanatory, systematic, intensive phonics book that works! Not a how to video but is designed to help parents decide if they want to use this system. $15.00

AUDIO TAPES

☐ **"Has the NEA Become Politicized? What Affect Has It Had on Education?"** From a Symposium on Education, St. Paul, Fall 86. Excellent summary of Dr. Blumenfeld's exposé of NEA and update on his book *NEA Trojan Horse in American Education* One tape, 60 minutes. $7.00

☐ **Blumenfeld's Major Speech on Education in America — Chattanooga, 1985.** Two tapes, 2 hours. Tells it all! $12.00

The BlumenfeldEducation Letter...
A monthly newsletter which assists parents in tutoring their children, evaluating their schools, texts, and curricula, and generally assuring that their children actually become educated.
☐ 3 months: $9.00
☐ 6 months $18.00
☐ 1 year $36.00

☐ **Free Information Packet.** Send me complimentary information on the many other education _____ No Charge resources Sam offers for concerned parents and taxpayers.

Idaho Residents Add 5% Sales Tax.
Add $1.50 postage for each video or set of audio tapes.
For U.P.S.: **Add** $2.00 to postal $1.50 = $3.50.
Canada: **ADD** $2.00 to U.S.Postal $1.50=$3.50 total.

CALL (208) 322-4440
24 HOURS — 7 DAYS
(Ans. Mach.)

Name _____

Street _____

City _____ State _____ Zip _____

Phone No. _____

Make Checks payable to:

The Paradigm Co.

P.O. Box 45161— Boise, Idaho 83711

Sorry, NO refunds on audio or video tapes.
Please Turn Over

Enclosed is my check for $_____
Charge my: VISA ☐ Master Card ☐
Discover Card ☐

Exp. Date _____

☐ **Alpha-Phonics: A Primer for Beginning Readers**.............................$29.95
  Complete systematic, intensive phonics reading program. All
  you need to teach any one to read. Priased by thousands. Anyone can teach with it.

☐ **Alpha-Phonics Audio Tapes** (2) 60 min audio tape set.....................$20.00
  All 128 lessons verbally sounded out, all 44 speech sounds
  reproduced. Tapes make Alpha-Phonics easier than ever for anyone
  to effectively teach reading. Tapes meant to aid, not replace teacher.

☐ **Alpha-Phonics on CD ROM: Phonics Tutor.***   Alpha-.................$139.00
  Phonics now on computer. Interactive, all 128 lessons,
  most with 7 extra practice screens for drill without boredom.
  Price includes a copy of the Alpha-Phonics book.

☐ **Phonics Tutor Demo Disk.*** Look at the first 4 lessons of.............. $5.00
  Alpha-Phonics on computer. See for yourself how great it
  is on computer. Light year advance in teaching phonics.

☐ **Blumenfeld Oral Reading Assessment Test**.....................................$19.95
  How well does your child read? Find out easily in privacy.
  Determines grade level. 5 sets of Pre-tests plus 5 After (re-
  mediation) tests.

☐ **Reading Test Pronunciation Audio Tape**..$5.00
  25 min. audio clearly reproduces all 380 words of both tests.

☐ **Alpha-Phonics Readers: Set 10 Little Companion Readers**..........$19.95
  to accompany first 77 lessons of Alpha-Phonics. Kids love 'em.

☐ **How To Tutor**: Teach "3-R's" with one book...................................$19.95
  Reading, cursive handwriting, arithmetic (Gr. 1-6) complete.

How To Tutor Arithmetic Workbooks:
  ☐ Addition, Subtraction..$24.95
  ☐ Multiplication, Division, Fractions.................................$19.95

☐ **Is Public Education Necessary?**..$14.95
  The true history of how we got Pub Ed starting in the 1830's.

☐ **NEA Trojan Horse in American Education**....................................$14.95
  The first full length exposé of National Education Assn.

☐ **NEW: The Whole Language / OBE Fraud**....................................$19.95
  "America had better heed his warnings" on these topics, says
  Dr. Walter E. Williams.

For Shipping Add $3.00. **Add** $1.00 for each extra book or set tapes. For UPS **Add** $2.00 to your total. Canada: **Add** $2.00 to your total (No UPS to Canada). Idaho residents **add** 5% tax.

* Specify: Macintosh _____
                  Windows 95 _____

Name _____
Street _____   Charge My: VISA ___MC___
City_____ State:___ ZIP:___   DISCOVER____ Exp. Date:_____
Phone:_____
          ☐ Send free information packet.
Make Checks payable to:

The Paradigm Co.
P.O. Box 45161 - Boise, ID 83711 - (208) 322-4440 - 24 hr/7day Ans. Mach.
Please Turn Over

☐ **The Whole Language/OBE Fraud...Brand New...1996.........$19.95**
The shocking story of how America is being dumbed down by its own
educational system. Lauded by Marva Collins, Dr. R.J. Rushdoony,
Prof. Patrick Groff, Dr. Walter E. Williams, Dr. D. J. Kennedy, and
others..Add $3.00 shipping.

<u>VIDEO TAPES</u>
☐ **Affective Education.** The dangers of "non directed" education: sex-ed, drug-ed, self-esteeem, values clarification, etc. Dr. Wm. R. Coulson, Samuel L. Blumenfeld. Detroit, September 1990. 2 hours. $30.00

☐ **Whatever Happened to Old Fashioned Education?** Samuel L. Blumenfeld. Missoula, MT, September 1989. Video of Fri. night & all day Saturday Conference on both home-schooling and general discussion of the current American Educational Scene. Edited to 2 hours. Very informative. $30.00

☐ **May 1988 Speech on American Education.** 2 Hour Color Video. An in-depth talk on problems of Public Education. Information gained from hundreds of speaking stops across the U.S. up through May. 88. $30.00

☐ **Blumenfeld Explains Difference Between "Look/Say" and Intensive, Systematic Phonics.** 25 minute color video. Makes difference between the two methods easy to understand. Short enough to facilitate showing to service club, church and home school groups. $10.00

☐ **Two Workshops on** *Alpha-Phonics: A Primer for Beginning Readers.* 90 minute color video. Filmed at Teaching Home National Convention, Portland, OR, Oct. 1988. Each workshop approximately 45 minutes and includes extensive questions and answers. Tells about this highly successful, self-explanatory, systematic, intensive phonics book that works! <u>Not a how to video</u> but is designed to help parents decide if they want to use this system. $15.00

<u>AUDIO TAPES</u>
☐ **"Has the NEA Become Politicized? What Affect Has It Had on Education?"** From a Symposium on Education, St. Paul, Fall 86. Excellent summary of Dr. Blumenfeld's exposé of NEA and update on his book *NEA Trojan Horse in American Education* One tape, 60 minutes. $7.00

☐ **Blumenfeld's Major Speech on Education in America — Chattanooga, 1985.** Two tapes, 2 hours. Tells it all! $12.00

The BlumenfeldEducation Letter...
A monthly newsletter which assists parents in tutoring their children, evaluating their schools, texts, and curricula, and generally assuring that their children actually become educated.

☐ 3 months: $9.00
☐ 6 months $18.00
☐ 1 year $36.00

☐ **Free Information Packet.** Send me complimentary information on the many other education _____*No Charge* resources Sam offers for concerned parents and taxpayers.

Idaho Residents Add 5% Sales Tax.
Add $1.50 postage for each video or set of audio tapes.
For U.P.S.: **Add** $2.00 to postal $1.50 = $3.50.
Canada: **ADD** $2.00 to U.S.Postal $1.50=$3.50 total.

CALL (208) 322-4440
24 HOURS — 7 DAYS
(Ans. Mach.)

Name _____

Street _____

City _____ State _____ Zip _____

Phone No. _____

Make Checks payable to:

The Paradigm Co.

P.O. Box 45161— Boise, Idaho 83711

Sorry, <u>NO</u> refunds on audio or video tapes.
Please Turn Over

Enclosed is my check for $_____
Charge my: VISA ☐ Master Card ☐
Discover Card ☐

Exp. Date _____